S0-BQW-721

RENEWALS 458-2440

The Social Construction
of Public Administration

SUNY series in Public Administration
Peter W. Colby, editor

The Social Construction of Public Administration

Interpretive and Critical Perspectives

Jong S. Jun

Foreword by
Frank P. Sherwood

WITHDRAWN
UTSA LIBRARIES

State University
of New York
Press

Published by
State University of New York Press, Albany

© 2006 State University of New York

All rights reserved

Printed in the United States of America

No part of this book may be used or reproduced in any manner whatsoever without written permission. No part of this book may be stored in a retrieval system or transmitted in any form or by any means including electronic, electrostatic, magnetic tape, mechanical, photocopying, recording, or otherwise without the prior permission in writing of the publisher.

For information, address State University of New York Press,
194 Washington Avenue, Suite 305, Albany, NY 12210-2384

Production by Susan Geraghty
Marketing by Michael Campochiaro

Library of Congress Cataloging-in-Publication Data

Jun, Jong S.
    The social construction of public administration : interpretive and critical perspectives / Jong S. Jun ; foreword by Frank P. Sherwood.
        p. cm. — (SUNY series in public administration)
    Includes bibliographical references and index.
    ISBN 0-7914-6725-2 (hardcover : alk. paper)
    1. Public administration—Social aspects. I. Title. II. Series.

JF1351.J87 2006
306.2'4—dc22

2005014020

ISBN-13: 978-0-7914-6725-1 (hardcover : alk. paper)

10 9 8 7 6 5 4 3 2 1

Library
University of Texas
at San Antonio

To my wife,
Soon Ye Regina,
for her support

CONTENTS

FOREWORD

The first priority in this introduction is to ensure that readers of this book are fully aware of the credentials of its author, Jong S. Jun.

He may be the most outstanding theorist in public administration today. The quantitative evidence is his remarkable output of scholarly work. Perhaps more important, though, is the perspective he brings to his studies and resulting publications. His roots are in the Far East, but he has spent his entire working career of thirty-seven years teaching in the United States. He is unique in that he brings to his philosophical considerations both a Western and an Eastern orientation. That meshing of the two worlds is very evident in this book, as in many other works.

While his rich background allows him insights that most of us can only envy, it is also important to recognize the profound wisdom of this book, which he regards as the capstone of his long and productive research efforts. It is his effort to summarize what he has discovered in nearly half a century of research.

Jun is a native of South Korea and received his early schooling there, including a Bachelor of Laws degree. In 1961 he came to the United States and has lived here ever since. He studied political science at the University of Oregon with a man well known to us old timers, Bert Wengert, who was highly influential in developing the case method of teaching in public administration. Wengert undoubtedly saw Jun as having a promising future and urged him to secure his doctorate in Public Administration.

With a master's degree in hand, Jun enrolled in the PhD program at the School of Public Administration, University of Southern California. His thirst for work and learning quickly became evident, particularly to one of the school's senior professors, William B. Storm. Jun came to him one day and announced, "I want to work with you and learn from you. I don't care about money. I just want to work and learn." It was such enthusiasm that caused Storm to enroll him as a graduate assistant and to serve as his mentor. It was an extremely fruitful relationship in which the two collaborated on two books, both published within five years after Jun had completed his doctoral work.

One of those books, *Tomorrow's Organizations: Challenges and Strategies* (Jun and Storm, 1973)[1] enabled me to become fully aware of Jun's capacities. Since I knew this was a real collaboration between Jun and Storm, I was very much struck how these two had combined to produce one of the few outstanding books of the last half-century. Shortly after it came out in 1973 and I had read it, I quickly assigned it to my graduate students with this observation, "If you read this book carefully and understand it fully, you will know about all that anybody knows about organization theory in the public sector." It was that good. My sense is that *Tomorrow's Organizations* never achieved the reputation it deserved because it was a collection of readings. That characterization results in an automatic discounting. In reality, though, Jun and Storm produced a book within a book. The introductions to the four sections of readings were absolutely brilliant. They could have comprised a book by themselves.

As a result of that fine volume, I never took anything Jun wrote lightly. He certainly had my attention. I do not want to imply I have read everything Jun has written. He has been far too prolific. He has published eight books, including three collaborated volumes. My count shows that he has published over fifty articles, book chapters, and symposium issues, roughly half of them dealing with ideas that appear in this book. He has been primarily a philosopher of public administration, as the content of this volume and the many articles and papers attest.

The mixing of the East and West is also very evident in an examination of his intellectual output. Various papers focus on South Korea, Japan, and China. When you examine all the unpublished papers, panel presentations, invited speeches, and consulting assignments, you quickly realize how international is his presence. He lists at least thirteen countries in which he has made intellectual contributions, the larger bulk of them in the Pacific Rim. Also, however, he lists a wide range of countries around the world where he has given lectures or been involved in other activities: Russia, Brazil, Italy, England, Austria, France, Australia, and the Netherlands.

South Korea has been, of course, a particularly frequent object of his attentions. The numerous involvements there are simply too many to report here. I have heard, however, that Jun's reputation in South

Korea is simply immense. Japan has also received a considerable amount of his attention. He spent more than a year there as a visiting scholar and has written insightfully about those experiences.

While he has lived a highly cosmopolitan life, it is extremely interesting that Jun's US. teaching responsibility has been at only one institution, the California State University at Hayward, California. He went there as a young assistant professor in 1968, rose through its ranks, and took partial retirement in 2000, thirty-two years later. Without wanting to depreciate the overall quality of Cal State-Hayward, I think it is fair to say that Jun, with some remarkably fine colleagues he recruited, gave the public administration program a reputation far beyond that of the university as a whole. He helped create a stimulating intellectual environment that he had little interest in leaving.

Further, Hayward provided him opportunities that might not have been so easily available elsewhere. While his research might have led him to increasing abstractions, he was always grounded by his students. They tended to work in state and local governments, and thus much of Jun's teaching had to be immediate and practical. This book reveals that Jun has never strayed far from these moorings.

Aside from having an appreciation of the quality of the author, it is important to develop an understanding for the departure point of this book. To summarize his feelings, Jun is profoundly disappointed with the way things are going in "mainstream" public administration. He is particularly troubled by the tendency of newly minted PhD's from non-Western countries to make the incorporation of Western ideas their basic agenda. He feels there are severe limitations to the notion that non-Western countries can be transformed by Western ideas. In fact, he makes it clear that the consequences of such efforts are often negative.

While he counsels that culture ought to play much larger part in our thinking about public administration, Jun is particularly concerned about two facets of the field. In both areas, he feels an urgent need for change. We have to understand these shortfalls before we can process fully the exquisitely reasoned approaches to change offered by Jun. (I should note that I want to be sure they are understood because I am so much in agreement with him.)

One is the decline in the importance of the qualifier *public*, in public administration. That is important because public administration is not concerned with *any* type of administration. It is specifically about handling matters of public consequence. Second, we seem to have only one way of organizing for any kind of collective action, a structure of top-down command. The approach has many dysfunctional consequences, which Jun emphasizes in this book. That is why he seeks to change our thinking and discover new alternatives for handling collaborative tasks.

The problem with 'public' seems a more geographically discreet problem than hierarchy, the label we typically attach to top-down approaches. In the United States we are perilously close to a disappearance of 'public,' with a generic *administration* taking over. That does not seem to be occurring in Asia in the same degree. Jun writes that culture makes a big difference. In Asia the sense of community is much stronger, influenced in great degree by the Buddhist religion. Both *community* and 'public' convey the idea of other-regarding events, and thus the modifier continues to have significance in Asian public administration.

In the United States, where the emphasis is much less on the community and far more on the individual, public administration is now regarded only as a minor variant in the variety of ways in which people get together to do common tasks. The general assumption is that administration (or management) is the same in any purposeful context. No values attach to the process.

The situation is made murkier by differences in the way public administration is practiced and ways in which it is taught. For the last thirty-five years governments in the United States have been increasingly politicized. In the federal bureaucracy, for example, there are virtually no career civil servants in top leadership positions, which are occupied by political appointees whose accountability is to political interests not to public. Such officials tend to see administration in highly instrumental terms. They have spearheaded a tremendous movement toward the contracting out of government activities, once again emphasizing that there is no public in their concept of public administration.

In the institutions teaching public administration, there is a substantial number of professors who share Jun's views. Yet the product they deliver is remarkably aligned with approaches in the practicing world. The typical courses taught are reflective of an instrumental orientation: budgeting, personnel and human resources, organizing, policy analysis, information management, and positivistic research. It is becoming increasingly rare to find even a course in behavior in the curriculum. I am not sure these are the courses many professors would chose to teach, but they remain pillars of public administration curriculums. That is what the clientele demands.

In the non-Western nations there is a tendency to retain structures that appear to be public. Such bureaucracies have been influenced, however, by Western approaches and thus have honored rational technologies. Such value-neutral instruments have the advantage of preserving for the bureaucrats an independent position of power in the society. Sadly, that independence and isolation preclude any real interest in involving citizens in their activities. So they operate relatively free from an engagement with the polity they are expected to serve.

Jun summarizes the problem of publicness in public administration in the following terms: "The professional bias of public administration toward rational analysis, efficiency, planning and goal maintenance means that public administration is largely administration, that is, it serves mostly to govern and manage the public. The ideas of participation, deliberation, civic engagement, citizen empowerment, and democratic process are secondary to public administration." That is a condition which, he feels, urgently needs changing.

Throughout his book, Jun points to the great dysfunctions that arise from the worldwide addiction to top-down systems of organizing, which we characteristically label "hierarchy." Because Max Weber viewed a bureaucracy as rooted in hierarchy, the word *(bureaucracy)* tends to be used synonymously with hierarchy. While the concept of 'bureaucracy' incorporates a number of other features, it is the command feature that is honored and adopted. It is a notion of centralization where someone is put in charge, given authority, and held accountable. Things reached an extreme in the United States when the Department of Homeland Security was created. Over eighty thousand employees of widely divergent agencies were put under the command of one person. There seems general agreement that the result has been chaos. What was undertaken for rational reasons turns out to be highly irrational.

There are many problems in applying the concept of 'hierarchy' to complex human organizations, as Jun has so ably reported. In my thinking, two have rendered hierarchy exceedingly vulnerable. In an organization with eighty thousand people, it has to be recognized that there is no simple set of goals to be pursued. Deciding what is most important to do involves delicate negotiations among all those who have a stake in the organization. In reality it should be accepted that negotiations must occur with all eighty thousand employees because each wants different things from the organization. Certainly no single boss can process those claims. To reduce these kinds of stresses, hierarchical organizations are typically reified as technological machines with fairly standardized parts, subject to orders from above. The effect is to depersonalize what is an intensely human situation and to act as if those in it were not people at all. Not only is this a defiance of reality, but also it is stupid. People are still people.

Even more significantly, hierarchical organizations are extremely poor learners. That is a fatal flaw because, in the last analysis, learning paves the way for change. Despite the fact that the complex organization must be learning in a host of ways, the premise of the hierarchy is that the person in charge is the principal learner. We need only to recognize that those at the periphery of the organization are engaged in the real work and have direct contact with those in its environment to see where the real learning must occur. The boss and his advisers back at headquarters are not close enough to the action to know what is really happening. Things tend to emerge upside down. The boss, with precious little information, is doing the telling, whereas he or she ought to be listening, and folks on the periphery do the telling. In the overall, Jun is absolutely right that there ought to be a determined assault on an organizational strategy that gives us nothing but trouble. As I have indicated, Jun has laid out ways to think about these problems and how to proceed toward at least more tolerable solutions.

Finally, it may be of some value to provide a small case experience that, at least in part, bears upon the strategy he espouses. The Federal Executive Institute, intended to serve as the staff college for the senior career service in the federal government, was established in 1968. This was a time of extreme turmoil and unrest in the United States, triggered in major degree by the Watts riots. It was also a period when the most elemental assumptions of our social organizations were under severe criticism. Mario Savio, from the University of California at Berkeley, led much of this assault. He was convinced that everyone over thirty had sold out to the establishment and could not be saved.

Though the federal government was the bulwark of the establishment, there were stirrings within its ranks, particularly among careerists. They were not about to buy the Savio line, but they really felt the government was too fragmented, unable to see the whole, and glacial in its pursuit of change. They believed that the people with the best prospects for bringing about change were the top careerists, who, up to that time, had not had formal development opportunities available to them. These federal executives were, on average, forty-five years of age, had been out of school about twenty years, and had another ten to twenty years of government service ahead of them.

The challenges to all the key actors in our complex, huge public systems were many. As Jun observed, the 60s and 70s were turbulent, but they were much more receptive to change than the decades that followed.

It is within this context that the origins of the Federal Executive Institute must be viewed. The roughly 350 executives who annually came to a residential campus in Charlottesville, Virginia, were expected to internalize two messages, one that the government could do much better and the second that they were agents charged with bringing this about.

It is clear that *change* was the word in good currency. But I remember that much of the original thinking for the institute was that the executives should be instructed how that new world would look. The premise was change, not (as Jun has eloquently noted) changing. We on the faculty saw the problem a bit differently, namely, that it was our job to help executives embrace the idea of changing, both personally and organizationally. In all honesty, I do not think any of us felt we were smart enough or wise enough to instruct senior executives on how the world should or would look.

We decided on two things: (a) to focus on individuals, not their roles in organizations or the organizations themselves; and (b) to heighten their learning interests and then to help them improve their learning capacities, all as a prerequisite to a greater commitment to changing.

The goal was pursued in a variety of ways and had clear consequences at the institute. A substantial number of executives told me personally that the institute was the first situation in their federal careers in which they thought of themselves as individuals. One small thing we did was to eliminate from our rosters any reference to civil service rank, which varied from GS-15 to GS-18. Because we eliminated the virtually obligatory "pecking order" rules, the way individuals were perceived and regarded had little to do with their civil service rank. Generally, the people from the field got the most attention. They were seen as knowing the most about the real world, though they were typically the lowest ranked. This seemed to support my view that the greatest learning resources in an organization are those closest to the action, not those in headquarters.

The concepts of the individual and learning were closely tied together, as our interest was in building a learning commitment and capacity in the individual and not the organization. For many this was a totally new experience. They said they had not thought about personal learning since they left the university. Conceptually, it did not occur to them that learning was a part of living, and changing. Life for them was much more a matter of behaving in terms of learned routines, carrying little excitement and even less growth.

The learning model we embraced was a very simple one. Exposure and feedback are required. People learn when they open themselves by exhibiting an attitude or behavior and thus provide data to others, drawing feedback. We found that the model was easy to articulate but hard to implement. Federal bureaucrats had generally found that the less they exposed themselves the better, and they were similarly reluctant to give feedback to others. One of our great accomplishments was to turn things around. By the time executives left the institute, they were particularly disposed to give feedback, recognizing it as an obligation to their colleagues. They had also become more comfortable with the idea of exposure.

Another highly important outcome of their experience was that the executives came to care for each other genuinely. They were extremely close emotionally and felt the obligation to give each other support. That was a new experience. It was vastly different from their work environment, where competition and disdain for personal needs and interests were the order of the day.

Research on executives who had left the institute about a year earlier (performed by an independent organization) produced a finding that we had never conceived or anticipated. A substantial majority of respondents declared that the Federal Executive Institute had significantly increased their self-confidence. While that gain may seem deeply personal, it has enormous organizational implications because personal confidence is the key to delegation. Moreover, delegation is about the best way we know to introduce flexibility into muscle-bound hierarchies. People who do not trust themselves are highly unlikely to trust others. They do not delegate, and the result is the kind of top down behavior we see in most hierarchies. A most important outcome of the FEI experiences, then, may have been a greater willingness to delegate.

In writing about some of the ways in which the eight-week residence at the Federal Executive Institute at least opened up the thinking and behavior options for many executives, I certainly do not want to claim that these changes carried over in any significant way to the federal government. In another time and circumstance, these executives might have made a real difference. But Washington was changing. The career service was losing ground, and politically loyal operatives were assuming the levers of government. There was no difference among the parties. Both wanted their politically loyal people in command. Further, the effect was to reinvigorate the dedication to hierarchy.

I hope this foreword will be regarded only as a precursor to Jun's book, with its thoroughly researched inquiries into the really daunting dilemmas governments face today. As I have sought to emphasize, we do need radically new thought, and I believe Jun is leading us in a fruitful, positive direction.

Frank P. Sherwood

PREFACE

Countries in the East and West are in the midst of a great transformation: the democratization of the governing process. The Western countries, the United States in particular, are working to renew democratic ideals and practices by strengthening the process of deliberative democracy. Because of the need for government intervention to solve complex social and cultural problems, Asian countries—which are relatively new to the great democratic experiment—are ineluctably immersed in the improvement of political democracy through strong government. But despite the dynamic transformation taking place nationally and globally, public institutions in both the East and the West are slow to change their practices, instead continuing to try to solve complex human issues with traditional management concepts and techniques.

To cope with a paradoxical, ambiguous, and continuously changing world, we need a new framework for dealing with a multiplicity of realities. There are, I believe, more possibilities in participation and communication among people collectively and in individual growth and change than in managing programs and people or typical efforts at the rearrangement of organizational structure, functions, and processes. The latter, however sincere, represents domination by management, which has often proven unresponsive to and ineffective in resolving contemporary dilemmas. The social construction of reality introduced in this book is neither a new concept nor a new idiom in social sciences, although it is not widely known by students of public administration.

In this book, I present conceptual perspectives whereby we may gain greater comprehension of our situations, realities, organizational efforts, social design, action and behavior, the self, ethics, and so on: this is a vital step in understanding the public and people. As people become better able to engage in their personal and organizational worlds, they learn to take joy in their empowerment, in challenging inhibiting formalisms, management-driven projects, rules, directives, and so on. They learn to find meaning in reconstructing organizational order and exploring alternatives without sacrificing either organizational goals or functional obligations. We are unlikely to return to the type of turbulence that we experienced during the 1960s and early 1970s in the United States, a period in which individuals rebelled against authority, demanding individual freedoms and rights.

Considering the present circumstances of institutional control, dwindling resources, demands for performance and delivery of service, information technology, and local and global politics, we must work with both management and the public. We will, however, be more effective if we act collectively in questioning the unintended consequences of hierarchical governing, problem solving, and change. Working through democratic process of participation, dialogue, and sharing interests is likely to offer more possibilities than if we each act alone. My emphasis is on the interpretation of the different meanings of objects that we create and the individual experiences that people bring to a situation, by critically exploring possibilities through the collective empowerment of the people who are affected by particular policies and actions.

This book is intended for a broad range of readers who have an interest in their relationships with themselves, with management and organizational members, with decision makers and marginal people, and with citizens and their problems. To be as inclusive as possible, I present social construction as a framework so that all of us may think about whether construction of action strategies is possible through the engagement of people and communicative action. More important, I try to relate the self to the interaction process, that is, to an individual's contribution through sharing his or her interests with others, learning which interests are mutual. People feel more comfortable once they learn to take risks in a group, to be experimental, flexible, optimistic, and imaginative. Group members learn to challenge existing ways of thinking, doing, and finding satisfaction in seeking new possibilities. I hope through this book, students of public administration will learn the hazards of oversimplification and develop some action skills as "complexifiers," divergent thinkers, reflexive facilitators, and critical agents of change.

In this book, I try to show that the management orientation emphasized by mainstream public administration is grossly inadequate. Instead, I attempt to reconstruct the study of public administration as a part of social, political, and democratic practice. Thus my most immediate concern transcends the idea of the strong administrative state, bureaucracy, and a single discipline or field of study. My point of departure is the social and political processes of confronting problems and searching for solutions and alternatives to them. I do not reject the importance of management or the technical necessity of public administration: efficient management as well as implementation of techniques largely depends upon the collaboration of the people who are affected by them. If we want to improve the adequacy and effectiveness of public administration, then we must change our perspectives. We must use different ways of knowing that are interpretive, critical, and qualitative. We must also understand the social, cultural, and political contexts in which problems originate and the meanings that people attach to them. In this regard, my approach in this book may be considered critical pragmatism because my arguments in different chapters emphasize the pragmatic possibilities grounded in human praxis, as argued by Richard Bernstein in *Praxis and Action: Contemporary Philosophies of Action* (1971). I consider the functionalist and positivistic approach to public administration to be largely instrumental pragmatism that aims to maintain rational control of the organizational process.

This book also represents my own agonized efforts to understand, explain, and bridge the administrative cultures of the East and the West. Thus my endeavor is to apply the perspectives and problems of administrative theory to different administrative contexts and to draw some theoretical implications from cases and examples, comparing and contrasting different cultures and experiences. The arguments in this book are as much a reflection of my understanding of the cultural contexts of public administration in different countries as they are critical analyses of the politics, policies, administrations, and people discussed. I speak as a person who has lived in several Asian countries and who has lived most of my academic and adult life in the United States. I think that therefore I have a sympathetic ear for and an understanding of people in different administrative cultures in various countries. At the same time, I do not hesitate to discuss the problems in those countries. My experiences in visiting different countries have greatly furthered my intellectual development.

At annual meetings of the Public Administration Theory Network and in the journal *Administrative Theory and Praxis*, a wide range of significant theory issues has been introduced and debated. Although I have immensely enjoyed my participation in dialogue with my theoretically oriented colleagues, I have also struggled with the fact that we are talking among ourselves, not reaching out to our students or to mainstream public administrators. Other fields in the social sciences face a similar problem in conveying alternative ways of knowing to those who are more accustomed to positivistic and scientific inquiry. One important theoretical contribution of the Public Administration Theory Network is the exploration of different ways of knowing, particularly the interpretive, critical theory, and postmodern perspectives; this exploration helps to encourage open dialogue among scholars. This book is the product of my own learning as I worked with international scholars who were intellectually sincere about studying the effects of theory on practice and the effects of practice on theorizing.

I am inevitably aware, in a book of this kind, of discussing superficially diverse topics that many other scholars know more about than I. My only plea is to show the need for going beyond the traditional influence of hierarchical governing and management. We need to pay attention to ways of enhancing the responsibility of people in the process of changing organizations and policies through practicing social and democratic alternatives. To understand the complexity and change the institutions, we need to seek ideas and concepts that are often the opposite of the assumptions of dominant theories and approaches. The philosophy and the new conceptualization of public administration need to accept the idea that administrative actions are embedded in and overlap with the complexity of social practices that involve the public and the individuals.

I am greatly indebted to Frank Sherwood for his gracious foreword to this book. His distinguished achievements as former dean of the School of Public Administration at USC, founding director of USC Washington Public Affairs Center, founding director of the Federal Executive Institute, and former Jerry Collins Eminent Scholar at Florida State University inspired me to learn the importance of integrating theory and practice. Raymond Pomerleau and Richard VrMeer read the complete manuscript and offered invaluable criticisms and suggestions. They have been the source of my learning the intricacies of American culture for nearly forty years. A number of people read chapters in various forms, including Ann Cunliffe, Dvora Yanow, Richard Box, Budd Kass, my graduate students, and the anonymous reviewers for the publisher. To all these people, I owe more gratitude than I am able to express.

CHAPTER 1

Introduction

We live in an "age of paradox," in which our good intentions to progress and our efforts to improve the quality of life produce unintended consequences and often contradictory results (Handy, 1994). This paradox results when policy makers put forth a strong argument for pursuing one policy and neglecting another, less pressing, one, such as preferring development over environmental protection, administrative efficiency over effectiveness, or organizational goals over individual needs. Although economic progress has meant material bounty for the individual in industrialized and postindustrialized countries, it has also produced numerous negative consequences nationally and globally, such as inequality, high consumerism, social divisiveness, and alienation. Because of the growth and spread of industrialization and modernization, people in the workplace and in society are often connected in a merely functional way: they lack intimate, social, or authentic relationships. Because of a desire to manage society and institutions in order to cope with turbulent changes, organizational goals are seen as more important than democratic governance, participation, human growth, or social justice. Although bureaucracies see progress and the management of complexity as necessary for human cooperation, bureaucratic organizations have been hostile to the promotion of democratic ideas. Since the latter part of the twentieth century, however, we have witnessed centrifugal forces working to renew greater human purposes in governing, development, change, and problem solving.

A public administration that relies on conventional pluralistic politics and modern management theories is inadequate for understanding today's crisis and complex human phenomena. Furthermore, mainstream public administration, which overly emphasizes the role of management, is incapable of developing democratic ways to resolve conflict or generate socially grounded solutions. What is required in the current crisis is a creative awakening to the dialectical social process—to the ability to join what is, what can be, and what should

1

be—in order to alter the social and administrative structure and processes. In other words, an appreciation of social processes, of the interplay of instrumental and technical elements, and of collective and democratic means of creating a more humane and hopeful society is needed.

When we examine the conceptual orientation of public administration today, we see that the dominant approach to its study, as manifested in the educational curriculum, in research methods used to collect information, in administrative operations, and in reform efforts, is both intellectual and pragmatic. Mainstream public administration reflects this orientation in seeking administrative knowledge and concepts grounded in the positivistic and functionalist tradition of epistemology.[1] But a true understanding of social reality and human relationships requires more than instrumental and rational ways of investigating human knowledge.

This book explores constructive ways of understanding the complex phenomena of public administration by introducing the interpretive and critical perspectives. The concepts applied are a hybrid of phenomenology, ethnomethodology, hermeneutics, critical theory, and postmodern ideas. The interpretive approach focuses on social practice: public administrators act in a social situation by listening to other voices. The primary concern of administrators is not to use a theory (or theoretical knowledge) to guide administrative action: rather, their effort is to understand and interpret people's experience and form a sense of mutuality by sharing "intersubjective meanings" (Taylor, 1985b; Schutz, 1967). The critical theory perspective, however, critically reflects on established assumptions, theories, values, and methods and reconstructs possibilities that are democratic and socially acceptable without dismissing the importance of theoretical knowledge and "technical interest" (i.e., the use of instrumental knowledge to control the environment) to administration (Habermas, 1971). The field of public administration needs a critical, self-reflexive practice if it is to improve current practice, which is largely influenced by the people at the top. Members of this elite work hard to justify their ideas and activities, which have produced the current crisis. Western public administration (U.S. public administration in particular) has become a rational-instrumental model for most non-Western countries to keep pace with industrialization and modernization. The growth of bureaucracy in both the Eastern and the Western governments has produced the management and professional capability. The bureaucratization of public institutions, however, has generated various unintended consequences and faced limitations.

THE LIMITATIONS OF MODERN PUBLIC ADMINISTRATION

The characteristics of modern public administration are adequate administrative guides in a stable organizational environment in which services and everyday operations do not require much innovation, in which people's values and needs remain persistent; and, in which external elements, such as politics, clientele, technology, and economics, remain predictable. In today's globalizing world, however, no organization is so placid. In a rapidly changing society, social phenomena do not remain stable: they are dynamic and continuously changing into new values, new meanings, new structures, and new networks. Coping with turbulent and evolving conditions of the postindustrial era is, nowadays, an inevitable task for organizations. The complexity of environments, organizations, information technology, and people's values requires new ways of understanding and collaborating with people through interaction, dialogue, and information sharing.

A complex public bureaucracy is designed to maintain organizational order, to suppress activities that are disruptive to organizational policies and goals, and to coordinate functional processes in order to assure productivity. Organizational order and survival are stressed by a group of top executives and managers, who exercise power and authority. The establishment of a new government agency, public policy, or goals is social construction because many officials from the executive and legislative branches are involved in the design and passage of the new legislation and policy. For example, the Homeland Security Act of 2002, which created the Department of Homeland Security, brought together twenty-two diverse agencies to help prevent terrorist attacks in the United States, reduce the vulnerability of the United States to terrorist attacks, and minimize damage and assist in recovery if an attack should occur. The demands imposed by management often create the false impression that dehumanizing organizational control and order are justified. Organizational members are expected to be loyal, committed, and able to manage crisis situations, no matter how strict or depersonalizing the atmosphere in which they function. One of the most difficult issues facing a complex organization such as Homeland Security is how to establish trusting relationships among a wide variety of federal, state, and local agencies so they can share information regarding vulnerability to and incidents of terrorism. Furthermore, changing the administrative cultures of twenty-two agencies into that of one new cabinet-level department requires the participation of employees from different professional backgrounds in order to strengthen the process of change, allowing employees to share their experiences and shape policies.

The major limitation of modern public administration is the unintended consequences of the elements that are supposed to contribute to the efficient management of agencies. In today's changing environment, these elements tend to hinder human action and undermine participation, horizontal relationships, and human collaboration. Various authors criticize the limitation of both old and contemporary public administration (for example, see Denhardt and Denhardt, 2003; McSwite, 1997; Farmer, 1995; Fox and Miller, 1996; and Kass and Catron, 1990). In this section, I briefly summarize seven common characteristics of traditional public administration and their limitations. They are as follows: (1) vertical governing; (2) professional dominance; (3) instrumental-technical rationality; (4) reified bureaucracy; (5) complexity; (6) placating citizens; and (7) dualistic thinking.

Vertical Governing

Public administration is vertically governed. That is to say, administration in every country is hierarchically organized in order to manage the basic functions of the agency and to enforce rules and regulations in relation to the agency's policies and goals (Goodsell, 1983; Stillman, 1987; Kaufman, 1981; Richardson, 1997). Because authority and power reside at the top of organizational echelons, executives and managers often make important decisions without consulting the people below them. Power is essential for executives and managers in maintaining a bureaucracy: it is a means of controlling the behavior of its members (Hummel, 1994). From the bureaucratic point of view, power must be exercised in order to accomplish established goals. Moreover, power is relational, in that the effective use of power by one actor depends on the perceptions of and cooperation of other actors in interpersonal and interorganizational situations. The traditional way of governing is gradually being transformed into the democratic process of horizontal governance, which puts federal government agencies in a more collaborative role with state and local governments, nongovernmental organizations (NGOs), international organizations, and businesses (Kettl, 2002; Sirianni and Friedland, 2001; Nye and Donahue, 2000).

Professional Dominance

Public administration is greatly influenced by groups of professionals: these include scientists, engineers, health specialists, systems analysts, policy analysts, planners, computer specialists, and economists. Frederick Mosher points out that government creates professionals, legitimizes professions, subsidizes all forms of professional endeavors, and employs an everincreasing proportion of professionals. The professions provide knowledge, training, and leadership to public agencies; influence public policy; and shape the structure of many public agencies (1968, p. 104). The most obvious path to power for professionals in public service is through their specialized training and knowledge. With the command that professionals have of the specialized language and information of their disciplines, they naturally tend to control the decision-making processes and the creation of policy for the public agencies that they represent. Professionalism in a public bureaucracy often impedes the political process. Agencies dominated by professionals often attempt to avoid public debate or the scrutiny of past or future decisions in, for example, dealing with sensitive environmental issues. The narrow focus of most professionals in public service, combined with an impatience and a lack of sensitivity toward the real world of politics and clientele interests, creates an atmosphere of tension and conflict that is inconsistent with the higher moral aims of public service and the ethics of democratic government. Jethro Lieberman, in *The Tyranny of the Experts*, warns that overdependence on professionals in an industrial society hampers the prospect of a more open and democratic society (1970).[2]

Instrumental-technical Rationality

Further, modern public administration operates under the assumption of instrumental-technical rationality, which Max Weber characterizes as the rationale for the ideal bureaucracy (1947; Gerth and Mills, 1946). For Weber, instrumental rationality is attained by the elaboration (on the basis of scientific knowledge) of rules that try to direct, from the top down, all behavior toward maximum efficiency. Weber's rationalization is the product of the scientific specialization and technical differentiation peculiar to Western culture, and Weber sometimes associates it with the notion of intellectualization. Guerreiro Ramos (1981), in his critique of the assumptions of the functionalist theories, points out that bureaucratic institutions confront the problem of administrative order by embracing the instrumental requirement of administration (described as instrumental rationality), which denies the potential of individuals to create a new administrative order (or substantive rationality), and focuses mainly on the economic needs of large organizations. Weber, however, is concerned not only with causal explanation and generalization of institutions from an instrumental-rational point of view but also with an interpretive understanding of the subjective meanings that people attribute to their actions (Weber, 1947, p. 88). As Julien Freund describes it, Weber stresses "meaningful relatedness . . . through which we are able to understand, quite apart from objective development, the subjective meaning which a social relationship holds for man and by which he is guided in his social conduct" (1968, p. 89).

Modern bureaucracies adopt various technical means of accomplishing the established goals of management. Individuals in a bureaucracy, however, do not always behave rationally, as top executives and managers expect them to do. Perceptions of employees and clientele are different from those of policy makers. As a result, a supposedly rational bureaucracy is, in practice, often irrational, inefficient, and incapable of understanding the situation or of solving many nonroutine or unanticipated human problems. As Weber argues, in order to understand how people behave in their community and society, we need to understand how they create and destroy various relationships through their actions.

Reified Bureaucracy

When we attempt to understand a bureaucracy by means of Weber's ideal construct, we are conscious of its existence as an objective phenomenon with basic characteristics. Presenting typical functions of a bureaucracy, such as hierarchical relationships, specialized role performance, application of technical skills, and enforcing rules and regulations, is itself an example of objectifying the institutional process. We explain administrative phenomena by adopting words and abstract concepts for analytical purposes. As time passes, we tend to forget the original intention of constructing such metaphors, accepting them as real things that control bureaucratic life. In other words, we tend to reify the bureaucracy as having a life of its own.

Peter Berger and Thomas Luckmann illustrate reification as the process whereby human beings so lose consciousness of their potential—and their past—as creators of society that they treat a social institution as if it had a life of its own, above and beyond human control (1968, p. 89; also see Gabel, 1975). If changing the undesirable characteristics of bureaucracy is to be possible then understanding the process whereby bureaucracy is reified is of the utmost importance. None of the troublesome elements of bureaucracy apply to Weberian bureaucracy. Rules, roles, and job classifications are historically and culturally constructed as people interpret and accept them as the necessary requirements for maintaining organizational order and operation.

Complexity

The bigness and complexity of public bureaucracy have become another broadly accepted idea in public administration, although not all bureaucracies are large. As society has become more technologically and economically advanced, we have also witnessed the growth of a number of large organizations, along with the rapidly increasing expectations of citizens. In fact, in all industrialized (and postindustrialized) countries, people's lives are very much affected by large organizations, such as government agencies, schools, hospitals, business enterprises, military establishments, and prisons. Complex organizations are networks of social interaction, with socially constructed meaning and collective action (Czarniawska-Joerges, 1992).

In addition to the large size of many public organizations, the explosion of information technology and the globalization of all areas of human activity have also contributed to the expansion of networking and interaction, domestically and globally. In dealing with social and political complexity, professionals and policy analysts, however, tend to rely on "excessive rationalism," which ignores effective public deliberation and is unable to realize "failures of rationality" (Bohman, 1996, p. 157). James Bohman argues that in a public situation that involves "hypercomplexity," which means that full knowledge of the situation is impossible and that there are multiple nonlinear interdependencies between the system and its environment, rational public decision making is impossible. Because of complexity and hyperrationality,[3] public organizations tend to emphasize the technical and informational necessity of managing organizations and are thereby less open to the public and less responsive to public criticism.

Placating Citizens

In a democratic society, citizen participation in the political process is essential (Pateman, 1970; Barber, 1984). Since the late 1960s, American public administration has recognized the importance of citizen participation in federally assisted programs. Government agencies that administer programs are supposed to teach citizens how to participate in and influence the many government decisions that affect their lives, as well as to improve government efficiency at all levels.

Unfortunately, although many administrators view citizen participation as an element of democratic administration, they are more interested in placating citizens than in taking citizens' ideas seriously. Government officials and professionals often see citizen involvement (or citizen governance) as "threatening to their interests" (Box, 1998, p. 157). Because bureaucracies at the federal and state levels are so large and complicated, ordinary citizens are not commonly involved in national or state government policy processes. Because of this lack of participatory opportunity in the policy process, more and more citizens are now questioning the effectiveness and competence of policy makers and public administrators. Because citizens are particularly conscious of political issues that affect their lives, administrators often try to influence the attitudes of interest groups and individual citizens. At the same time, public bureaucracies at the local level have become more sensitive to citizen involvement.

Although the idea of citizen participation in democratic countries has become increasingly important, many non-Western countries still control citizen movement by, for example, legally restricting the formation of NGOs. Even in Japanese public administration, although the internal administrative process seems to be more participatory than that of the United States, and many important decisions are made by Gacho (Japanese for "department heads") with the involvement of employees, status-oriented Japanese bureaucrats are less open to citizens' ideas (Muramatsu, 1997; Jun and Muto, 1995).

Dualistic Thinking

Dualistic thinking is still common in public administration. As I discuss in chapter 2, managerially oriented administration has a tendency to separate the public from the governing, or administrative, process. For example, the new public management movement of the 1980s and 1990s emphasized the need for providing efficient services to customers ("citizens as customers"), assuming that public administrators were the active agents, serving clientele. Serving the public efficiently is paramount, and yet in order to improve services, administrators also need to work with citizens. The citizens are the "owners of government" and, as such, have the right and the obligation to question and inform administrators about ways of improving their governance and services (Schachter, 1997). Citizens should be encouraged to be critical and active human beings, not passive recipients of government services. Dualism is also evident in the study of public administration, most conspicuously in its epistemological and methodological approaches, which pit functionalist epistemology against interpretive epistemology, empirical and quantitative research against human science and qualitative research, and objective reality against subjective reality.

Any serious student of mainstream public administration needs to realize its limitation and develop the organizational capacity to overcome those limits, possibly by facilitating the democratic and participatory process of governance. Social and administrative phenomena are so complex that the current practice of rigid bureaucracy, in which most decisions are made at the top, is inadequate, in that it does not reflect the complexity of socioeconomic, political, or human contexts. Furthermore, the dominant emphasis on the structural and functional necessity of administration grossly undermines the importance of understanding the problems and experiences of people throughout the organization, the community, and the world.

SOCIAL CONSTRUCTION IN A DEMOCRATIC CONTEXT

In this book, I introduce a fresh perspective on the study and understanding of public administration by depicting it in a large social and global context. To broaden our perspective, I apply other people's ideas largely from other academic disciplines put into my framework and into my interpretation in order to help students realize the value of learning new ideas that are different from those of mainstream public administration. I also attempt to explore problems of public bureaucracy and instrumental rationality that have preoccupied public administrators for a very long time. Thus, the social constructionist framework discussed throughout the book is broad in scope, covering problems of public policy, bureaucracy, administrative action, change, rigid hierarchy, and ethical responsibility.

As people engage in activities of mutual interest and coordinate their efforts, a form of social construction that entails human relationships emerges. Not all social constructions, however, are democratic social constructions. On the contrary, most constructions in government are either political, involving pluralistic, exclusionary politics and an autocratic attitude on the part of top executives and managers toward people at the lower echelon of bureaucracy, or they are rational-economic and technical with experts sharing scientific and analytical interests. In this book, the democratic nature of social construction is discussed as a critique of the prevalent modes of construction. Democratic social construction is grounded in the idea of multiple actors sharing, learning, deliberating, and contesting. This type of social construction provides a new perspective on public administration, distinguishing it from current practice by relating it to broad political, social, and cultural contexts. It goes beyond the limitations of modern (and traditional) public administration by emphasizing the views of critical modernism and even embracing fragmented ideas of postmodernism in light of a global perspective.

Through social construction, we shape our social (and administrative) world. Thus social construction is a framework for transforming reality, rather than explaining how bureaucracy works in a historical, legal, or political context or promoting new management strategies in order to improve organizational efficiency. The following is a synopsis of the social constructionist approach and its relevance to public administration. A conceptual exploration of this approach and examples of its application are discussed throughout the rest of the book.

My first assumption is that we should reflect critically on the accomplishments of policies and administration in the twentieth century and the limitations of the theories and methods that are the foundation of modern public management. We need to explore the possibilities of reconstructing public administration in the twenty-first century, based on the lessons that we have learned from the past. Administrative ideas such as efficiency, functional rationality, hierarchical governing, and the role of experts, which may have been appropriate in a time of industrial and economic development, are now constraints to the democratization of public service, that is, to working with the people, realizing their values and needs, and helping them to self-govern. Thus public administration should face its critical function of examining the past and the present and actively facilitate the process of constructing policies and action strategies through public engagement with the enlarged role of public administrators.

Perhaps the essential idea of social construction is the process of reality construction. In everyday administration, we do not question what reality is or what we perceive reality to be. The inquiry into the relationship between people and reality raises the ontological issue[4] of people's existence in the organizational world. We have a tendency to define and interpret the situation according to our experience by applying a stock of knowledge and do not realize that our experience and knowledge may be the "result of social construction" (Holzner, 1968, p. 1). In organizational and social situations, how reality is interpreted and defined affects our course of action. Because perception is largely influenced by administrators' personal interests, needs, and past experiences, the way that situations are viewed will vary from individual to individual: our view of reality is subjective.[5] The question is, how can we come to a common understanding of reality or a social situation, that is, to a shared view of the division between self and significant others, the division between self and the social world? In the social construction of reality, the concepts of both 'reality' and 'objectivity'[6] are constructed according to the intersubjective experiences of the actors in a shared world. The shared consciousnesses of relevant actors can eventually provide a common ground for identifying and defining the nature of a particular problem. By sharing their thoughts and experiences, participants begin to give structure and meaning to issues that were previously incomprehensible. This process forms the basis for an exploration of possible solutions to problems and an evaluation of possibilities as they develop.

One challenging alternative is the enhancement of public administration, linking it closely with the public both nationally and globally. Today the world has become so interdependent and interconnected that nation-states increasingly depend on one another economically, politically, and technologically (Mulgan, 1997). More important, the connectedness between citizens and government and among people globally through economic exchanges, media, the Internet, e-government, and networking has greatly increased, allowing people to choose from a wider variety of options. Face-to-face interaction and collaboration among people, however, has not improved; thus the social constructionist approach aims to help people develop relationships in order to share their experiences and interests, learn from one another, and work together on common agendas. Executives, managers, and professionals can be far more effective when a diverse group of people is involved in solving nonroutine and difficult problems. In addition, citizen groups appreciate administrators when administrators facilitate the process of making connections among citizens and helping citizens explore possibilities of effective self-governance.

The social constructionist approach emphasizes a process of deliberation, dialogue, and discourse, and argumentation as people discuss issues and problems (Bohman, 1996; Dryzek, 2000; Fischer and Forester, 1993; Forester, 1999; Guttmann and Thompson, 2004; Hajer and Wagenaar, 2003). In the literature on interpretive policy analysis, deliberative democracy, and participatory planning, the process is grounded in social practice, which stresses that people work, learn, and act together through sharing their knowledge, stories, agreements and disagreements regarding the issues and problems at hand. In this deliberative process it is crucial to minimize hierarchical relationships, work toward horizontal collaboration, and promote communicative action and intersubjective understanding.

Finally, social construction is practiced more effectively in decentralized organizational units or in local government than in centralized management. Centralized governing tends to limit the participation of people in decision making; decentralized governing offers a possibility for nonhierarchical and collaborative forms of governance by linking organizational units and people through open interaction, dialogue, and the sharing of socially distributed knowledge. Although arguments are often made against decentralization and citizen participation, citing their fragmented nature, current trends suggest that democratic social construction offers the potential to improve public services and develop a more responsive public administration.

DIALECTICAL POSSIBILITIES

This book is also about the divisions in administrative theory today and how to weave disparate concepts and ideas into a useful conceptual framework by exposing the interdependence of different perspectives in order to see the totality of public administration. I attempt to help the reader understand the concepts and ideas of dialectic; the relationships among the individual, the organization, society, and the world; each entity in its multitude of contradictory relationships; and the consequent implications for the coexistence of opposing elements. Hegel's discussion of "master and slave" in his book *Phenomenology of Mind* provides an example of dialectical thinking. The master according to Hegel is independent and therefore enjoys life; the slave is dependent, so he or she does not partake in enjoyment, but instead carries the load of labor. The master's identity comes to depend upon the slave, whereas the slave, through labor, gains consciousness and thus independence. Each side can be described in an unambiguous fashion. Although this discussion is abstract, this dependency in authority relationships may be found in many bureaucratic organizations. This dialectical analysis presents the contradictions inherent in the activities of public administration.

The conceptual and practical tools that are germane to the improvement of public organizations can be found in various management approaches. Each approach has its own merits, and each has its own inadequacies in explaining and understanding the social world and the operations of public organizations. In this book, I first critique the dualistic approach to administration and the individual, and the effect of this approach on administrative theory and practice. Dualistic thinking can be seen in a number of administrative theories: the functionalist or the interpretive perspective, positivism or antipositivism, and objectivity or subjectivity. Second, I discuss the meaning of the self and how organizational members share their experiences and mutually learn how to confront personal and organizational issues.

Third, I explore the task of reconceptualizing opposing perspectives in light of a dialectical alternative: the social constructionist approach. Conceptualizing, or theorizing, is a social production in which a theorist, researcher, or practitioner reflexively generates ideas and knowledge through interaction with individuals in a social setting. This is different from deductive theorizing, in which a practitioner is guided by a set of rules. These rules specify ways that the researcher accomplishes self-conscious activity. The social construction of public administration helps us go beyond one-dimensional thinking and consider the possibility of a critical synthesis of seemingly polarized, contradictory perspectives. I do not assume that every issue is socially constructed or can be dialectically resolved. Because each theory or paradigmatic perspective is based on a set of assumptions about the social world, theoretical integration is difficult if not impossible. However, as we engage in a critical examination of each theoretical perspective, we may gain new ideas by avoiding its pitfalls. But current public administration practice tends to rely on one learned frame—an institutional, structural, functional, or political perspective—rather than to use multiple frames or to critically synthesize frames. In a time when many citizens see government as their protector against terrorism, questioning the role of government, emphasizing alternative approaches, or demanding the participation of people in the policy-making process is not important to voters. In the future, however, if policy makers want to promote policy agendas, and public administrators are eager to improve the administrative process, then they will have to find ways of working with a broad spectrum of people who have different ideas and theoretical perspectives.

Because each methodological perspective offers both advantages and disadvantages, different approaches are necessary for advancing theoretical and practical knowledge. At the same time, however, there is the problem of excluding important elements of other areas of social phenomena because a particular theory or frame encompasses only those aspects that lie within its theoretical boundary. But as we engage in social interaction and discourse about the strengths and weaknesses of each perspective, we begin to see what is problematic and what is possible. Furthermore, as one political scientist points out, "[A public administration] that wants to produce valid knowledge needs many knowledge regimes, and the different voices that women and minorities are bringing" (Rudolph, 2002, p. 195). In other words, the field of public administration needs to generate broad social knowledge based on many voices, including the voices of the members of marginalized groups.

Throughout this book, I focus on the importance of interpretive and critical social theory approaches without stressing a functional, structural, conservative communitarian, or rational approach. The interpretive and critical perspectives on social construction are most relevant to understand the problems and processes of human and organizational activities. I try to reconcile the need for organizational order and stability with the social construction of reality and the flexibility that are common characteristics of social phenomena in contemporary society. I would like to see the significance of humanistic and liberal thought reflected in the study of public administration, not pushed aside by a mainstream notion of pragmatism.

LEARNING FROM A CROSS-CULTURAL PERSPECTIVE

In the course of this exploration of change, other important themes emerge. For example, the book explores the sociocultural and political aspects of change and the influences that comparative, transformational, and global changes have had on the understanding of public administration and contemporary public organization in various countries. I also relate my arguments to modern and functionalist concepts in order to compare and contrast them with democratic and late (or critical) modern perspectives. Because public administration in many countries is engaged in reform and change projects, such as governmental reorganization, reinventing government, performance measurement, improvement of client services, and democratization, high-level executives push their people to comply with management-driven goals of change and reform. These goals often exist in remarkable contrast with the concepts of participatory administration and democratic governance. Therefore, in this book, I urge public administrators to reexamine the meaning of public administration and to reconsider the need for reflecting on the values and experiences of people both within and outside of large organizations. Today's public administrators and mainstream public administration scholars are visibly committed to institutional and functional solutions to problems of policy, administration, and human cooperation. Despite their intention to improve institutional processes and services, however, most change efforts have not had a sustainable impact.

Public administrators in the East and the West accept that any radical changes in organizations must be supported by the power and authority of executives and managers, whose influence dominates the politics, economics, and processes of governing organizations. Those at the top must also collaborate with the people who work for them, as well as involve citizens in the policy process. Thus ongoing interaction and discourse between the people at the top and the people below them are vital. Those in management who are not willing to empower people below them will continue to exercise their organizational power to control the process. I believe, however, that any innovation originating from top management will be difficult to implement, unless the members of organizations and citizens in the community appreciate the meaning of the change and are committed to the process of change. It is also true that any idea for change initiated by the people from below is unlikely to bear fruit unless those in authority are receptive to it. This implies that the issues of participation in and resistance to development and change must be critically examined, particularly by the people who will be affected by the change. Those projects that are successfully implemented tend to be ones on which people collaborate, that is to say, projects that are broadly understood and whose participants share a purpose, share goals, and share action strategies.

This book introduces students of public administration to examples from different countries to illustrate theoretical and practical problems of designing and implementing public policy as well as transforming organizations. I also emphasize the critical application of theories and knowledge to different cultural contexts. Because most texts and articles on administrative theory or organization theory address the issues of public administration in the West, their concepts and ideas should be critically examined before they are applied to a cross-national context. I have two concerns here. First, when a foreign student or scholar visits the United States or another Western country for study or research, he or she is interested in learning contemporary approaches to management and policy analysis. Upon returning home, the student or scholar is eager to use what he or she has learned by imparting this newly acquired knowledge to students or applying it to governmental, business, or social problems. In most cases, however, Western models cannot be readily applied to indigenous conditions, due to political, administrative, cultural, or historical differences. The most common tendency for non-Western academics and practitioners is to transform the techniques of rational-comprehensive planning, budgeting and finance, performance measurement, and new public management into their administrative setting. In most cases, the use of a Western model results in complete failure and produces negative consequences. The application of any techniques or theories must be critically examined in the context of a particular social reality (Rosenbloom, 2002).

My second concern is that when a Western professional goes to another country to work, he or she tends to look at the problems of the host country from his or her cultural point of view. If the Western professional is to understand the complexity of politics and administrative culture, then he or she needs to interpret the indigenous problems from the local point of view, considering the hidden dimensions of socioeconomic and political operations. As we approach another culture, we often attempt to explain and understand it through the application of our established categories and mental frames, which are derived from our past experiences. But because each society has developed a language, categories, procedures, and roles through its own process of social construction, ideas and frames developed in one country are not necessarily acceptable to people in another cultural context. To understand the reality of other administrative cultures and the experiences of strangers, we must try to understand their reality from their own point of view. If we impose our own frame on them, then we are likely to get descriptions of reality that only fits into our established categories.

For example, the employee performance criteria used in many U.S. government agencies might not work if they were applied to administration in Japan or South Korea. Both of these Asian countries have begun to adopt performance evaluation systems. But performance measurements used by the U.S. federal government emphasize results and face numerous problems, such as methods used, the criteria for measurement, reliability, objectivity, and trust in people. This stands in direct contrast to the administrative cultures of Japan and South Korea, both of which value employees for their willingness to work with others and their commitment to assigned tasks. This process is valued particularly in Japanese administration in order to accomplish organizational goals. If we public administrators consider results to be the primary goal, then we will miss out on significant tacit knowledge that is indispensable to an understanding of policy implementation in foreign cultures.

The bracketing of our own biases[7] could help us understand the experiences of people in other cultures. Complete bracketing of presuppositions regarding other cultures and other people, as presented by Edmund Husserl (1975), is a difficult task. Nonetheless, because many aspects of the social world are not easily subject to causal explanation—

are not obvious—we need to engage in the task of seeing, describing, explaining, and understanding experiences in the context of the world in which others live (Jun, 1986, pp. 71–73).

To understand the hidden aspects of administrative culture, I attempt to bring out some similarities and differences in Eastern and Western views on the self, human relationships, and social reality by drawing on philosophical ideas and administrative traditions. For example, Eastern thoughts, such as Buddhism, Confucianism, Hinduism, and Taoism, are devoted to the development of the self, authority relationships, and our relationship to the nature. The prevalent view of the self in the West tends to value individuals' self-interest. Both Eastern and Western thoughts, however, are concerned with ways of dealing with conflicts, opposites, and contradiction. Although there is a conceptual difference between the Lao Tze's view of polarity and the Hegelian dialectic, we may be able to link Eastern and Western ideas in order to develop constructive possibilities. Western synthesis happens when two opposing things combine to make a synthesis. The Eastern perspective sees the two sides as already connected. A common concern between these two views is the importance of mutual arising and going beyond duality. This discussion is further explored in chapters 8 and 10.

THE ORIENTATION OF THIS BOOK

In this book, reconstructing the grounds of the various beliefs and positions, I discuss supporting arguments and counterarguments associated with different theoretical perspectives. I am interested in a critical evaluation of these views, as well as constructive ways of approaching problems and issues. The underlying theme of this book is that an understanding of public administration ideas requires a broad and critical attitude with regard to the theory and practice of mainstream public administration. My approaches can be characterized as self-consciously value laden and normative, rather than nominally value free and descriptive. Such an orientation involves a contextual analysis of public administration theories and ideas—an analysis that penetrates to the underlying values and image of public administration that are presupposed and reinforced. Such interpretive and critical approaches go beyond the reified appearance of ideas and concepts, revealing their social, historical, and cultural contexts. In this way, it is possible to evaluate the relevance of administrative ideas to administrative settings and complex reality, rather than relying on a blind empiricism or a rational analysis of policy and administration.

My exposition in this book is intended to reveal idiosyncratic characteristics of administrative cultures in different countries as well as to provide my own interpretation of the problems of various change efforts designed to improve public institutions. Furthermore, my subjectively theoretical slant is toward a comparative, interpretive, and critical analysis of public administration, particularly public administration and policy in the East and the West. I apply phenomenological, interpretive, and critical theory perspectives to the social constructionist framework, but I do not provide an overview of the history or various theoretical traditions of this framework. I discuss them only in the context of comparing and contrasting them with my arguments.

The phenomenological and critical theory perspectives in particular have led my interest in the concept of social construction as an alternative perspective that is dialectical and interactive in studying complex issues of public administration. I discuss other administrative theories, such as incrementalism, rational choice theory, and management theories, for the purpose of comparing and contrasting theoretical positions on the explanation and understanding of social phenomena. Ideas of postmodernism challenge our thought patterns; unfortunately, they tend to confuse students of public administration because of obscure language. In addition, I find that the lack of constructive suggestions and somewhat negative implications of postmodern arguments are not always helpful to either students or practitioners. Nonetheless, ideas such as deconstruction, fragmentation, difference, critical reflexivity, and decentering the self help us critically examine the reified and centralized operations of public administration as well as to understand the changing nature of multicultural society.

Perhaps my most important task is to convey abstract concepts and philosophical ideas to students of public administration and organization theory so that they see the possibility of applying interpretive and critical theories in order to better understand public administration and the changing responsibilities of public administrators. I want to convey these subjectively and dialectically oriented perspectives to students and academics who are unfamiliar with or who reject the importance of, interpretive and critical understanding, as well as to those who are familiar with, or who are profoundly interested in learning about, other ways of knowing.

This book may be of special interest to those who are beginning to feel some tension and disillusionment about the popular approaches used in mainstream public policy and administration, as recently manifested in new public management, public choice, rational policy analysis, reinventing government, performance management, and result-oriented administration. It may be stimulating to those who are seeking a broader understanding of the social, political, and cultural contexts of public administration. It is most appropriate for courses in theory of public administration, administrative theory, organization theory, or a capstone class in public administration; it is also appropriate for other public administration courses at the upper undergraduate and graduate levels.

Thus the purpose of this book is to provide a conceptual guided tour of public administration without deeply delving into the history and the legal context of U.S. public administration. It focuses on the dialectical processes and interactions between public administration and the public, between the individual and public administration, and between administration and the social world. I hope that its contents are applicable to both Western and non-Western countries as students and academics search for a broader conceptual frame that will help them understand their responsibilities to the public, to society, and to the world.

CHAPTER 2

The Changing Context of Public Administration

The primary objective of this chapter is to briefly explore the successes and the failures of public administration in the twentieth century and their lessons for the new century. The conditions of political, socioeconomic, and cultural contexts have greatly contributed to the growth of public institutions and the scope of public policies. My purpose here is not to review historical developments in detail but rather to show how past policies and administration have generated unanticipated consequences and how they can contribute to our present understanding of today's problems, as well as provide useful lessons for improving and innovating public administration. One important lesson for coming decades is that the concept of 'public administration' should be broadened by relating it more actively to public participation and social relations to seek public input to policy making, implementation, and problem solving.

UNANTICIPATED CONSEQUENCES IN THE TWENTIETH CENTURY

The twentieth century was a time of enormous progress in science and technology, industrialization, and the growth of nation-states. For some developed countries, it may be characterized as a period of great transition from the industrial era to the postindustrial era, or from the modern period to the so-called postmodern period. The transition from an agrarian economy to an industrial economy is, of course, still a struggle for most non-Western countries. Since the 1990s, economic globalization has further contributed to market rationality and competition, which is a basic characteristic of global free trade: it maximizes the economic gains of each country but ignores the price paid in human suffering.

Both industrial and postindustrial countries in the twentieth century and today have emphasized rational, scientific, and technocratic activities because these have led to discoveries, increased production, bigger profits, and a higher standard of living for an everincreasing portion of the world's population. The emphasis on rationalism has inevitably conditioned our perceptions of the world. Now the logic of science and technology is the dominant force in our lives. This way of thinking is so omnipresent that we fail to recognize that it permeates everything we do: how we communicate; how we travel; the shape, style, and goals of our organizations; our aspirations; our perceptual processes; our worldviews; the television that we watch; and even our human interactions. The very way that our minds work is affected by these values. Our contemporary civilization is so much the product of the technological revolution of the twentieth century that we barely sense that any other perspectives or values exist—nor can we easily imagine life without rationalistic-linear thinking or the physical products of the technological revolution. Moreover, as industrialized societies become more materialistically oriented, people become more reluctant to ask broad philosophical questions, such as questions about values, relationships, dialogue, distrust and trust, equity, and democratic governance.

To keep up with industrialization and the political and economic crises of the twentieth century, the field of public administration focused much of its efforts on the development of management and professional capability, applying an organizational approach that emphasized efficiency and rationality. This organizational (or management) approach, however sincere, represented either the status quo or only incremental changes in policies designed by policy makers and top administrators, which too often proved to be outmoded, unresponsive, or ineffective in resolving political or societal dilemmas. The strong management emphasis assigned more responsibility to the top echelon of complex organizations, which ensured institutional domination over the people below. Management adopted instrumental and rational approaches to administrative reform and organizational changes in order to improve efficiency and productivity (Jun, 2002, xii–xvii).

There were many unanticipated consequences of development and progress that were negative, such as inequity, injustice, environmental disasters, wars, holocaust, and hunger. Major changes were brought about not only through the active role of government—although there were many side effects of government intervention—but also through the collaboration of the people in the construction of socially viable alternatives. Many centralized projects, such as the New Deal programs during the 1930s and the War on Poverty programs in the 1960s in the United States and many developmental projects in industrializing countries, are examples of how projects can be implemented under the guidance of the national government, in cooperation with multiple actors representing different levels of society. Although human actions occurred in a context of social and intergovernmental relations, the relationships within the frame of centralized planning were, by and large, vertical and manipulative in the sense that policy makers and bureaucrats pressured local people to participate in the implementation of national policies and projects. Without broad participation, government officials could not have accomplished projects. Numerous successes and failures may be largely construed as the social construction among higher level policy makers, professionals, administrators, private organizations, and citizens. And yet the ideas emphasized by various scholars, such as people-centered development, citizen governance, public deliberation, participatory democracy, and the construction of social reality, were neither widely realized nor developed into useful theoretical frames as we began the new century. Instead, administrators and managers of government agencies continued to play the dominant role in governing society, controlling the processes of policy making, designing alternatives, mobilizing people, and performance measurement by relying excessively on instrumental and technical solutions to problem solving and change. As Kenneth Gergen points out, "When the world turns instrumental, no one can be trusted" (1999, p. 18).

The Failure of Government Programs

A problem that was once solved may create new problems due to changing circumstances. Russell Ackoff's example of the problem of private transportation illustrates this point: one may solve a problem of getting to work by purchasing an automobile, but having a car presents some new problems, such as obtaining insurance, maintenance, finding parking places, and so on. Therefore, in order to avoid undesirable consequences, he or she needs to anticipate critically future problems (1978, pp. 189–93).

The most puzzling aspect of public problem solving is that because of the diverse nature of the public, few complex problems remain solved. Although some solutions accomplish anticipated consequences, others tend to produce unanticipated negative consequences, many of which are as severe as and as enigmatic as the original problem. Certain unintended negative consequences of public policy formulation and implementation are numerous throughout the world. In the early stages of development in Japan, Korea, and Taiwan, for example, national government played a key role in promoting rapid economic development. But centralized planning continued for several decades, and local governments were not able to develop a self-governing capability. National policies are implemented through the cooperation of local jurisdictions: civil servants and citizens at the provincial, county, city, town, and village levels react to the orders of the national government. They are not given the opportunity, autonomy, or freedom to develop local financial capability or to concentrate on local needs or interests.

The paradoxes of centralized government present various tensions between efficiency and public participation, honest government and corruption, conflict and loyalty, national and local development, and a free market and civil society. In the case of public bureaucracies in Korea and Japan, the central government exercised control over policy making, planning, and allocating financial resources for several decades after World War II. Although Japan began the process of improving local autonomy much earlier than Korea, because of the role of strong national bureaucracies in both countries, local governments and bureaucrats still struggle to govern autonomously. This phenomenon is more conspicuous in Korea, because local governments lack the financial means necessary to govern themselves.

In the United States, for instance, the social welfare issue has been a sticky policy dilemma since 1935. A seemingly useful social welfare program such as Aid to Families with Dependent Children (AFDC) generated many enduring administrative problems, such as overpayment errors, escalating costs, fraud, an intergenerational cycle of welfare dependency, and an increasing number of recipients, all of which are subject to continuous (and ineffective) sets of solutions. Until 1996, AFDC was the nation's oldest and largest welfare program, guaranteeing cash benefits for poor families. Recipients also automatically qualified for food stamps and health insurance. With the widespread impetus for welfare reform in 1996, President Bill Clinton abolished AFDC, changing the program to Temporary Assistance to Needy Families. Most welfare benefit programs have now shifted to the states. The local government receives a block grant and is responsible for devising welfare programs and controlling welfare costs. More authority is granted to state governments in order to encourage innovation in welfare programs, job training, and job search assistance. Local governments must deny welfare benefits to noncitizens, and there is a two-year time limit for recipients who are able-bodied and childless. Job training programs, however, have so far had little success. At the time of this writing, there are few jobs to be had, particularly for minimally skilled workers. For example, in the year 2002, fifty-eight counties in California had more job seekers than jobs. Even the most richly funded job-training programs have had only modest success in helping mothers work their way off welfare; none has had any proven success with unwed teenage mothers, the core of long-term recipients; and paradoxically, welfare reforms have not saved money. For example, when welfare mothers are forced to take full-time jobs, if there is no one to care for their children, the government subsidizes day care services for these women and their children. The recent studies on the 1996 welfare reform, however, seem to produce some positive effects on family structure and children, moving welfare recipients to work, hard-to-serve populations, immigrants, and racial and ethnic groups, but long-term consequences are still too early to predict (Weil and Finegold, 2002).

Another disastrous example of social welfare in the United States is public housing programs; these programs were based on rational decisions and political expediency. During the first Franklin D. Roosevelt administration (1933–1937), the federal government assumed a major role in the development of public housing by providing jobs, clearing up slums, providing inexpensive housing for the poor, and helping the construction industry. The U.S. housing policy since 1933 has been described as the accumulation of "mindless incrementalism" (Meehan, 1979). Many significant legislative changes have been made. With the passage of the 1937 Housing Act, the federal government undertook major responsibility for constructing numerous housing projects, allocating resources for new projects, budgeting, auditing, and monitoring operations. However, housing management was left to local housing authorities. Housing authorities at local levels tended to consist of conservative, middle-class people, including businesspeople, lawyers, and realtors (largely white men). Local authorities had a voice in selecting housing location, architectural design, project size, and facility staffing. They were also responsible for such daily operations as maintenance, tenant selection, repairs, legal action against tenants, staffing, and general administrative matters.

Housing programs were targeted at very low-income populations, and the maintenance of buildings was totally dependent on rental income. Most projects were large high-rise apartments, poorly designed and located, badly managed, and built for occupancy exclusively by the poor. When rising costs led to higher rents, many poor tenants became unable to meet their payments. Housing authorities, however, could not evict and replace tenants, because the housing had deteriorated beyond repair. These apartments, with their leaking roofs, broken water pipes and windows, and piled-up garbage, became a target for vandalism; often, they were finally abandoned.

Another cause for urban ruin was the inefficient administration of the Federal Housing Authority (FHA). Administrators and staff personnel were inexperienced in handling housing programs. Corrupt officials helped contractors, large speculators, and urban redevelopers with mortgage and real estate interests. In the spring of 1972, George Romney, then U.S. secretary of Housing and Urban Development, finally stopped the subsidized mortgage interest program for the urban poor, although the poor were not the abusers. By late 1972, between 240,000 and 250,000 units were foreclosed upon. Detroit alone had about 25,000 units in default. Bryan Boyer argues that when we consider the foreclosures, defaults, interest subsidies, and tax breaks for the rich, "we are talking about a $70 billion slum," with the federal government being a slum landlord. By 1975, the federal housing program had, without a doubt, failed, and many buildings were bulldozed (1973, pp. 6–8). So far, every study on public housing indicates that many of the federal housing projects for the past half-century have failed, not because of the nature of the programs themselves, but because of administrative incompetence in solving fiscal deficiencies, correcting administrative mistakes, anticipating implementation problems at the local level, and most of all, ignoring the problems of poor tenants.

High-rise apartments built in the 1950s and 1960s are symbols of America's urban policy failures. However, units built in the 1940s, low-rise town houses and garden apartments, are still decent living quarters for many since the 1970s; these housing projects have been on a small scale, having buildings with attractive landscaping and open space.

Unanticipated Consequences of Societal Successes

Perhaps the easiest way to understand unanticipated consequences is to look at various accomplishments of our technological society. Certainly, at societal and institutional levels, the impact of unintended consequences due to technological advancement is diffused and difficult to evaluate because a new consequence is often connected to other issues. Table 1.1 is a modification of a list developed by Willis W. Harman. He argues that unanticipated consequences that are negative are ultimately unsolvable within our present worldview because their origin and accumulation lie in the very success of that worldview (1974).

TABLE 1.1
Societal Successes and Their Unanticipated Consequences

Successes	*Unanticipated Consequences of Success*
Advances in biotechnology	Prolonged life span; regional over population; and medicineproblems of the aged; shortage of social security fund
Highly developed science	Hazard of mass destruction through nuclear or bio-logical weapons technology
Machine replacement of manual and routine labor	Exacerbated unemployment and urbanization; more service-oriented jobs
Advances in telecommunication and transportation	Increased air, noise, and land pollution; complex society, which is more vulnerable to breakdown
Internet and information technology	Digital divide; information overload; lack of privacy; gradual loss of individual rights
Efficient production system	Dehumanization of ordinary work; inability to create challenging jobs for people
Affluence	High consumerism; increased consumption of energy and goods, leading to pollution and depletion of the Earth's resources; destruction of natural environment; inequality

(continued on next page)

TABLE 1.1 *(continued)*

Successes	*Unanticipated Consequences of Success*
Satisfaction of basic needs	Worldwide revolutions of "rising expectations"; rebellion against no meaningful work; desire for freedom and full participation in society; demand for individual rights
Expanded wealth of developed nations	Increased gap between "have" and "have-not" nations; Frustration of the "revolution of rising expectations"
Centralized rational planning	Implementation problems locally; expert dominance; lack of citizen input; lack of trust
Globalization and economic growth	Growth without job in highly industrialized countries
Professionalization of management	Excessive reliance on rational analysis; lack of citizen participation; passivity of citizens; Specialization and compartmentalization; individual competition

The unanticipated consequences listed in the right column relate to societal successes in medical science, the physical sciences, industrial technology, improved production systems, economic development, and management. The rapid economic development of industrializing societies, such as Brazil, Mexico, Korea, and China, means that these societies are experiencing many contradictions and inequalities that lead to societal conflicts and unanticipated negative consequences. Ironically, most of their current problems stem directly from rapid economic growth. Thus the continued success of industrializing nations depends largely on how well they can cope with problems that are emerging from that very success. In the irresistible, fast-paced change of the global economy, many advanced countries face at least two unpleasant economic realities: economic growth does not guarantee a decreasing rate of unemployment; and restructuring companies and entire economies to make them more competitive commonly require job cuts, with those laid off often unable to find equally good jobs utilizing their present skills. Mounting concerns about complex economic and social problems require cooperation among government organizations and all sectors of society in order to develop effective ways of coping with crisis and innovating alternatives.

LESSONS FOR THE NEW CENTURY

A common source of unintended (or unanticipated) negative consequences is related to what Robert Merton calls "latent system functions" (Merton, 1957, pp. 60–84). Organization-as-system tends to focus on objective consequences: manifest functions that aim at expected behaviors, task performance, and hierarchical coordination of authority. However, an organization's ability to accomplish organizational goals is related to its ability to cope with various latent elements: subjective considerations, such as individual personalities, perceptions of clients, and employee compliance. For example, managers and staff at lower echelons of a bureaucracy do not always follow the policies and procedures ordered by headquarters. Unanticipated consequences are inevitable when employees do not behave in ways top executives and policy makers expect them to behave.

Public institutions must develop that organizational capability not only to solve problems but also to maintain and control the implementation of those solutions. Effective problem solving requires administrators to study the nature of unanticipated consequences by critically examining the original problems, theoretical assumptions, values, and goals, rather than reinforcing implementation strategies that produce anticipated results. According to Donald Schön and Chris Argyris (1978), this process requires a different mode of organizational learning, double-loop learning. This type of learning demands that the problem definition, goals, assumptions, and norms be critically reexamined in light of errors that show up in the environment.

In order to identify new problems and develop new goals, administrators must learn how to understand the successes or failures of solutions and how to develop new alternatives that have the desired socially effective impact. Continually looking at problems afresh and being willing to support creative change may help administrators to reformulate the knottiest problem, thus allowing broader and more sustainable solutions. This learning and changing process can be much more effective when many stakeholders (multiple actors) are involved, depending upon issues with which people are concerned. An issue such as sustainable community development requires the broad participation of citizens because their voices need to be reflected in the creation of a community if it is to be viable. This is social construction that relies on social processes and interactions.

In the process of implementing a solution (i.e., public policy), unanticipated consequences tend to crop up when one or more of the following occurs:

- The interpretation or understanding of an anticipated problem is inaccurate.
- The problem is conceptualized in overly simple and narrow terms. This problem is often caused by political expediency or rational analysis by experts.
- There is a mismatch between the problem and the solution.
- Conditions are inadequate for implementing a policy or decision (e.g., lack of financial resources, lack of management support, or lack of political support).
- The goals and objectives of the policy are inefficient.
- The organization is unable to foresee negative effects of the policy or decision. There is an inability to control latent functions (i.e., conflict or deviant behavior).
- Forecasting procedures are less adequate than the state of the art would allow for the problem.
- Professionals and managers play the major role in deciding the goals of change or development.
- The most important factor that leads to unanticipated consequences is lack of a public participation or cooperation.

What public administration needs in the twenty-first century is the active involvement of citizens in promoting public values (Gawthrop, 2002; King and Stivers, 1998; Box, 1998; Denhardt and Denhardt, 2003; Kettl, 2002). If we continue to rely on the powers of government and bureaucrats to impose changes on society and the world, then we will not realize the human potential of creating an appreciative system of governance in which participants take collective action to meet the challenges of public issues, such as equality, social equity, justice, inclusion, multiculturalism, participation, environmental sustainability, and the quality of life. Rather than continuing to impose politically driven or management-driven projects on people, we must design and redesign work organizations and policies for ourselves. If we critically reflect on past experiences, then we can learn, relearn, and recreate public administration.

REINTERPRETING THE MEANING OF PUBLIC ADMINISTRATION

During the past half-century in Western and newly industrializing countries (NICs), the study of public administration has developed into something of a large professional enterprise. This trend has been most noticeable in the past few decades. In the process of rapid development and modernization, public administration (particularly public administration of large bureaucracies) has emerged out of the need for more economy, efficiency, and productivity. The growing influence of public administration also attests to the spread of professionalization and management development in public service through the strengthening of educational and training programs, as well as through the development of journals and professional associations. To understand how public administration has developed throughout the years in a particular country, we must look at the increasing role of public administration in the social, political, and economic contexts of that country. For many years, public administration was concerned with the problems of society, economic development, and national defense. The impetus for expanding the functions of public administration was inevitably caused by these demands. As the role and power of large institutions grew, forces external to bureaucracy, such as citizens, came to be perceived as things, as objects that stood in the way of the design and management of development projects. Citizens and civic organizations were perceived as hindrances to governing society and developing a market economy. The public was understood to be an objective phenomenon that exists over and above the subjective reality of citizens' experiences and perceptions. When administrators perceive the social world in a reifying manner, it is difficult for them to understand the reality of citizens and community or promote the democratization of society. Furthermore, when administrators objectify reality without including the public, particularly of nongovernmental organizations (NGOs) and citizens who will be affected by administrative decisions, they deny citizens the ability to participate in constructing social reality; in this way, administrators underestimate the power of constructing alternatives that are grounded in social practice.

If we are to understand the truest and deepest meaning of public administration, then we must include the importance of the public in any conceptualization of it. It may be argued that anything that public administration does is for the betterment of the public. The instrumental and rational orientation of public administration, however, frequently produces unanticipated negative consequences, largely due to a poor understanding of complex social phenomena. A good understanding of these phenomena is essential if we are to gain a clear and vivid picture of the interactions between public administration and the public. Because the public is made up of networks of people, groups, and organizations, the dynamics of the interactions among them are unpredictable and constantly changing. When we examine the conceptual orientation of public administration, we see that the dominant approach to its study, as manifested in the educational curriculum, in research methods used to collect information, in administrative operations, and in reform efforts, is both intellectual and pragmatic. Mainstream public administration reflects this orientation in seeking administrative knowledge and concepts grounded in the positivistic and functionalist tradition of epistemology.[1] However, a true understanding of social reality and human relationships requires more than instrumental and rational ways of investigating human knowledge. Public administration strongly emphasizes the administrative side of public administration implementing and managing programs and functions, thus neglecting social innovation and imagination. Various case studies demonstrate that innovative community problem solving and change occur as a result of collaborative efforts among public administrators, citizens, business organizations, and civic organizations. Furthermore, the inclusion of people outside of public administration can put public administrators on the right track in carrying out their public obligations in an ethical and responsible way. To understand the complexity of society, we need to reframe our approach to the study of public administration. One of our tasks is to reexamine (and reinterpret) the concept of public administration by considering at least two important dimensions of public administration: (1) public administration is carried out in the context of the public, particularly in the context of democracy and civil society; and (2) administrative activities need to be conducted, and design choices need to be made through the participation and interaction of multiple actors who will be affected by policies or projects.

By administrative organizations I mean an organization of individual positions and roles—a group of people whose activities are designed to meet specific challenges or solve specific problems and whose behavior and actions are influenced by rules and expectations regarding each member, politics, symbols, and human relations. The public sphere, which encompasses citizens, groups, voluntary associations, and many NGOs, is the arena for entertaining problems, ideas, agreements and disagreements, and possibilities for change. Administrative organizations are socially constructed to provide services, maintain social order, and learn from the public. If public administrators are to emancipate themselves from strong administrative and management ideas in order to realize public values, then practitioners and academics alike must critically reflect on the institutionalized professional and epistemological bias of the field.

The Vulnerability of Administration

Public administration emphasizes the importance of administration over the *publicness* of public administration. The assumptions of efficiency, instrumental rationality,[2] professionalism, positivistic and functionalist epistemology, and managerial leadership are the foundation of mainstream public administration. These assumptions serve the purpose of public administration in terms of managing the functions of agencies, but they do not capture the full complexity of a phenomenon that involves the public. The rationale behind mainstream public administration's focus on economy, efficiency, performance, goal maintenance, and conflict management is that this focus helps provide better services to the public. This rationale, however, underestimates or neglects to consider the important role that citizens, businesses, NGOs, and grassroots organizations can play in identifying local problems and solving them. Citizens and organizations in civil society are viewed as passive entities: they receive governmental services and intervention.

The first and most obvious reason why public administration should manage the public is the fact that the field is professional and specialized. Because functional specialization is the bread and butter of public administration, public administrators have an organizational and a social interest in drawing attention to the advantages of specialization in ensuring organizational survival, maintaining functional autonomy, providing technical skills, and collecting information about public problems. This specialization is, unfortunately, at the expense of public involvement. It is not that public administrators have not tried to promote citizen participation and networking, but their efforts have been largely reactive ones: they have merely responded to external forces for political reasons. This phenomenon is particularly conspicuous in non-Western countries. Public administrators in those countries have obscured the importance of the public, thereby depoliticizing their activities and disengaging themselves from the public—until a crisis occurs or the public makes loud demands. In an undeveloped and chaotic society—Afghanistan and Iraq are current examples—organized institutions are necessary in order to provide basic governmental services and maintain social order. But in an early stage of development, it is important to listen to and learn from the public rather than unilaterally imposing rules and regulations. To develop a good society, it is important to promote effective and efficient administration as well as a viable civil society. As these two countries struggle to form democratic governments under the influence of the United States, the Iraqi Governing Council member and the fragile Afghan government find their own ways of bringing order and normal services to their citizens and communities. Achieving legitimacy in the eyes of citizens is a slow process of social construction.

The professional bias of public administration toward rational analysis, efficiency, planning, and goal maintenance means that public administration is largely *administration*; that is, it serves mostly to govern and manage the public. The ideas of participation, deliberation, civic engagement, citizen empowerment, and democratic process are secondary to public administration. In their everyday administrative activities, practitioners only peripherally take these ideas into consideration. Despite the argument that contemporary public management recognizes the importance of the participatory process, in actuality, management-driven projects gloss over not only the participation of employees at the local level, but also the participation of those citizens who will be affected by their activities.

The commitment of public administration to administering and governing internal and external affairs focuses on the organizational responsibility of managers and employees to efficiently perform their assigned tasks and solve problems in a professional manner. Administration governs from the top down: decision making, administrative reform, and problem solving are largely hierarchical, are not participatory, and do not disturb the status quo. Thus governing is the conventionalizing process of organizational change.[3] Managers and professionals in large bureaucracies do not think beyond their own areas of specialization. In many countries, rigid bureaucracies operate under the traditional assumptions of managing functions within their jurisdiction. Thus administrative theories focus more on describing the aspects of administration than the characteristics of the public and their influence on public institutions. Accordingly, theoretical approaches to governing and managing pay little attention to the importance of horizontal relationships, participation, access to decision making, dialogue, discourse, public deliberation, or civic engagement. Administrative theory for mainstream public administration takes these democratic elements into account only when they are seen as the means to achieve organizational ends.

A Renaissance of the Public

The word *public* has a much broader meaning than the one assigned to it by public administration practitioners and academics in governing community. Public administrators often are insensitive to the needs of the public and unaware of the possibilities for social innovation in the public sphere. This phenomenon is more conspicuous in non-Western countries. For example, because the politics in most non-Western countries do not take the needs of citizens into account, in recent years NGOs in some Asian countries, such as Japan and Korea, have emerged as an important force for societal change by critiquing government policies, politicians, and bureaucrats. In Western countries, the conception of a public entails the egalitarian quality in which "members of a public stand on an equal footing and do not regard themselves as a privileged few. In addressing each other, members of a public address each other as equals, with no claim of intrinsic authority" (Richardson, 2002, p. 184). This ideal assumes that in a multicultural and democratic society, the public should be inclusive of realizing the rights and freedom of people with diverse backgrounds.

If the recent revival of the literature of deliberative democracy, civic engagement, and participatory management teaches us anything, it is that the radical transformation of public administration is possible through the social construction of new governance processes and citizen participation in the public sphere. In order to expand the mainstream meaning of public administration, public administrators have begun to accept civic engagement on the part of citizens as well as the enhancement of civil society. Although in the 1980s and 1990s, management-driven projects for new public management and reinventing government gained considerable popularity among executives and bureaucrats in many countries, we have also witnessed a great deal of criticism from upper-level management and limitations put upon reform projects. Numerous studies have shown a discernible shift away from the conventionalizing approach to changing organizations to the renaissance (or divergent) approach, with change occurring from the bottom up and through horizontal interactions.

I am not arguing that in the near future, strong management or professionalism will wither away. In fact, current trends suggest that most large organizations will continue to operate under the assumptions of twentieth-century organizations. The current emphasis in the U.S. federal government on performance measurement, performance budgeting, and management use of human capital confirms the increasing role of management. The opposite trend, however, is also gaining popularity. This more participatory trend offers exciting possibilities: many organizations are actively transforming structures and processes in ways that construct meaningful community. This transformation is influenced by the critical role played by citizens, NGOs, grassroots organizations, and associations that represent civil society. Civil society is alive and vital, and it, not government and not business, plays the major role in creating democratic community. What is the evidence for my optimism? Following is a list of some significant changes that have occurred in the public sphere:

- Critical citizens are recognizing that the democratic process, the use of democratic means, is the best way to strengthen democratic institutions.

- Effective and responsive government is realizing that citizens are "the beginning point of *public* and that citizen influence and participation are essential to effective public policies and programs" (O'Connell, 1999).
- Policy deliberations are increasingly open to the public (Bohman, 1996; Richardson, 2002; Dryzek, 2000).
- Although the majority of citizens may not be inclined to participate in community problem solving, many good citizens do want to engage in public deliberation. Participation in deliberation, citizens are discovering, has not only an instrumental value of public policy making but also an intrinsic value to the individuals (Christiano, 1997; Guttman and Thompson, 2004).
- Local citizens are particularly interested in critical discourse concerning issues of community planning, sustainable development, and local democratic governance.
- Local forces for critiquing the assumptions of public management are helping people to seek democratic alternatives.
- Many good citizens are concerned with global issues, such as economic globalization, sustainable development, human rights, global warming, hunger, and pollution.
- Active networking without a strong center of authority is contributing to networking participants, increased awareness of problems and the development of horizontal relationships.
- Empirical evidence on civil society indicates that a country with a strong democracy is likely to have active civic republicanism.
- Technological innovations are not only informing people in remote areas about world changes but also serving as vehicles through which people can connect, sharing their ideas and experiences.

The preceding trends suggest profound implications for the future of public administration and administrative theory, as well as the possibility of exploring alternatives in the public sphere. I discuss trends just mentioned in different chapters in the book. Although these indicators might be proven by collecting empirical evidence, the normative implications for the changing responsibility of public administration and even a new way of conceptualizing the study and purpose of public administration are what is most important. Considering the rapid transformation of domestic and global politics, along with democratic changes, we can expect that the role of the strong administrative state in many postmodern societies will decline. At the same time, we can also anticipate that in less industrialized and developing countries, special emphasis will be placed on building strong government, emphasizing administrative centralization and efficiency, and meeting basic public services. Development experimentation in those countries because of their socioeconomic and cultural conditions, however, will be different from the experiences of industrialized areas in Asia that saw periods of authoritarian and undemocratic governance, with the growth of civil society.

DIALECTIC IN ADMINISTRATIVE ACTION

Although public administration and the public exist in different social spaces, if public administration does not relate to the public, then it may serve only the goals of bureaucracy and lose any opportunity for correcting its internal limitations. Without efficient public administration, citizens are not likely to receive good services. As Frederick Mosher (1968), Emmette Redford (1965), and Dwight Waldo (1948) point out, without efficient administration, democracy cannot be functional. Thus it is important to realize the problem of overstating the significance of either public administration or the public, because an overstatement of administrative efficiency and the strong administrative state can result in as much reification in public administration as can a stress on the public. However, a public administration that assumes that the public can be served better when internal management is strong misses out on the transformation that can emerge in the public sphere when alternatives are constructed. This strong internal management creates the strong government and strong administration currently advocated by many Asian countries and the Scandinavian countries; it also creates an imbalance among government, business, and civil society. Public administration can no longer be understood outside of the public, and the public cannot be served well outside of efficient administration (Ventriss, 2002).

The assumed dualism between administration and the public, with public administration focusing on the instrumental, functional, and rational aspects of administration as efficient governing, has misled public administration into ignoring the dialectical relationship between the two as well as the possibility of the construction of social alternatives in the public sphere. Furthermore, in large bureaucracies, rationality grounded in instrumental thinking is never achieved, because people do not always behave rationally or predictably. This is one reason why performance measurement of programs and the use of objective and quantifiable criteria can never reveal the true causes of a project's success or failure.

In the literature of public administration, numerous attempts are made to discuss these dynamic changes by synthesizing macro and micro issues into the change process. Such efforts are manifest in the terms that the authors employ, such as *employee participation, citizen involvement, customer service, empowerment,* and *consultation.* But these words are often hollow: no corresponding action takes place. Thus the result is a reification of the social phenomenon. The language intended to describe public participation also tends to reify the phenomenon. We rely on language to represent and characterize the various aspects of the social world. To reinterpret the language used in social practice, we inevitably rely on dialogue and discourse to share the meaning of our experience.

Throughout this book, I emphasize the dialectical nature of public administration by stressing the improvement and responsibility of individuals in the administrative process, rather than the imposition of structural changes on organizational members. Without dialectical understanding, it would be difficult for administration to function, let alone develop a viable democracy. Perhaps humanly meaningful understanding, synthesis, or collaboration can occur only when an individual is able to act reflexively and critically. Marshall Dimock attempts to put the study of public administration in a philosophical perspective, arguing that public administration is more than a science and more than an art: it is a philosophy. He states the following:

> Philosophy is a body of belief and practice aimed at achieving better performance. A philosophy of administration is a thought-through and viable pattern of survival and influence for individuals and for institutions. It is good policy and good technique. But most of all it is a real integration, a blending of everything that is important. (1957, p. 1)

Dimock's goal is to integrate the administration with the individual, that is, to integrate organizational goals and objectives with social values and individual growth. To integrate many polarized elements, he insists that "people at all levels be encouraged to develop a philosophy of administration" (p. 6). Although Dimock's observation is insightful, his illustration of a philosophy of administration does not address the importance of the individual's responsibility to critically reflect upon institutional goals, structure, functions, unintended consequences, and, most of all, conflicting theoretical frames and epistemologies. Furthermore, it is very unrealistic to think that we may be able to synthesize every polarizing issue. Dimock's intent, however, is to emphasize the need for integration and the appreciation of mutuality among opposing elements.

In several chapters in the book, I emphasize the need for critical awareness of the limits of different conceptual issues and for constructing alternatives through social interactions. The assumption is that our understanding and appreciation of the ideas and experiences of others could lead to new ways to promote the public good and improve the processes of public administration. For example, some major dichotomies in studying public administration, such as theory and practice, facts and values, objectivity and subjectivity, ends and means, efficiency and effectiveness, and explanation and understanding, require a critical analysis of these seemingly opposing dimensions.

Last, among the many responsibilities of public administrators as they interact with the public is the civic obligation to facilitate the growth of civic capacity so that citizens, NGOs, associations, and community-based organizations can be actively involved in public discourse. Because potentialities in the public sphere can be further developed through relationships, participation, discourse, and deliberation, public administrators need to develop a civic consciousness and engage in collaborative action with the public so that citizens in turn develop a civic consciousness and meet their civic obligations. Through the Internet and direct contact with citizens and NGOs, public administration produces knowledge that helps us to understand public problems better. At the same time, citizens can assist policy makers and administrators to make more effective decisions and to think effectively and compassionately by engaging in public deliberation, seeking public reasons for collective action. Democracy and a strong administrative state are often viewed as mutually exclusive. The commitment to bridge these two processes of power in society has important implications for the workings of public administration. If the dialectical linkage is not realized, then the potential for utilizing people's ideas and energy will remain unrealized.

CONCLUSION

Public administration has, correctly, emphasized the importance of administration. But there is a point beyond which administration becomes a caricature of itself, with an exaggerated emphasis on administering and governing the public. Because mainstream public administration in the twentieth century was obsessed with the managerial and technical aspects of administrative operation, it did not pay much attention to broader issues, such as values, complex realities, hidden cultural and symbolic aspects of organizational life, social equity, the public good, democratic governance, or other value-laden topics. Current trends seem to indicate that the field of public administration is becoming more oriented toward managerial and professional knowledge development. For example, changing the name of the academic degree program from public administration to public management would be a commitment to increasing the scope of professionalization, power, and responsibility of public administrators. To call the program "public management" would be to emphasize the increasing role of public administrators in improving efficiency, productivity, and performance measurements of organizations. The down side of strong professional management is that it tends to perceive citizens as passive, thereby losing the opportunity to energize their potentials and self-governing ability. Enhancing the responsibility of public administrators is unquestionably important, but their new role in the coming decades should be to work with the people as well, to construct socially meaningful alternatives. To understand the unanticipated consequences of administrative action, administrators must take on the role of facilitator, involving citizens and learning from their interpretations of problems and issues through dialogue and discourse.

The "publicness" of public administration challenges the discipline to transcend its parochial focus on administration, going beyond its limits and exploring possibilities in the public sphere (Jun, 1986, pp. 27–28). Taking into account the effects of the public on administrative activity would broaden the notion of public administration beyond its governing and managing emphasis, which has been its major emphasis since the early twentieth century. We should reconstruct administrative theory to situate the public explicitly in its context in the processes of democratic governance. The public, culture, and the broader participation of organizational members and citizens are the least explored subjects of research in public administration. If public administration continues to focus on administration and management, seeing the public as having only minor importance, and if it retains a positivistic and functionalist orientation, then it will not be possible to use public administration concepts to understand the dynamics of the social interweaving and cultural constructions that people and organizations form in the public sphere. Therefore, a renaissance of public administration should situate the field in the context of the public and social relations without slighting its traditional commitment to the promotion of public services.

We are beginning a new era of democratic experience in which we will encounter new social forces and relationships. Our attention to the language, communication, discourse, culture, and local knowledge that we encounter every day gives us a way of exploring possibilities and relationships. Many times, public administration is criticized for being inefficient, bureaucratic, and insensitive to the needs of the public, underestimating the value of public participation. Public administration, however, is slowly changing in response to the wider forces in society. Effective administration from civic-minded administrators can enable citizens and civic organizations to become self-governing. Thus it is time to bring the public into the study of public administration in a rigorous way. The social construction frame, as stressed throughout this book, is perhaps the most effective approach to use in seeking public collaboration.

CHAPTER 3

The Social Constructionist Approach

In a public administration that places much emphasis on a positivistic, empirical, and bureaucratic culture, only that which provides practical results and serves management interests is taken seriously. As practicality becomes an important measure, theoretical approaches and ideas are judged in terms of their applicability to immediate issues, such as organizational efficiency, productivity, customer services, and measuring performance. As a result, those who advocate structural, functional, empirical, and rational approaches have adopted a positivistic epistemology in pursuing knowledge, establishing a causal connection between the desired ends and the means of achieving those ends. But theory or approach requires more than objective and positivistic means to deliver adequate results. When the demand for an immediate result and the practical concerns of organization are put to one side, good ideas may arise. Actors in a social situation may begin to open their minds, exploring possibilities, rather than focusing their thought, dialogue, and discourse on the intended outcome. This chapter introduces the social constructionist approach, which can help us to achieve a better understanding of ourselves and to design alternatives on the basis of this understanding. When people engage in social interaction and discourse, a practical solution may not emerge immediately, but the actors involved in the process are likely to come away with a better understanding of the problems and issues with which they are confronted. I am not stating that the social constructionist approach is not concerned with immediate results or practical solutions. In fact, as organizational members collectively discuss the problems at hand, they are more likely to discover a practical solution than a manager or a small group of experts is. In fact, a decision based on the shared knowledge of many stakeholders has a better chance for successful implementation.

THE LIMITATIONS OF THE
FUNCTIONALIST PERSPECTIVE

In recent years, there has been an inordinate amount of confusion and tension among scholars in public administration with regard to the basic presuppositions underlying different theoretical frames. Liberal theorists, who are concerned with the inadequacies of the current theoretical and management orientations, seek alternative ways of understanding the complex dimensions of public administration. Mainstream theorists, however, feel comfortable with the theoretical and management orientation, which is largely built on the epistemological perspectives of functionalism, institutionalism, systems theory, rational decision-making, public choice, pluralistic incrementalism, and contingency-management theories. The functionalist and positivistic approach was popular throughout the twentieth century; this was, perhaps, due to the powerful influence of bureaucratic institutions and their demands on people.

In terms of the scope and methods adopted by public administration academics and practitioners, the institutional, rational, or functionalist approach is the most dominant perspective. Positivistic and management-oriented thinking are particularly conspicuous in public administration research and writing. This orientation is inseparable from the tradition of strengthening the role of the administrative state within the constitutional frame, in that the responsibility of the state is to implement rules and regulations for assuring administrative efficiency, performance, and rationality in an intergovernmental context.

The positivistic and functionalist approach has been prevalent in the philosophy of public administration ever since the publication of Woodrow Wilson's article entitled "The Study of Administration" (1887). It proceeds from the assumption that administrative efficiency and productivity can be achieved through the application of the scientific method and a set of management principles, such as accounting and budget control, planning, systems analysis, the efficient allocation of organizational resources, and recently, performance measurement and result-oriented management. The functionalists put their emphasis on the institutional, structural, and functional coordination among administrative units and also on the adaptation of the organization to its environment. The decision-making process is carried out within hierarchical relationships. The positivistic and functionalist way of studying administration also assumes that because people are by nature rational and self-interested, also human motivations and behaviors are predictable and can be empirically explained by testing a set of hypotheses and variable relationships. It also assumes that external forces determine social reality and that rational explanations can be given. All we need to do is to uncover and measure the truth by determining the causal relationships that exist in objective reality. Change is seen as a linear process moving from general to specific or from theory to action and using a set of principles to induce and guide human action.

Positivism and functionalism emphasize that the characteristics of objective reality (e.g., objectified elements in an administrative culture) are taken for granted and are developed throughout the organization's history, possibly long before an individual member becomes part of it. The underlying assumption is that administrative culture is historically constituted for the individual. In the "culture-as-constituted" theory (Sahlins, 1982, pp. 35–44), administration has the following characteristics: hierarchical relationships; a collective consciousness of organizational members oriented toward goal accomplishment; symbolic process in functional coordination; organizational language, rituals, and norms of behavior; and a stable structure. Finally, the positivistic and functionalist approach as the foundation for mainstream public administration aims to explain and predict social phenomena, by generating explicit knowledge as opposed to tacit knowledge, which is qualitative and hidden.

Although the functionalist perspective has numerous shortcomings, it has become an important theoretical foundation of public administration and should not be misunderstood. In fact, a large body of administrative functions involving routine work is nevertheless maintained through the application of rules, procedures, and hierarchical relationships; organizational accountability also depends upon loyalty and obligation of organizational members particularly at the lower echelon of bureaucracy. In order to explore other ways of knowing, we need to understand the positive and negative aspects of the functionalist perspective so that we realize that what may seem to be obvious to us about managing public organizations can become problematic.

THE INTERPRETIVE, CRITICAL THEORY, AND POSTMODERN PERSPECTIVES

The social constructionist approach, as illustrated in this book, relies heavily on interpretive and critical theory on the study of public admin-istration and organization theory. The interpretive perspective is an alter-native way of understanding complex phenomena based on the points of view of organizational members, stakeholders, and citizens by focusing on their experiences, values, dialogue, and discourse and by interpreting their language and stories. Despite the strong intellectual influence of interpretive inquiry across the social sciences, it is largely liberal theorists who have a vested interest in exploring the subjective and intersubjective nature of democratic administration who carry out interpretive research in public administration. The critical theory perspective incorporates the value-oriented and socially grounded aspects of social reality by critical-ly examining the objective, value-neutral, and rational aspects of institu-tions, power, and authority. At the same time, it is critical of the subjec-tive tendency that is common in the interpretive inquiry. As a way of cri-tiquing the tradition of public administration theory, the postmodernist views are also introduced in this section. The fragmented contribution of the postmodern perspective to social construction is that it begins with the critical-reflexive task of examining the traditionally biased assump-tions and norms of public administration.

The Need for Interpretation

The interpretive approach[1] is not an explicit paradigm, a theoretical position often taken by structural and functional-oriented theories; that is to say, it does not include a set of constructs and assumptions that aims to explain and predict social phenomena. The interpretive perspective is, instead, a set of ideas and methods that helps us to understand social practices at various levels of organizational analysis. In the eyes of practitioners, the interpretive concepts do not provide practical guidelines for solving the problem that they face in their everyday work.

To understand the interpretive approach, we must realize the lim-its of a positivistic and scientific way of explaining social reality. Wilhelm Dilthey (1833–1911), a German philosopher who introduced a new method of studying society and culture, argues that there is a fundamental difference between, on the one hand, the natural sciences and, on the other hand, the humanities and social sciences in terms of the methodologies that their scholars use in investigating social phenomena. Natural science scholars attempt to explain a phenomenon by applying general laws; humanities and social science scholars try to understand a phenomenon by means of an experience of a certain sort, depending upon the object of study (Dilthey, 1961; 1977; 1996). Dilthey brings hermeneutical theory into "a philosophy of historical knowledge and the human sciences" in which the method of explaining human activity is basically psychological or intuitive (Gunnell, 1987, p. 106). Although Dilthey emphasizes the significance of understanding, Hans-Georg Gadamer (1977) is concerned with understanding meanings in terms of the values, purposes, assumptions, common sense, and objects from historical contexts that condition them. The essence of understanding is *interpreting* texts (1989, p. 252). Gadamer also claims that a misunderstanding resulting from disagreement with the text can be as important an influence as understanding an agreement in human life. His hermeneutical inquiry stresses the linguistic nature of our relationships with other people and the world, stating that "language is a medium *(eine Mitte)* where I and world meet, or rather, manifest their original belonging together" (1989, p. 474). From this, we may infer that public administrators in an organization use language as a medium in their interactions. Thus an important task for public administrators is to understand the meaning of linguistic expressions, reflecting on past and present contexts.

Edmund Husserl (1859–1938) criticizes the natural sciences (or empirical science in the social sciences) as having a "naive objectivist" (or realist) view of social reality (1973). He was particularly critical of "naturalism" (empiricism/positivism) in establishing truth in philosophical study. Husserl emphasizes the importance of understanding the "life-world," the world of ordinary, immediate experience, which is experienced by means of perception. The life-world is seen as the living and worldly horizon and is described by Husserl as the context within which we experience changing things, expectations, emotions, ideas, and so on (Husserl, 1973; Natanson, 1973). This worldly horizon, this life-world, precedes all reflection and must be understood as that which gives meaning to all other possible experiential horizons that take place within it.

Dilthey and Gadamer, as hermeneutical philosophers, and Husserl, as a phenomenological philosopher, have greatly furthered the development of the interpretive perspective. Other Western thinkers who hold an interpretive perspective include Max Weber, Martin Heidegger, Jean-Paul Sartre, Maurice Merleau-Ponty, Alfred Schutz, Harold Garfinkel, and Paul Ricoeur. They argue a difference between natural and human sciences by critiquing the presuppositions of scientific inquiry and developing new ways of understanding history, culture, language, tradition, and human phenomena in general. What makes the interpretive approach unique and particularly relevant to public administration is its constructionist stance with regard to the social world. This constructionist view emphasizes the dialectical possibilities in a nondeterministic (noncausal) way, and in such a way that goals, projects, or solutions legitimize collective action based on the sharing of ideas and experiences among participants (Schutz, 1967; Berger and Luckmann, 1967; Winch, 1958; Douglas, 1970; Garfinkel, 1967; Habermas, 1984; Ricoeur, 1991; Collin, 1997; Polkinghorne, 1983; Yanow, 1996).

The interpretive approach offers a number of ideas (or assumptions) that can help in understanding social (administrative) phenomena. First, the interpretive perspective, which is particularly grounded in phenomenology, seeks to understand and explain the social world primarily from the viewpoint of the actors in a social situation. It seeks explanation within the realm of individual consciousness and subjectivity, that is, within the frame of reference of the participants, not that of an observer of the action. It sees the social world as an emergent social process that is created by the individuals concerned. Human beings are creators of social reality. People construct meaning in the social world through social interactions. Through social interaction and the sharing of meanings, a revised (negotiated) meaning of action emerges.

Additionally, an understanding of social reality begins with an act of interpretation that, if successful, produces understanding. As Silverman points out, "The task of interpretation is to understand that which is to be interpreted. To produce an interpretation is to come up with an understanding of the interpreted" (1984, p. 21). An interpretive approach focuses on "the human capacity for making and communicating meaning" (Yanow, 1996, p. 5). With regard to an examination of administrative communication, for example, phenomenological (or hermeneutical) interpretation concerns itself with understanding the meaning of communicative experience between subjects through the act of interpreting the content of the communication and generating a meaning. Interpretation is a qualitative description in the sense that meaning can be investigated and described according to the interpreter's relationship to the text (or message). From this relationship, meaning is produced (Jun, 1997, p. 22).

Also, because an individual exists both for himself or herself and for community with others, an understanding of the intersubjective relationships that constitute all forms of organizations and community is necessary, even though the person is often in conflict with others. For example, in the workplace, an individual acts not only in his or her self-interest but must also have an association with others because he or she is not only an atomistic being, but also a social being.

Finally, interpretive theorists argue that functionalist explanations of human action fail to see the theoretical presuppositions and limitations of the positivistic and empirical epistemology. The failure lies in functionalist assumptions about persons and actions. The functionalist concept of a person assumes that a person is largely a passive and reactive object, subjected to environmental influences, such as organizational, economic, political, and social factors. Interpretive theorists' concept of the individual is that he or she is an active, purposive, and creative subject (Harmon, 1984; Silverman, 1970). The interpretive approach may be viewed as "practical" because it is always directed at or applied to some intentional objects, such as language, story, theory, thought, symbols, and various human activities. In order to increase interpretive validity, the different methods of interpretation are applied to specific situations (Hiley, et al., 1991, pp. 11–13). Interpretation, however, also faces some serious issues, such as choices among equally acceptable interpretations, misinterpretation, or misunderstanding by interpreters.

In summary, the interpretive approach seeks to understand shared (though often implicit) assumptions about why events happen as they do and how people are to act in different situations. Merleau-Ponty says, "To understand is ultimately always to construct, to constitute, to bring about here and now the synthesis of the object. Our analysis of one's own body and of perception has revealed to us a relation to the object, i.e., a significance deeper than this" (1981, pp. 428–29). To interpretive theorists, understanding the social world from the subject's point of view is fundamental to all human activity and is the means by which social life and collective action are realized.

The Need for Critical Reflection

Critical theory offers a theoretical perspective that helps us examine not only political, economic, and institutional concerns but also the humanistic, cultural, and social dimensions of complex social phenomena. Critical theory has become the focus of the interdisciplinary dialogue among scholars of all the theoretical perspectives—functionalists, structuralists, and interpretive theorists—as well as informing a broader range of social practices, such as management practice, modernization, development, environment and sustainability, globalization, and civil society in the public sphere. It has become an important intellectual force in critiquing the presuppositions of mainstream social theory. The critical perspective is also evident in the arguments advocated by poststructuralist and postmodern social theory (Kellner, 1990, p. 12). As Kellner implies, critical theory (including the original Frankfurt school) and postmodern social theory bring a multidisciplinary orientation to public administration theory, introducing perspectives from philosophy, sociology, political theory, psychology, cultural theory, political economy, and history. Critical theory makes a significant contribution to the critique of public administration (Harmon, 1986; Abel and Sementelli, 2003; Forester, 1985; Zanetti, 1997) and (not without controversy) critiques mainstream public administration theory and methods. It could do even more to promote change by offering new theoretical alternatives for transforming today's institutions as well as promoting democratic actions grounded in a collective understanding between public administration employees and citizens.

Although critical theory is not fully developed, the ideas advocated by various theorists, such as Theodore Adorno and Max Horkheimer (1979), Jürgen Habermas (1984), McCarthy (1981); and Martin Jay (1973), are directly relevant to an understanding of the problems of public administration. Public administration that is grounded in the critical theory perspective supports efforts to effect fundamental institutional change, advocating a critical synthesis of institutional issues and human value issues, subject and object, empirical-analytical science and hermeneutical (historical-interpretive) science, a value-neutral stance and a value-committed stance, and the active and passive aspects of human nature. Critical theory also rejects a qualitative distinction between subject and objects or between researcher and subjects.

Critical theory is value-critical in conducting administrative research. For example, because the selection or design of a theoretical framework and the analysis of facts are both influenced by the personal values of the researcher and ultimately objectify social reality, it is necessary to interpret the limits of theory (or hypothesis) testing and the empirical data derived from research objectively and to reexamine the supposed value neutrality (as Weber points out) critically (Weber, 1947). To this end, the interpretive perspective and the critical perspective could make significant contributions to alternative approaches to the issues of public administration. Another important aspect of critical theory is that it recognizes the strengths and limitations of multiple explanatory perspectives, critically integrating them into a broader and more inclusive interpretive framework. In this respect, critical theory offers an interpretive quality for public administration, rejecting the inhumane institutional domination of people (Schroyer, 1973) and the habitual behavior of administrators. Critical public administration understands and interprets existing behavior and actions in terms of how ethical the behavior is and how responsible the actions are. Change occurs through a dialectical process in which old and new interpretive schemes interact, resulting in a synthesis.

In summary, neither functionalist nor interpretive epistemologies provide a comprehensive view of complex social reality. Although functionalist theories focus on the influence of objective elements in administration, on the behavior and action of individuals, interpretive theories stress the understanding of reality (objective phenomena) as essentially a subjective process. Functionalist and interpretive theories may be viewed as one-dimensional administrative theories, because neither provides an adequate picture of the totality of administration (Alexander, 1982). Thus there will be little advancement of theory development if public administration is approached primarily through either the functionalist or interpretive epistemology, or if the functionalist necessity of the administrative state is justified mainly in terms of the instrumental values of maintaining administrative efficiency, order, and survival. This is not to argue that theory for legitimizing organizational survival is unimportant. But because both functionalist and interpretive theory aims to explain only part of complex administrative phenomena, each produces empirical and conceptual problems (Laudan, 1977).

Critical theory perspective provides a framework for discovering theoretical alternatives and exploring possibilities for action that are

more congruent with public problem solving and changing organizations. I would like to think that critical theory as a dialectical perspective is an alternative approach to going beyond the inadequacy of present administrative theory by liberating ourselves from a one-dimensional epistemology (or theory). Even when we are not able to achieve
a creative and critical synthesis, our reflection on opposites and conflicts among different perspectives could lead us to a heightened level
of theoretical understanding. The dialectical aspect of critical theory
such as developing intersubjectivity through communicative action
(Habermas, 1984), is a constructionist approach to understanding the
dynamic processes of public administration.

Dialectic is a process of searching for a critical synthesis among
contradictions, conflicts, and discontinuities in the social (administrative) world. It is a way of thinking about alternative possibilities by
critically examining different epistemologies, social relationships,
methods, and techniques. It is a method of dialogue (Plato) and criticism (Aristotle). As I discuss later in the book, 'dialectic' is a concept
that has a long philosophical tradition in both Eastern and Western
philosophy. Critical-dialectical analysis requires an explanation, interpretation, and understanding of opposing elements and conflicts, tangible and intangible aspects, and facts and values; it also requires a relationship between nature and human beings. The process of understanding administrative phenomena can be enriched by attempting to
resolve various opposing perspectives, such as functionalist epistemology and interpretive epistemology, positivism and antipositivism,
objectivity and subjectivity, efficiency and participation, centralization
and decentralization, stability and change, passivity and activity. When
critical synthesis is not possible, we may still gain a better understanding of our problems, differences, and social reality.

Postmodern Ideas

Throughout the history of public administration in modern times,
there has been an amazing continuity of one theoretical idea, namely,
rationalism. Extensive discussions of rationalism in institutional activities and in human action can be found in the literature of public
administration and organization theory. The fallacy of instrumental
rationality, rational discourse, and foundationlessness has been pointed
out by public administration theorists, such as O. C. McSwite (1997b),

David Farmer (1998), Charles Fox and Hugh Miller (1996), and Michael Harmon (1995). The idea of postmodernism, I like to think, provides a kind of critical reflection on administrative rationality. Of course, there have always been antirationalists in other disciplines, particularly those who critique the tradition from a postmodern perspective. Postmodernists are critical of rationalism, positivism, metanarratives, rational communication, and the centralizing tendency of administration. Antirationalists act as the countertradition. Although they have not been successful in overcoming the theoretical pitfalls of irrationalism, their skepticism and negative interpretation of the tradition of public administration is an intellectually energizing force as scholars are confronted with the task of "negating administrative-bureaucratic power" (Farmer, 1998, p. 5). Postmodernists as antirationalists are also not interested in reconstructing traditional ideas; instead they are concerned with the issues of deconstruction, multiplicity, difference, fragmentation, power relationship, and critical reflexivity. Despite the lack of a constructive effort, I am inclined to think that postmodern theorists in public administration are not arguing for irrationality but for a more adequate account of rationality by critiquing the foundational problem of public administration (McSwite, 1996).

To understand the rather fragmented ideas of postmodernism, we need to listen to the postmodernist critique of modernity (Hassard and Parker, 1993; Marsh, Caputo, and Westphal, 1992; Rosenau, P. M., 1992; Albrow, 1996; Jun and Rivera, 1997). The project of modernity, formulated in the eighteenth century by Enlightenment philosophers such as Kant, is associated with objective science, universal morality and law, and autonomous art. Modernity is associated with the Enlightenment project, in which the positivistic epistemology of the scientific method is the basis for establishing causality in explaining human behavior and in regulating social interactions. It is concerned with the role that reason may play in building a humane society. Postmodernists criticize modern priorities, such as career, office, individual responsibility, bureaucracy, humanism, egalitarianism, evaluative criteria, neutral procedures, impersonal rules, and rationality (Rosenau, 1992, pp. 4–6).

Although postmodernists have emerged as the countertradition to rationalism, they concern themselves with the problem of interpretation, such as the deconstruction and interpretation of text. Largely based on the work of Jacques Derrida (1973; 1981) and Jean-Francois

Lyotard (1984), deconstruction is a process of critical interpretation that works with a text, using its own terms and contradictions to uncover subtexts, thereby paradoxically elevating texts and lending them dynamism while denying them any final meaning. The concept of 'textuality' thus extends beyond literature: the world can be viewed as a text, and social practices, as well as interlocutions, can be viewed as narratives. Derrida also argues that whether we deal with literary text or social narrative, "the hermeneutical effort to decide among all the possible interpretations inevitably fails because of the essential undecidability of textual meaning" (Hoy, 1985, p. 54). Deconstruction as an element of postmodernism provides an alternative perspective on the functionalist grand narratives present in modern administration (Linstead, 1993). As applied to public administration, the participants (i.e., administrators and citizens) may play the active role in the deconstruction process.

Perhaps the most important contribution of postmodernist thought is its characteristic insistence on the plurality and multiplicity, as well as the diversity and difference, of human social experience. In phenomenology, this is described as recognition of the difference in the lived experiences of the reflective subject and its object (or the other). Postmodern theorists would argue that administration should be dispersed and fragmented, capable of accommodating conflict, multiplicity and difference, and decentralization and autonomy. Postmodernists, such as Jean-François Lyotard, Jacques Derrida, Jean Baudrillard, and Michel Foucault are evidently not interested in resolving issues of dispersion and fragmentation; on the contrary, they implicitly, if not explicitly, assume that fragmentation and multiplicity promote creativity.

Although most postmodern arguments seem to support pragmatism and social constructivism (Bogason, 2002, p. 70), they fall short of offering constructive alternatives for dealing with some fundamental concerns of positivists and functionalists, such as social order, authority relationships, efficiency, productivity, policy design, organizational change, and problem solving. Rather, the process of reflexive and critical questioning is the beginning of exploring possibilities of transforming institutions. This, as Richard Peterson points out, for postmodernists, "is a matter of self-conscious irony" (1996, p. 194) as they challenge authority relationships, rationality, antiadministration, and centralized modern projects. I expect that postmodern thought can be reconstructed into a force that transforms traditional institutional practices into pragmatic and culturally based alternatives by reasserting the critical role of individuals in organizations, the inclusive aspect of discourse analysis, the importance of plurality and difference, and the significance of citizen participation in the process of making public institutions more democratic.

THEORIZING THE SOCIAL CONSTRUCTIONIST APPROACH

Until this chapter, the social constructionist approach has been discussed implicitly, mostly through a discussion of opposite tendencies in public administration during the twentieth century. Why social construction? Public administration is in relationship with social reality, that is, a reality that is constituted from human ideas and interactions (Roy, 2001, p. 6). When people consider that realities are socially constructed, they accept that there is not one reality or one version of the truth. Rather there are multiple realities and truths constructed and experienced by people in their everyday interaction. By assuming that there are many possible ways to understand the nature of reality and diverse interpretations of any situation, management no longer dominates the governing process, and the experiences, ideas, and divergent views of other organizational members are valued. This is the case in many effective organizations. For example, from a social constructionist perspective, a manager thinks that he or she has the best way of solving a particular problem but that other members may have different interpretations of the same problem. The social construction of public administration concerns itself less with how policy makers and managers make certain decisions and control people in agencies and more with how people construct and attach certain meanings to their experiences and how these meanings become objectified aspects of public administration, such as rules and regulations, positions, roles, institutions, organizational acronyms, symbols, categories, and specialized tasks. These objectified elements would not exist without people's understanding and enactment of them.

The social construction of public administration acknowledges that the members of an organization create organizational realities through interaction, dialogue, and discourse; they are continually working on a sense of themselves and their surroundings in their everyday interaction and can construct alternative solutions on the basis of this understanding. Social and organizational realities are constructed, or created, by how we as humans define, understand, and interpret the world in which we live. Thus, communication must exist between and among the parties attempting to share their reality. We humans use language and dialogue to build our relationships with other people and to describe our relationships with our world. In this way, we articulate and share our understanding of the world around us and of other humans who occupy our world with us. I shall lay the framework for such understanding by providing a set of concepts that are more or less accepted by those who advocate the ideas of critical construction and democratic possibilities. The basic concepts are already introduced in various literatures in public administration and other disciplines.

Many characteristics of the social constructionist approach are discussed in the literature of participatory democracy, deliberative democracy, governance, and the sociology of knowledge (Pateman, 1970; Guttman and Thompson, 1996; Bohman, 1996; Dryzek, 2000; Berger and Luckmann, 1967; Gergen, 1999; Searle, 1995; Young, 2000; Collin, 1997; Roy, 2001). Here, I briefly introduce a set of common assumptions that are essential to the social constructionist frame, by bringing out the somewhat fragmented viewpoints of those who support constructionism.[2]

The Value of Social Knowledge

Social construction asserts that social knowledge is socially distributed everywhere in an organization, in a community, and in the world. This everyday knowledge relates to how we live our lives and make meaning in our world. It is often taken for granted because it is shared by others as a common sense we integrate into our daily actions. We communicate with other humans through our sense of knowledge; we make sense of the world around us and organize our lives within this framework of knowledge. Because knowledge is a complex and ambiguous entity, there is much controversy about that which we call "real knowledge" (knowledge grounded in a social situation) and knowledge that is other (knowledge of an objective thing). Each person's knowledge belongs to the realm of real and true knowledge, within which he or she attempts to construct a reality in which to live and relate to the world and to other people. According to Berger and Luckmann, every individual lives in a world of social knowledge, but only a few individuals concern themselves with "the theoretical interpretation of the world." They point out that "the sociology of knowledge must first of all concern itself with what people 'know' as 'reality' in their everyday, non- or pre-theoretical lives" (1967, p. 15). Social knowledge reflects social (and organizational) conditions that are in turmoil and that are diverse and changing and is also concerned with the relationship between human thought and the social context with which it arises. Thus, social knowledge is the basis for the social construction of reality.

Whereas traditional and scientific forms of knowledge are often regarded as being crucial to the efficient functioning of bureaucratic organization, an understanding of common sense or social knowledge increases both the quality and the extent of administrative activity by aiding an understanding of organizational and human problems. The more we know, the more deeply we feel; and the more we know about people and external problems, the better chance we have of understanding them and thereby making better decisions that reflect social, political, and human conditions. If we are not able to solve the differences among participants, we are, at least, able to move toward a better understanding of their conflicting positions. Increasing our understanding through sharing knowledge broadly seems to be the best way to improve an organization, both its policies and members' commitment to those policies. As we attempt to understand the complex nature of the administrative world, we are also better aware of the limits of the organization in which we work and the limits of theoretical analysis we apply. Berger and Luckmann point out in their analysis of the sociology of knowledge that the theoretical articulation of administrative reality will continue to play an important function in public administration, but it is not the most important activity: we are also concerned with democracy, people, interdependence, and diversity. Therefore, knowledge shared through social interaction increases the range of our involvement, understanding, conflict resolution, and possible alternatives. Through the mutual construction of goals and strategies, we can take action to shape our collective destiny, creating a future that is different from the present.

Vertical governing of government agencies as well as central-local government relationships in many countries certainly marginalize the use of social knowledge that is embedded in an intricate network of organizational and human relationships. Each human relationship in a social situation involves different values, facts, experiences, energies, and creative forces. Public administrators who are confronted with nonroutine decisions must explore possibilities through the use of social knowledge and an interaction process that is less hierarchical (or nonhierarchical) if they are to find a socially acceptable course of action in which the greatest collaboration occurs at the level of implementation.

Social Order through Relationships

How do we manage to make sense of our world and one another in the face of conflict, ambiguity, and crisis? One prevailing view is to allow management authority to maintain or restore organizational order through the enforcement of rules, regulations, and procedures, ensuring the compliance of organizational members. All formal organizations require employees to follow certain procedures and forms, not only to bring order, efficiency, and uniformity but also to protect the organization, its employees, and its clientele. The organizational necessity for maintaining order is close to the Hobbesian view of a social contract. Thomas Hobbes (1588–1679) maintains that when a contract has been formed between the governed and the individual who governs, it must place absolute authority in the hands of the ruler (1946). As applied to the context of public administration, after an individual joins an organization, he or she must abide by the decision of the governing authority, that is, the management. Thus, Hobbes's antisocial view of the individual is concerned with social order and stability: there is no room for democratic governance.

The social constructionist approach stands in contrast to Hobbes's view of the rational authority of government (i.e., the authority of management). It champions organizational members' ability to self-govern, that is, to sustain social (and organizational) order through interaction. We cannot understand reality in a chaotic situation or reconstruct organizational order alone but find ways of dealing with disorder and tensions as we engage in actions with other human beings. By interrelating and responding to others, we create new ways, new possibilities, and new solutions for dealing with the disorder and differences in our world. As human beings, we have created and recreated by the world in which we live through our joint efforts, through our thoughts and knowledge, through our interactions with one another. Our sense of social being and social order exits only as a product of our human activity. Our most important experiences take place within our social interactions, our face-to-face encounters. How we relate to one another is how we construct our social order and the future world in which we will live. An administrator as a person (a being) in the social (or the administrative) world shares the world of other people, and this makes it possible for the administrator to turn to other people.

Social Learning and a Plurality of Values

The functionalist approach, which is largely rational and instrumental, in contrast, takes a deterministic view of learning, assuming that organizational learning is the process of establishing causal relationships between theoretical knowledge and desirable outcomes (e.g., the relationship between the use of certain technology and an increase in productivity).

Social construction is a learning process in which organizational members are engaged in a continued sharing of ideas and experiences so that they may acquire a better understanding of the views of others. In the social learning process, past and current events are reinterpreted in light of participants' diverse values and beliefs. As an individual critically reflects on and interprets others' experiences and ideas, he or she may develop a new understanding of the world of others as well as "create alternative systems of values and beliefs to counterpoise his or her own values and beliefs" (May, 1996, p. 20). The individual's exposure to the values of others is essential to organizational learning. According to Donald Schön, public organizations must be viewed as instruments, or agents, for "inquiring into public problems affecting society as a whole" (1971, p. 176). An organization's problem-solving effectiveness depends on its ability "to engage in public learning." To this end, the social constructionist approach to organizational learning provides the opportunity for innovation and creativity through the active learning and participation of members. It assumes the possibility of learning, understanding, conflict resolution, and problem solving by emphasizing critical reflection on both social and rational knowledge. Because social learning is continuously evolving, the process is nonlinear, open-ended, and dialectical. Social learning generally arises from sharing practical experiences and available knowledge; the use of established theory is less useful to an understanding of complex, nonroutine problems.

The effective functioning of the organization therefore depends greatly on the learning ability of its members (Williams, 1982, p. 91). Learning in democratically designed organizations involves a consciously creative process as organizational members deliberately reconstruct existing procedures, processes, and tasks to create new meaning in their workplace. As members respond to external problems and negative feedback, they are interested in maintaining stability; more important to them, however, is their opportunity to discover alternative possibilities for correcting mistakes by reflecting critically on their assumptions and norms. As members take increased responsibility for transforming rigid bureaucracies into democratic and decentralized organizational arrangements, their organizations can become settings for innovative and creative human interaction.

Awareness of Diverse Cultures and Multiple Realities

From a social constructionist perspective, all administrative (social) cultures are constructed from diverse aspects of the multiple realities of different individuals and the organizational context. As we move from one culture to another, we experience different relationships with others, just as an individual travels around from the workplace to the community organization or from one country to another. As an individual engages in each organizational setting with other members, he or she is aware of different ideas that other members bring to the discussion. Each person's subjective interpretation of an organizational (social) situation might be different from others' points of view. As an individual encounters others through interaction and dialogue, that individual might be able to transcend his or her original thoughts, coming to a new understanding. Merleau-Ponty calls the process of this understanding an "analytical reflection" which begins "from our experience of the world and goes back to the subject as to a condition of possibility distinct from that experience, revealing the all-embracing synthesis" through exercising of the subject's cognitive powers (1962, pp. ix–x).

In a bureaucratic culture, the management seeks to assimilate and downplay the different experiences and ideas of members for the purpose of accomplishing established goals. In a multicultural organizational environment, comprising diversity, ethnic minorities, and marginal groups, a critical issue is not to assimilate all members into a dominant hierarchical culture but to recognize the potential contributions of different individuals and groups and at the same time, to discover a commonality that respects difference (Jun, 1996, p. 350). As we interpret the organization from the view of Merleau-Ponty, the organizational world consists of clearly identifiable objects, such as structure, hierarchy, rules, procedures, and people. In this setting, each organizational member has a certain view of what the organization is like, what these objective elements mean to him or her, and what kind of relationships exist between them (Merleau-Ponty, 1962, p. 71).

The contemporary idea of multiculturalism stems largely from postmodern thought, which tends to question rationalism and universal truth (Melzer, Weinberger, and Zinman, 1998, pp. 1–12; Glazer, 1997). Postmodern thought suggests we expose the dominant culture and the ways in which it marginalizes and suppresses other groups and cultures. Multiculturalists argue that actual representation and participation of ethnic minorities and marginal groups are good for society as a whole and for democratic governance because this offers a chance to learn from perspectives, ideas, and experiences that would not otherwise be available (Boxill, 1998). Although we do not have clear ideas as to how to resolve issues of multiculturalism in liberal democracy and in administrative organizations, our active attention to diversity and multiple realities could serve as "a means for preserving the fundamental goal of constitutional democracy" and promoting participatory organizations (Boxill, 1998; Cox, 1993) by preventing majority tyranny or hierarchical dominance by people at the top level of administration. Stanley Deetz suggests that "balanced responsiveness" is one way of doing this—for example, responsive decision making, which means "seeking the moment with care and moral direction, rather than with instrumentality and decisional rules" where one responds to others, takes responsibility for one's action and complicity (1992, pp. 337–38).

Dialogue, Discourse, and Intersubjectivity

Because social construction is interactive and focuses on how people come to produce a sense of commonly shared reality, interaction involves all forms of communication, such as face-to-face dialogue, interviews, commentaries, and formal expression of ideas in speech, conversation, or writing. According to Martin Buber's "principle of reciprocity," through a reciprocal relationship between I and thou, a relationship that is not necessarily symmetrical, people talk to each other, both passively and actively (1961). Although Buber does not illustrate the existence of diverse dialogue, such as in a multicultural context, his dialogical approach implies that a person can work in the organizational world only through another organizational member. A possibility of change arises in dialogue between I and thou. Dialogical communication is particularly essential to the process of social construction as the participants engage responsively in expressing their ideas and listening to the views of others. Through dialogue people can see how an alternative arises for them in the dialogue between them, and change occurs as a result of new understanding. Thus the dialogical process is essential for constructing intersubjective reality.

The social construction of intersubjective reality may be viewed from two different perspectives. Edmund Husserl (1859–1938) is concerned with the constitution of an individual's intersubjective life as the transcendental ego connects with the experience of other egos, with alter egos, and with the other in general. His main concern is how the experience of the other person helps an individual to find his or her own transcendental experience, the transcendental subjectivity (Husserl, 1962; Ströker, 1999). Husserl sees the intersubjective nature of people's experience but always grounds it in the subjective; his interest lies in how the other enters into an individual's consciousness. Husserl's view of the "life-world"[3] is always an important part of the consciousness of the subject. He, however, does not expand on how people jointly develop a mutually shared reality, and overlooks the possibility of constructing intersubjectivity through dialogue and practical discourse between the self and others.

Another assumption underlying intersubjectivity is that people will be transformed as a result of sharing ideas and experiences. Organizational situations present a possibility of constructing an intersubjective reality in which the actors try to share their ideas and experience by mutually tuning into one another's consciousness (Zaner, 1970). By reflecting upon one another's biases and experiences, the actors can produce a socially meaningful project. Alfred Schutz (1889–1959), a student of Husserl, emphasizes intersubjectivity in the interactive and reciprocal process. According to Schutz (1967), in face-to-face situations, the actors can produce socially (mutually) shared phenomena, that is, an intersubjective reality in which, through a face-to-face encounter, its members share a sense of "we-relation."

Because the foundation of the administrative organization is the assumption of rational action in relation to ends and means, Jürgen Habermas attempts, in his critical theory, to achieve rationality through communicative action, going beyond Max Weber's view that reason is manifested in scientific rationality. Intersubjective relationships can be developed through dialogue and discourse in social situations and in the public sphere in general. Because the discourse ethics of Habermas (1987; 1998) emphasize moral learning over technical-instrumental learning, the social practice of these discourse ethics could help administrators to realize the negative effects that their actions have on others. Although individuals' reflexive actions are important to Habermas, the postmodern argument is suspicious of the role of the subjects (individuals) in postmodern discourse, rejecting reality construction based on intersubjective communication. For example, Michel Foucault (1969 and 1981) argues that the individual subjects are constituted by the power relationships that are inherent to all social relationships as well as hierarchical power relationships. However, both Habermas's view of intersubjective discourse and Foucault's analysis of relationships among economic structures, social and administrative structures, and various discourses help us to understand the changing relationships among government, business, and civil society, and between administration and the public. In this book, I emphasize the responsibility of individual administrators as they work and interact with other human beings in the organization and the community.

Facilitating Process without Neglecting Product

The social constructionist approach is concerned with the processes of creating meanings and knowledge as people share experiences and develop strategies for human collaboration. Because social construction always involves human relationships, the process becomes another important means for connecting actions, purpose (or goals), and intended (or desirable) outcomes. It is evolutionary and dialectical as interactions between them generate new possibilities for action and change. Process is also viewed as a deterministic path toward a realization of intended goals. To David Edwards, the term *process* generally implies "an individual or group activity that is moving through a succession of acts or stages toward some form of arrival or completion." He views a process as a "series of actions or events, with a pattern or regularity and an effective automaticity, sometimes dynamic" (1973, pp. 61–62). A process is a means that could lead to accomplishment of a solution or completion of a product; a product is seen as a realization of organizational goals or public program objectives.

A process may encompass a conspicuous, ongoing activity, such as the process of public policy formulation and implementation; a slow, hardly discernible action, such as the process of organizational learning and adaptation; political action, such as the budgetary and policy-making process; or collective bargaining and dispute resolution, such as the negotiating process. Describing a process in terms of a product entails linear and rational thinking moving toward a desired end. Thus the intended product is the realization of the substance of the actor's belief and his or her predetermined course of action.

Process emphasized in social constructionism can also be conceived as nonlinear and open-ended interaction among people who participate in dialogue and are engaged in an exchange of different viewpoints concerning problems and issues that are related to their organizational or external concerns. Particularly in public problem solving, process may be the most important product. This in no way detracts from normal goal achievement. Indeed, goal achievement is also a vital human experience and an invaluable societal asset. Many goals, however, are achieved in a routine way: delivering human services in a welfare agency, meeting production quotas in a manufacturing organization, routing mail in an office, and so on. In a nonroutine situation, the process may not deliver the intended outcome. Although a process that particularly emphasizes interaction, dialogue, and the clarification of language used may produce no agreement on a difficult issue, participants may learn the opposing views of others and as a result transcend their original positions. Nor can we expect that everything that is done in a process will affect all aspects of a situation positively or always accomplish the intended goals. In other words, a process does not always lead to an efficient product (Wildavsky, 1979). The processes that we use for organizational activities may be positive or negative, transparent or secretive, inclusive or discriminatory, facilitative or destructive, or anything in between. Working on the assumption that an effective process leads to a desirable product, the social construction process aims to promote broad interactions and collaborations among multiple actors. In a participatory process, participants are responsible for expressing their ideas, openly sharing their views with others.

Dialectic between the Individual, Organization, and Society

Public administration is influenced by external conditions; at the same time, it influences society by the ways in which it solves present and future problems. The reality of public administration is determined by objectified societal elements, as well as by the subjective actions of public administrators.[4] Public administration exists in the context of the social world (i.e., the public): it is not an isolated entity in society. A social environment can change the direction of an administrator's thinking and plans, and public administrators interpret the social situation according to their own perception, knowledge, and experience. By interacting with the environment and with citizens, public administrators construct meanings of social situations. Thus public administration is an ongoing dialectical process that exists between society, institutions, administrative knowledge, and the individual. Society and public administration are inseparable and influence each other. Just as individuals play a major role in changing institutions and communities through social processes, they themselves can be changed by those processes.

The relationship between the individual and the organization can also be understood dialectically throughout changing and evolving organizational realities, such as an organization's budget crunch and its effect on employees; employee turnover and its effect on organizational performance; management-employee relations; and action research projects in changing organizations. Although management puts a heavy emphasis on structure, goals, policies, technology, tasks, and functions, individual employees are concerned with meeting personal needs, such as relationships, empowerment, job satisfaction, and self-development (Bolman and Deal, 1997; Argyris, 1964). For managers to be effective, they must have the ability to work with other members in resolving conflicts and changing work processes.

The relationships among the individual, the organization, and society are laden with values, conflict, tensions, crises, uncertainty, and fragmentation, and as these relationships change, they present the possibility of creating new social realities and different futures. For example, overcoming a budget crunch could lead to reordering priorities and exploring new ways of people working together with a changed consciousness. Raising people's consciousness about the deteriorating natural environment could help citizens to take action to achieve a sustainable environment.

The theories of public administration in general have inadequately treated the individual-organization-society (and individual-organization) relationships, as these theories were developed to reflect the needs of the organization in a period of rapid growth and industrialization. The overriding concern of bureaucratic theory and even modern management approaches is with ensuring instrumental and technical rationality in order to maintain efficiency and productivity (Ramos, 1981). Rational choice theory in policy analysis is assumed to maximize (or satisfy) policy choices in a way that is economical and political, considering existing resources and structures. An adequate understanding of a changing society (and a changing organization) requires dialectical thinking, which is particularly emphasized in the interpretive and critical theoretical perspectives. The dialectical perspective on the evolving relationships among the individual, the organization, and society not only appreciates the historical and cultural contexts that influence the ideas and values of people but also critically examines tradition in light of new social conditions and new human experiences.

GLOBALIZATION AS SOCIAL CONSTRUCTION

There are numerous signs that global politics and administration at all levels are undergoing enormous changes. Economic, social, political-structure, and administrative reforms are emerging, and old approaches are being transformed as technology and politics become more dynamic. The state-centered structure of world affairs, in which actions and interactions are dominated by the nation-state, is being rivaled by new structures and processes through which various transnational collectivities—from multinational corporations to small cities to global networks incorporating a vast range of new kinds of actors—engage in pursuits that are not confined within national boundaries.

Globalization influences different ways of connecting institutional and social relationships. Economists and business analysts are keen to explore the economic significance of the spread of transnational corporations as well as the rise of new global business strategies that promote smaller enterprises and local industrial conglomerates. Political scientists focus on the rise of supranational political bodies and their implications for the autonomy and sovereignty of regional and national institutions and world government (Luard, 1990; Rosenau and Czempiel, 1992).

Another possibility is to consider globalization as a process by which the world becomes a single place, not in the sense of homogenization, but in the sense that a common purpose emerges while the diversity of and differences in cultures is sustained, such as the movement toward the democratization of politics and society and the exchange of arts and cultural activities. Roland Robertson states that to a large extent all of international politics is cultural—that we are "in a period of globe-wide cultural politics" (1992). He focuses on the realm of culture in globalization, rather than the world-system perspective. He illustrates a comprehensive analysis of global social change around the idea of the relative autonomy of culture, stressing the significance of the reality of "nationally constituted society" and the need "to see where individuals and constructions of individuals, as well as humankind, fit into the picture" of global change (1992, p. 5). It is also evident that cultural change in global analysis is influenced by the international tourism, rapid transportation, global telecommunications, and the electronic mass media.

As we critically examine globalization, it can be described not only as the process of adaptation to international conditions but also as the creation of possibilities through people's interactions in sociocultural, economic, political, and technological spheres. Thus, globalization is a human construction of a social world in that it is an ongoing process of constructing and reconstructing ways of sharing the meaning of interdependence as well as developing alternatives to improve local as well as global socioeconomic and political conditions. In this respect, the globalization process is not a continuation of modernization, but rather is open-ended transformations of people, communities, institutions, and society, indeed, of the world. Albrow aptly points out that, unlike the project of modernity, "globalization is fraught with indeterminacy and ambiguity" (Albrow, 1996, p. 94).

To a large extent, however, economic globalization has been an extension of modernization and development. Modernity has to do with development and innovation in terms of a linear projection toward economic, social, and scientific progress. Globalization, however, is more than economic globalization. The term *global* (or a global perspective) implies an Earth space (a global space) in which political, economic, cultural, and social interactions take place in the international public sphere. When we conceptualize approaches to globalization, we emphasize the complexity of changing social and world phenomena into manageable methods. In dealing with interactions among people, we see two polarizing perspectives: globalization from above and globalization from below. When globalization is governed by central policies and rules, as is the case in newly industrializing countries, "grand narratives" as depicted by postmodernists, are extensively used in order to rationalize the goals of modernizing projects. Narratives and discourses controlled by policy makers from above emphasize a deterministic view of social change and the idea of rationality, as promoted by the modernists. The creation of the World Trade Organization (WTO) and international trade agreements are outcomes of globalization from above.

What is most important in the transformation, both globally and locally, is the need for critical discourse at all levels of social interaction. In the mid-1990s, we began to realize that orthodox discourses on global capitalism, industrialism, and rationalism inhibit not only social interaction and participatory problem solving but also the possibilities of social innovation at the local level. The economic crisis in the late 1990s in Asian and Latin American countries attests to the fact that the discourse on economic globalization has been largely controlled by economically powerful nations, who have focused on international trade issues. As the rich nations gain evergreater affluence, the poor nations fall further behind, unable to compete in global markets and facing more poverty and inequality. Those who criticize globalization from above argue that domestic policies toward globalization have been designed by policy makers and high-level experts who manipulate information in order to present convincing arguments for economic development. To this extent, economic globalization has been exposed to a critical social theory and a rethinking of hierarchically negotiated global trade policy and economic interactions.

The critical theory of Habermas (1984) can be used to analyze globalization policy. His communicative action theory is a means of developing a shared vision through a dialectical understanding and mutual learning, accepting even grand narratives if people understand the possible consequences. Habermas assumes that as long as a symbolic vision of policy makers is authentically communicated and shared, administrative action can be justified. Moreover, many postmodernists, such as Lyotard (1984), emphasize the use of "local narratives" over grand narratives, which are uncontrolled by modern institutions. Richard Rorty, as a postmodern pragmatist, also rejects the monolithic nature of grand narratives and advocates a pragmatic way of understanding local culture, in particular, through dialogue among local actors (1982). Although Habermas emphasizes a constructionist view of intersubjective learning as well as the possibility of unifying the subjects, the postmodernists as critical social theorists seem to stress "a critical understanding of self as a way of democratizing human community" (Keyman, 1997, p. 4). Both the critical theory of Habermas and the postmodernists' critique of grand narratives, however, reject the reduction of policy making, such as globalization policy, to instrumental and economic rationalism. From a normative point of view, critical discourse and dialogue improve the content of policy as citizens, and local policy actors become involved in the process of discovering the common good, as well as understanding consequences in relation to their own situations. In other words, without participatory discourse and dialogue among broadly represented actors, economic rationalism is not only incomplete but is also unable to formulate "public reasons" for promoting "globality," that is, human interaction and collective action with global forces (Albrow, 1996, pp. 82–85).

The outcome of globalization is, of course, unknown. When goals (or agendas) of globalization are stated, they are merely futuristic visions. Domestic goals for modernization and economic development may be formulated and implemented within a particular time frame, but globally oriented activities require more flexibility and diversity, as the actions of people from different cultural backgrounds are hard to predict. In addition, global activities require much more collaboration among multiple actors, who build a collective consciousness through discourse and dialogue. Global activities face unforeseeable problems, largely due to legalistic and cultural differences among nation-states and local communities. Global strategies are only incremental steps, and their outcome is unpredictable. On the way to the creation of a possible future, nation-states, institutions, and people continue to interpret and reinterpret old and new experiences, as well as create a different experience by exploring a commonality of perceived interests.

In summary, globalization means the interdependence and interconnection of nation-states, cultures, human activities, people's life experiences, and economic and material exchanges. It is an intensification of cultural, social, political, and economic interactions and interdependence among nation-states, institutions, and people (Jun and Wright, 1996, pp. 1–8). Each entity and each individual involved in globalization has a unique perspective on the process. Each explains a part of fragmented global changes through a particular lens and provides insights not obtainable elsewhere. The intensification of economic globalization continues to increase, and the asymmetries and discontinuities of sociocultural, economic, and political development are its common features. People globally are demanding more autonomy and participation at the grass-roots level. For example, the negative consequences of economic globalization have prompted the organized opposition of NGOs and millions of people internationally to the so-called Washington Consensus to build a homogenized, corporatized economy. Street demonstrations against the meetings of the WTO in Seattle, Washington, and Cancún have certainly slowed the momentum of economic globalization.

As various undesirable consequences of globalization emerge, one way of critically examining, understanding, and resolving paradoxical issues is to strengthen dialogical interactions between rich and poor nations, between central and local governments, and between policy makers and citizens. If globalization (particularly economic globalization) is to be meaningful to people, it must be part of a participatory, constructive process that works to enhance sustainable development and local democratic governance and that is grounded in critical discourse. The future of globalization, particularly economic globalization, requires a dialectical process between action from above and voices from below; that is, it must move toward social construction of critical and democratic possibilities through the processes of relating, sharing, learning, and compromising.

REFLECTION

In this chapter, I have argued that by means of social interaction and democratic participation, we can improve our understanding of problems, creating a new community and a new public administration. Traditional public administration tends to confine our thought patterns and relationships within a positivistic and hierarchical framework, thereby hindering our opportunities for understanding social reality, the use of social knowledge, and the democratic possibilities that are grounded in cultural, social, and political contexts. At first glance, a social constructionist approach might seem impractical, even impossible, because the dominant influence of the functionalist and positivistic orientation in managing public institutions prevents these institutions from developing democratic alternatives. As people become more critical of the ineffective governing of the administrative state, however, they will invite in alternatives that promote critical communication and debate. This new public administration will share some aspects with the old public administration: the objectified elements of the institution that its members have constructed throughout the years will not be totally discarded. The ideas of social construction in public administration can serve as the conceptual foundation of participatory public administration. The social constructionist approach is a reasonable candidate to fill the need of critical modern and postmodern public administration to engage in fully reflexive and critical thinking, relating, living, and working.

I have emphasized the utilization of social knowledge in public administration organizationally, nationally, and globally; this social knowledge largely entails people's values, experiences, beliefs, and ideas. It also implies that there are divergent views and interpretations of any situation that need to be taken into consideration. In addition, social knowledge reflects the conditions of sociopolitical, economic, and cultural milieux; an understanding of these conditions is essential to the design of socially acceptable alternatives and decisions. Social knowledge also assumes that inside an organization, innovation can occur through leaders, managers, experts, and other organizational members sharing knowledge; and outside the organization, social innovation can emerge as people share their knowledge, interact and communicate through a network of formal and informal arrangements, engage in relationships and learning, and interact with business and nonprofit organizations, associations, groups, and citizens.

Public administration is socially constructed and reconstructed through interactions, dialogue, and discourse. By realizing our ability to change, we can also deconstruct the reified aspects of institutions, rules, functions, roles, and procedures as we exercise our critical reflexivity, examining the established assumptions and norms of bureaucratic culture. If we fail to realize that reconstruction is our responsibility and within our power, public institutions will decay further: the result will be dysfunctional and dehumanizing practices in public institutions. It is people who make inflexible and control-oriented institutions the way that they are. Thus social construction (or social deconstruction) of public administration is a reflexive activity of administrators as they examine unquestioned beliefs and explore alternative ways of transforming ineffective and inauthentic institutional practices as well as meeting global challenges. Globalization is precarious as long as people at the top make important policies without listening to people from below. If administrators wish to pursue a meaningful existence, one beyond that of maintaining often vacuous order and being powerless individuals, then they need to participate in the active construction of meaningful realities. Policy development, whether it is national or global, is a social construction process in which the interests and needs of policy makers, executives, and managers who seek change, and citizens who are the targets of change, have to be taken much more seriously if we are to understand the basic problems and to achieve desirable results.

CHAPTER 4

Public Administration as Social Design

Traditionally, public administration has been considered to be either a science or an art, and these metaphors have substantially affected theory and practice in this field. When it is seen as a science, public administration uses the scientific method and quantitative information; when it is seen as an art, it focuses on functional coordination, leadership skills, negotiation, conflict resolution, decision making, and problem solving. I believe that both of these approaches often lead to unsatisfactory solutions to vexing problems. Accordingly, in this chapter, I attempt to apply the concept of social constructionism to the study of public administration by comparing the social design approach with the perspective of science approach and the art approach. The social design perspective, as discussed here, offers a socially grounded (or context-oriented) framework for understanding administrative phenomena and more effective human action. My reasons for suggesting this new approach are threefold: (1) to convey the hazards of overreliance on a one-dimensional approach (public administration is either a science or an art); (2) to emphasize the importance of the relationship that exists between the conceptual approaches that we use and what we actually think and do in our field; and (3) most important, to apply social constructionism to the field of public administration.

THE USE AND ABUSE OF METAPHOR

We often use metaphor to facilitate our understanding of administrative phenomena. Like a paradigm, a metaphor provides a framework for ordering, even constructing, social reality. At the same time, use of metaphor can hamper our understanding of an administrative world; this is because the particular metaphorical framework that we adopt tends to reflect only selected aspects of a complex reality. As Martin Landau points out, "[A] metaphor structures inquiry, establishes relevance, and provides an interpretive system. Hence it must be used with full awareness, and must be made fully explicit" (1972, p. 100). Metaphor is a typified form of knowledge, the symbolic representation of a given phenomenon. In this sense, metaphor keeps company with language and art, each of which is used to describe characteristics of the social world. These symbolic devices are helpful, but they are imperfect epistemological tools in that they provide no more than what Alfred North Whitehead terms "'useful functions for comprehending reality" (1927). This is to say that all conceptions of reality that are typified in symbolic form are essentially metaphorical. Thus, metaphor is the heart of the procedures that we use to develop concepts and express them objectively, but metaphor is not reality.

Indeed, in a minor sense, metaphor always creates falsehood. It is, after all, misleading to attempt to explain one fact or experience by using another: the second cannot be the same as the first, or there would be no metaphor. Colin Turbayne speaks of the possible misuse of metaphor: "There is a difference between using a metaphor and being used by it, between using a model and mistaking the model for the thing modeled" (1971, p. 22). Critical to the use and understanding of metaphor is the awareness that metaphor is selectively structured and risks making a false impression. According to George Lakoff and Mark Johnson, we perceive and experience much of the world through the use of metaphors: it is as much a part of our everyday functioning as our sense of being in touch with any particular situation (1980).

Most metaphors downplay some elements of a concept while emphasizing others. It is this selectivity, again, that leads to distortion and falsehood. The machine metaphor and organism metaphor for administrative organizations and their subsystems illustrate this limitation of metaphor well. A manager can rely so heavily upon a specific metaphor, defining himself or herself so rigidly in terms of that particular metaphor that he or she excludes other visions and alternative ways of perceiving.[1] The abuse of a metaphorical framework can lock an organization into a pattern of behavior that constricts its choices and limits its responsiveness to opportunity and difficulty. It is my belief that the field of public administration suffers significantly from this problem.

Metaphors reinforce paradigms and theoretical constructs. Using elements of administrative systems and structures as metaphors for organization, for example, reinforces the paradigm of functionalism, by which organizations are controlled, purposive, ordered, coordinated, and regulated. Such metaphors become significant statements about the intended nature of organizational reality, and they condition our thinking and behavior. They also have the capacity "to create ways of seeing and shaping organizational life" (Morgan, 1997, p. 348). The result may be that organizations are more functional and mechanistic but that unique qualities and needs of humans are neglected. In this example, a paradigmatic perception of organizational reality is heavily reinforced by an overly narrow, far too simplistic metaphor. Metaphors that reflect broad, multidimensional realities are difficult to develop and harder to comprehend. In the long run, however, they are more adequate, constructive, and reliable structures and can better help us to understand reality and solve problems. The social design approach, based on the social constructionist perspective, offers a framework for understanding multiple realities and facilitating innovative ways of dealing with issues, problems, and possibilities.

In this chapter, I develop the argument that two metaphors, often used as conceptual modes of studying public administration—public administration is a science, and public administration is an art—have seriously distorted the image of public administration, including many activities central to that field. The result has been a misdirection in both theory building and practical public administration. This distortion stems from a failure to treat the science and art metaphors properly, as parts of a larger, more encompassing metaphor: social design that is based on relationships, action, dialogue, and discourse. To rely on either the science or the art metaphor (or both) is tantamount to offering selected parts rather than the whole as the central conceptual metaphor for public administration. Ways in which the science and art metaphors misrepresent public administration are discussed in this chapter, and social design is introduced as a metaphor that is far more inclusive of what actually happens and what needs to happen in public administration now.

DESIGN: A BASIC CONCEPT

To reiterate, the metaphors that we employ in formulating our field are of vital importance in establishing the parameters and processes of public administration and its beliefs and actions. As a general metaphor that suggests a broader set of meanings and activities for public administration, I offer the concept and process of 'design.' In suggesting a different metaphor, I am attempting to broaden and enrich theory and practice in this essential part of the governance process.

In this era, an important activity of public administrators is not only to participate in active problem solving and change (or change making) but also to engage in interpretation and critical understanding of social and human problems as they are involved in the designing of the policies, programs, structures, functions, and processes of public programs.[2] Public administrators' involvement in change activities significantly affects the nature of their work, their environment, and their relationship with society. Most public administrators at the managerial level are actively engaged in some aspect of design most of the time. A contemporary public administrator may be viewed as a flexible, innovative social designer who critically participates in policy development with others while examining and adapting patterns of organizational life to make the process of conflict resolution and problem solving more effective.

Design is an elusive concept, one that relates to people in a broad range of activities. Such persons are involved in purposeful and creative actions directed toward the accomplishment of a project or goal. West Churchman says that "design, properly viewed, is an enormous liberation of the intellectual spirit, for it challenges this spirit to an unbounded speculation about possibilities" (1971). Design, according to Churchman, includes the following characteristics:

1. Design attempts to distinguish in thought between different sets of behavior patterns.

2. It tries to estimate in thought how well such alternative set of behavior patterns will serve a specified set of goals.

3. It aims to communicate its thought to other minds in such a manner that they may convert thoughts into corresponding actions which serve goals in the manner the design said they would. (p. 5)[3]

Churchman's view is basically rationalistic in that his design activity is aimed at realizing certain prescribed goals defined by a rational designer and the set of behaviors and actions that are needed to implement them. Thus the task of a manager who follows the rational design process is to convince others to see the value of his or her plan.

Design may also be regarded as that process of human interaction through which relevant actors work, sharing ideas and experiences, to define social reality more accurately. Erich Jantsch describes design as "a process of continuous learning through a multitude of interacting feedback relations linking ourselves and the world of our ideas to reality" (1975, p.100). This viewpoint says that we must create and recreate the social world through the process of communicating and sharing ideas. In this context, goals and alternatives are socially constructed and socially sustained; design is a continuous, ongoing accomplishment that emerges from the process of social interaction. Conscious, purposeful creative activities constitute the dynamics of public administration at its best.

Another important characteristic of design is a social process. The concept of social designing discussed by Donald Schön and Martin Rein can be summarized in the following:

1. The designer involves in the task of developing a "designing system," a coalition of actors, individual or institutional. For example, a public manager takes the responsibility of coordinating programs to help senior citizens, homeless people, transportation systems, and crime prevention. Interactions among multiple actors may be cooperative or hostile.

2. The social design process entails an external context, including a wide range of public opinion through which the meanings of a project, values, and complaints are debated and constructed.

3. Social designing is necessarily communicative. Multiple actors must communicate with one another in the form of language, dialogue, discourse, and action.

4. Social design is inevitably political because the participants have their own interests, knowledge, experiences, resources, and power. (1994, pp. 167–68)

Finally, design is a deliberate process, a process that involves a critical consciousness on the part of the actors involved in creating alternatives to understanding and problem solving. In particular, the social constructionist's view of design is to energize the participants through interaction and discussion, allowing disagreeable and agreeable, negative and positive aspects of design (or creating a project). The effectiveness of design depends on how well it understands the situation,

compromises conflicts, and solves the problem; thus, it depends largely on how well people with different interests and ideas work together.
Social design, as applied to the field of public administration, is a
framework of understanding conflicts and values and solving problems
through interactive processes, often including the external politics.

ADMINISTRATIVE SCIENCE, ART, AND SOCIAL DESIGN

Because it is interactive, dialogical, and creative, social design implies
much more than order or control, although it may be used to achieve such
objectives. The design concept is most challenged and most useful, however, where there is a need for developing processes and goals that are
evolving continually and dynamically; where nothing is stable, orderly, or
in control; and where possibilities are the critical resource in the search for
solutions. In that context, intersubjective relationships, individual and
organizational learning, professional opinion, communication, exploration, and imagination become paramount values and activities.

Those who practice rational design have trouble in such an environment. Their notion that problems must be solved with scientific
knowledge and techniques, that answers must be analytical and sys-
tematic, and that only a select few can make useful contributions to
solutions blinds their capacity to perceive, develop, and use possibilities. Since the "uncertainty is a threat" for them (Schön, 1983, p. 69),
the professionals involved in the analytical process have little problem
with reaching a consensus on defining the problem and selecting a goal
because of their shared professional interests and educational backgrounds. The incremental designer (the politically skillful administrator), whose art is finding the possible (that is, acceptable action in a
complex power field), is also blind to many possibilities in policy choices because of his or her nontechnical perspective and because of elements in the political configuration of each problem situation.
Moreover, social designers are, by definition, open to an acceptance of
scientific knowledge, professional expertise, political persuasion, and
other information. They rely on knowledge, intuition, and participation in the process of administrative problem solving through broad
social interaction and dialogue with other actors.

Administrative science, being rational and technical, has isolated
many potential actors from the design and problem-solving processes. In

so doing, it has created legions of experts who believe that ordinary citizens cannot tell what is good for them because, presumably, they lack any sense of how complicated problems are solved. The social designer, by contrast, views the administrative world as an open-ended context that presents multiple opportunities for learning something new from the environment and from other people's ideas and experiences. The social designer perceives the administrative world as becoming clearer as administrators carry on meaningful dialogues with employees, clients, and the public. Individual and organizational learning is paramount. This approach holds that by promoting open communication, social relationships, and participation, people begin to better understand the political and economic aspects of problems, including the possibilities and the limitations. If socially grounded change strategies are to be implemented, then the public administrator must play the role of a facilitator. In this way, people's interest in collective problem solving may be nurtured and sustained. The social constructionist perspective (as outlined in table 4.1) deals with the process of making conscious choices among various alternatives and selecting strategies that have meaning for human action. It attempts to integrate organizational needs and individual values. Because it is purposeful activity, the social construction framework generates its own dynamics, including the creation of alternative institutional processes and the design of new decisions and programs. It focuses on the "appreciative inquiry," in which the members of an organization focus on positive narratives or stories of value, thus allowing them to move forward and think futuristically by looking at how they can increase positive experiences, which, by default, automatically allows the previous problems to drift into obscurity (Gergen, 1999, pp. 176–78; Schön, 1983, pp. 272–73). Organizations and communities could benefit from appreciative inquiry by sharing positive (and even negative) stories and narratives regarding collaborative work with one another, thereby creating bonds based on compassion, caring, and mutual relationships. Discussing positive aspects with another person allows an opportunity to arise in which further dialogue could lead to learning exactly how the positive experiences came to be and how they can be created again. The methods of future search conference and action research strongly emphasize collaboration and learning across boundaries and among participants. The intent of such a method is not to hash out problems in order to alleviate disagreements but to create a forum that allows a common vision of a viable future to materialize.

TABLE 4.1
Social Design Compared with Science and Art

Public administration	Perceived As Science	Perceived As Art	Perceived As Social Construction
Conceptual Orientation	Rational design; technical rationality; political economy; normative	Incremental design; nonrationality; pluralism and incrementalism; descriptive	Social design; rationality through communicative action; descriptive & normative
Method of Inquiry	Theory and empirical testing; value-neutral; quantitative and positivic inquiry; explanation and prediction	Theorizing situational context; value-committed; qualitative and human science inquiry; describing and understanding	Critical of facts & values; appreciative inquiry of quantitative and qualitative analysis; interpretation and understanding
Conception of Reality	Objective reality as seen by a scientific researcher and a functionalist manager	Subjective reality and a narrow view of intersubjective reality	Intersubjective reality and authentic reciprocity
Activity	Scientific & empirical research; application of theory; measurement; standardization	Advocacy; leadership skills; consensus building; bargaining and compromising	Dialogue & discourse; sharing and learning; participation and deliberration; action research; future search conference
Process	Rational/mechanistic; deterministic process	Mythological/adaptive; disjointed process	Evolutionary/inventive; dialectical process

Because social design derived from social construction stresses possibility, it attempts to integrate facts and values and to consider both descriptive (what is) and normative (what ought to be) dimensions as appropriate to administrative inquiry. Martin Rein argues that a value-critical approach is needed to integrate facts and values and that such an approach helps us to understand purposes, societal goals, policy-relevant issues, and social processes because it treats "values not merely as accepted aims of policy, but as a subject for debate and analysis" (Rein, 1976 and 1983). A critical assessment of facts and values is also an important epistemological position taken by Jürgen Habermas (1984; 1998).

In assuming the existence of objectivity, administrative science adopts the rational approach to the design process. Administrators who perceive public administration as science attempt to define problems logically, based on factual information; they assume that reality is something that already exists in the external world and that therefore their basic task is to uncover the truth as objectively as they can. For example, in non-Western countries (and even Western countries) developing new community projects such as building parks, bridges, and dams, government planners and architects may determine their community's needs and design a blueprint according to what they think is best for the people in the community, without inviting the views of citizens. Research activity in rational design is, by definition, logical, quantitative, and controlled. The premise is that a phenomenon that can be described factually can be measured. According to this perspective, administrative—and human—behavior is of this nature: behavior can be predicted, and therefore it can be quantitatively ordered, tested, and explained.

Administrators who consider public administration as art assume that each actor perceives and interprets a problem according to his or her own interests. Thus, interpretation of social reality depends on who perceives, at what time, and in what context. This subjective view does not mean that objective elements of a situation are unimportant but rather that an individual's action reflects his or her vested interests, knowledge, and personality as in the legislative politics. Actors, however, take into consideration the views of others in formulating or reconstructing their original ideas. Consensual decision making by actors in negotiating a particular issue may appear to be an intersubjective phenomenon. Their agreement, however, tends to be influenced by a few influential actors; often there is little sense of shared interest among interested parties. Thus, the construction of intersubjective reality is narrowly reached.

Both subjective and objective views of organizational reality are important to consider when viewing social learning, collective problem solving, and change. The question posed by the social constructionist view is, how can we come to a common understanding of reality, that is, to a shared view of the problem? Realizing the nature of multiple realities of different actors and groups, social reality is constructed according to the intersubjective experiences of the actors in a shared world. The shared consciousness of actors can eventually provide common ground for identifying and defining the nature of a particular problem. By sharing their thoughts and experiences, participants begin to give structure and meaning to issues that were previously incomprehensible. This process forms the basis for learning, exploring future alternatives, and evaluating action strategies.

To distinguish further these perspectives on administration, we may compare their approaches to how social relationships are understood. For this, Erich Jantsch's illustration is appropriate. He explains the processes used in three types of systems—mechanistic, adaptive, and inventive—in their self-organizing behavior and their patterns of interaction with their environments (1975, chapter 5). Mechanistic systems, having rigid organizational structures, resist internal change; adaptive systems adjust to environmental changes with flexibility in their organizational forms; inventive systems "change their structure through internal generation of information in accordance with their intentions to change the environment" (p. 66). Their structures are more complex and diversified.

In explaining the design process at the human-system level, Jantsch introduces three approaches: rational, mythological, and evolutionary. These are based on different assumptions about the relationship between subject and object, between observer and observed:

1. The rational approach assumes separation between the observer and the observed, and focuses on an impersonal "It" which is supposed to be assessed objectively and without involvement by an outside observer; the basic organizing principle here is logic, the results are expressed in quantitative terms, and the dynamic aspects are perceived as change.

2. The mythological approach establishes a feedback link between the observer and the observed, and focuses on the relationship between

a personal "I" and a personal "Thou." Its basic organizing principle is feeling, the results are obtained in qualitative terms, and the dynamic aspects are perceived as process, or order of change.

3. The evolutionary approach establishes union between the observer and the observed and focuses on the "We," on the identity of the forces acting in the observer and the observed world; the organizing principle is "tuning in" by virtue of this identity, and the results are expressed in terms of sharing in a universal order of process. (namely, evolution, p. 84)

The scientific and functionalist view of public administration does not focus on the dynamic processes of human interactions and participatory problem solving. Instead, it explains quality in terms of quantity by measuring and analyzing organizational productivity and efficiency. Administrative art, on the other hand, may be viewed as an adaptive process, assuming the subjective relationship of the administrator to the external world. Our perception of social design, then, is as a synergistic (and integrative) process that contributes to the construction of shared realities (or intersubjectivities) and the establishment of "we" relationships between subjects and objects; it is a process that gains meaning only when there is mutual participation. Quality is a product of synthetic or holistic experiences in which the administrator engages in sharing, negotiation, and coordination of administrative activities. Social design is evolutionary in the sense that it includes appreciative (or "self-balancing") activities in relation to a situational context. It is developmental in the sense that design focuses on purpose, meaning, and future direction. It is inventive in that it learns and creates new ideas and explores relationship potentials.

In summary, the processes of administration as social design relate to consciousness, intention, participatory planning, deliberation of different views, and purposiveness; it also relates to formulating structures, forms, processes, policies, and goals. On both the public and the governmental sides of public administration, the social design perspective involves all of us directly in the processes of invention, evolution, and self-governance. As a metaphor for public administration, social design best describes what we are actually trying to do now to make public administration appropriate and workable for the needs of today and tomorrow in relationship to the changing contexts of the public sphere and the world.

THE MODES OF ADMINISTRATIVE
AND POLICY DESIGN

A number of different approaches to administrative and policy design are possible. For purposes of comparison, I introduce here four modes of design: crisis, rational, incremental, and social. Although all design activities involve a degree of interaction, the social design process is much more open and inclusive than others, involving many actors. Different modes of design activity are categorized in table 4.2 in relationship to two main dimensions: (1) a value appreciation of relevant actors; and (2) an orientation toward conflict resolution, problem solving, and change. The first dimension concerns an administrator's realization of the value of other actors in terms of the administrator's effort to listen to other voices, share in others' experiences, and gain new knowledge. An administrator who appreciates other voices integrates these voices into the new meaning of the situation, problem definition, and formulation of decisions, as well as strategies for implementing those decisions. The second dimension describes the administrator's orientation toward conflict resolution, problem solving, and change; the administrator's actions can range from proactive to reactive. Of the four general design approaches discussed here, two of them—rational and incremental—are now serving, under the science and art labels, as conceptual metaphors in the administrative arena. The strengths and limitations of each category are considered in the following discussion.

TABLE 4.2
Four Modes of Design

		Appreciation of other voices (listening, questioning, understanding, sharing & learning)	
		High	Low
Conflict resolution, problem solving, and change	Proactive	Social design	Rational design
	Reactive	Incremental design	Crisis design

Crisis Design

A low appreciation of the values of others and a reactive orientation to understanding, conflict resolution, problem solving, and change strategies have become more commonplace in public and private organizations since the mid-1970s. Many public bureaucracies are now experiencing management crises due to scarce resources and turbulent external conditions. Hardships in managing their organizations stem from rising social demands, budget deficits, tax cuts, confusing policy direction, declining productivity, citizen anger, and a depressed economy, among other matters. Many local governments, school districts, colleges, and universities offer case studies of crisis management: enrollment declined since the mid-1970s; education budgets have been cut in recent years; and state and local governments have seen their budgets slashed for fiscal year 2003 to 2004, owing to low economic growth and declining revenues.

Two California crises illustrate the reactive responses of government agencies. The first is the California tax revolt. In June 1978, a conservative real estate group gathered 1 million citizen signatures to qualify as their tax-cut initiative for the state ballot. This initiative, Proposition 13 on the ballot, had a simple message: property taxes must come down and government must be reduced.[4] California voters went to the polls on June 6, 1978, and Proposition 13 passed by a landslide (65 percent to 35 percent). The vote reflected not only the attitude of California voters regarding property tax relief, but also their distrust of how the government as a whole was operating. The voters clearly believed that government was inefficient in its use of taxes. The result of the tax revolt has been crisis management and unintended consequences in the local municipalities. Local government agencies have reached a critical point and become incremental in their everyday problem solving. This is largely a result of uncertain revenue sources, an increasing demand for services, and a dependence on state government for maintenance of such functions as schools, transportation, and social services.

Reflecting on the twenty-five years since the passage of Proposition 13, the need for improved efficiency and productivity has allowed managers and professionals to exercise more power. This, coupled with the centralization of relationships between state and local governments, has limited the participation of employees in making organizational decisions. University administrations have also become much more bureaucratic (and vertical governing) in allocating resources. At the same time, however, many cities unlike state university systems have become more innovative and proactive in seeking alternative problem-solving methods and citizen cooperation. Unintended consequences have occurred, such as an inequity in tax rates between homeowners who receive the benefit of Proposition 13 and new homeowners, who pay higher property taxes. Although the problem that created the impetus for Proposition 13 was a legitimate concern of homeowners, the solution created an even greater problem.

Another major crisis was the budget deficit for fiscal year 2003–2004 among U.S. state governments. This crisis was due largely to a cut in taxes, an increase in spending, and a decline in revenues, stemming from an economic and stock market downturn. Forty-seven state governments faced budget shortfalls. Struggling through their worst financial crisis in a half-century, the cutoffs varied from state to state. Some common measures included freeing prisoners, closing libraries, increasing college tuition, eliminating subsidized health coverage for hundreds of thousands of low-income residents, and even halting the prosecution of abusive spouses or minor crimes, such as shoplifting. The *Los Angeles Times* reports that at least a dozen states faced deficits equal to 15 percent or more of their annual budgets. In a few states (California, Nevada, Oregon, Texas, and Wisconsin), the deficit was an estimated 25 percent of the budget (December 29, 2002). In California, Governor Gray Davis and the legislators had to deal with a $38 billion deficit, largely caused by the huge loss of taxes on capital gains and stock options that the state enjoyed when the economy was booming in the late 1990s. In order to cope with the crisis, Governor Davis has eliminated more than 12,000 state jobs, canceled many contracts, stopped purchasing equipment, eliminated nonessential travel, and reduced health care and other essential public services for low-income residents. The budget crisis in California gave the conservative Republican politicians the opportunity to recall Governor Davis by gathering 1 million signatures, enough to qualify for a special election. The recall election was held on October 7, 2003, and 55 percent of the 15.4 million registered voters chose to remove him. The voters also chose as his replacement a movie star, Arnold Schwarzenegger, by a convincing margin (47.8 percent of the vote to support him compared to just 32 percent of the vote for the second place candidate).

In the face of turbulent environmental changes of increasing magnitude and complexity, many administrators have become reactive and conservative rather than proactive and innovative. Their approach to a budget deficit focuses on the survival of organizations and community, involving a small group of policy makers, experts, and high-level administrators. Their goal is to maintain the system and their jobs from one fiscal year to the next. The crisis design process underestimates the long-term implications of crisis solutions: attention is riveted on short-term needs.

Crisis design does not facilitate employee or citizen participation; neither does it facilitate organizational learning. Crisis administrators emphasize the importance of formalism, rules, regulations, and standard operating procedures. And they tend to make their decisions through the exercise of formal authority and power. Decisions affecting many people are often made by a few managers; they are made because a crisis situation demands an immediate response. Problems are dealt with on a short-term basis with an insufficient understanding of underlying causes and long-term potentials. For example, oversimplifying the budget crisis—an incremental solution for political gain—cannot help the California state government tackle the root causes of its malaise.

Although high-level officials are supposed to be responsible in time of crisis, the overly inhibitive bureaucracy at the federal and state levels often prevents an appropriate response to the disaster situation at the local level. On August 29, 2005, Hurricane Katrina hit the America's Gulf coast and caused several breaches in the levees protecting New Orleans, a city with a population of around 500,000. The subsequent flooding of most of New Orleans, a large part of which lies below sea level, resulted in catastrophic flood damage, many deaths, and a massive evacuation effort.

As many as 60,000 gathered at the Louisiana Superdome and about 20,000 people at the New Orleans Convention Center were without food, water, or health care. Even though pleading desperately for help on CNN, FOX, and other broadcast outlets, Michael Brown, the head of the Federal Emergency Management (FEMA), claimed to have no knowledge of the use of the Convention Center as a shelter until the afternoon of September 1. Homeland Security Secretary, Michael Chenoff, who was getting much of his information from Mr. Brown, was not aware of what was occurring in New Orleans. For two days, still, the evacuees' pleas were ignored. Vice President Dick Cheney remained on vacation in Wyoming and Defense Secretary Donald Rumsfeld was passive as he was preoccupied with Iraq. President George Bush returning from vacation in Texas later admitted that the federal government's response to the crisis was totally unsatisfactory. What happened in the Gulf coast and particularly in New Orleans has revealed some shocking truths not only about the inefficient bureaucracy but also about the racial divide and the lack of preparedness. The bureaucratic chain of command at the federal, state, and local governments were unreliable and unprepared to deal with crisis. The federal government blamed local government and local government blamed the federal bureaucrats. Networks of communication were slow, and no one seemed to take responsibility. The people at the lower level of bureaucracy were waiting for orders from above before taking any action to help the people who were desperate to survive. While the government agencies failed to deliver relief to its people, however, business organizations, nongovernmental organizations such as the American Red Cross, and thousands of volunteers have acted swiftly and helped the evacuees.

Continued crisis design also leads to a sharp deterioration in the quality of working life and a decrease in service to citizens. Organizational members are likely to experience decreased job satisfaction, alienation, anxiety, powerlessness, and hostility, along with reduced efficiency, productivity, morale, and collaboration among members. Services to citizens and the community tend to be delayed. Because the implications of survival strategies are not properly analyzed and debated, problems solved at one time may resurface later in new and possibly more awesome forms.

Rational Design

At the beginning of the twentieth century, an increasing concern with administrative efficiency led to rejection of the highly politicized public administration of previous centuries and experimentation with more rational design in administrative organizations. The rational orientation assumes the administrative ability to control all relevant aspects of the organizational environment, to render process and behavior objective and predictable. In this scenario, experts use professional knowledge to design knowledge-based processes to achieve prescribed goals. The experts' orientation with regard to conflict resolution, problem solving, and change is proactive to the extent that their design activity is related to future problem solving. The experts rely largely on their technical knowledge.

The emergence of management science since the early 1960s, the logic and processes of which have attracted—or entrapped—many public administrators, is a natural projection of rational design. Scholars and practitioners of management science are committed to searching for knowledge that will facilitate refinement of administrative systems and guidance of human behavior. They perceive public administration as an arena wherein scientific methods should be applied to determine procedures, solve problems, measure efficiency and productivity, and do much else that must be done. A major objective of management science is to explain administrative phenomena objectively and impartially and to control irrationalities of politics and human behavior as these manifest themselves in organizational action.

Management science uses rigorous procedures and techniques to generate knowledge that facilitates planning and decision making; objective indicators are used as bases for conflict resolution, problem solving, and change. The rational-scientific perspective in administration is different from incremental or social design in that rational administrators use sets of questions to guide their observations, and they use sets of categories to organize what they observe. Presumably, their observations are not influenced by their values, but scientifically oriented administrators often judge the importance of questions and findings in terms of their own beliefs and training, just as others do. The effect is a reinforcement of their own premises or mind-sets in their areas of investigation, findings, and applications (Taylor, 1947; Simon, 1957 and 1977; Quade, 1975; Allison, 1971; Stokey and Zeckhauser, 1978).

An example of rational design is the role of the expert in policy analysis, because the expert applies appropriate technical knowledge and skills to "enlightened decision making." The expert's approach to policy change normally favors long-term goal establishment to meet anticipated problems. The choice of goals is likely to reflect professional perspectives and values: the attitudes and experiences of citizens are given little weight. Rational designers tend to identify the value preferences of society according to their own frames of reference. Their approach to conflict resolution is calculative and often follows the logical rules of game theory. Problem-solving and change strategies often include such scientific-rational techniques as systems analysis, cost-benefit measurement, and various budgeting techniques. In recent years, the use of rational procedures in public policy studies has been pervasive in both theoretical and practical attempts to make policy choices and evaluations. Rational design is widely used in defense policy making and management, such as developing new weapon systems, using systems analysis and PPBS (Planning, Programming, Budgeting System) during the Vietnam War, and recently the invasion of Afghanistan and Iraq.

In rational decision making, an analyst or a decision maker follows steps to "maximize" the use of rational principles.[5] Thus an emphasis on rational choice postulates an "economic person" who, in the course of being "economic," is also "rational." Decision makers are assumed to have knowledge of relevant aspects of the environment, knowledge that, if not absolutely complete, is at least impressively clear and explicitly structured. They are also assumed to have a well-organized and consistent set of preferences (including policies and goals) and to have skills in rational calculation that enable them to measure the effects of alternative available courses of action. If their measures and judgments are accurate enough, then they will be able to reach the highest attainable goals.

In making rational choices in the rational design process, rational-economic criteria are the primary guides for calculation, prediction, selection, and achievement of a preferred choice. These criteria should summarize all relevant knowledge in the environment. Herbert Simon recognizes that this is literally impossible because of environmental complexity. In later revisions of his *Administrative Behavior* (1957), he refers to a "satisficing" approach rather than a "maximizing" one. Obviously, he is aware of limitations that decision makers face in being purely rational in the process of problem solving. Rationality is necessarily limited by each individual's capacity to grasp all relevant data and explore the most promising alternatives. However, his interpretation of satisficing is still considered a rational model of administrative decision making. Simon's works have had great effect on the field of public policy analysis.

The assumptions and biases of analysts also enter into the process of defining problems that involve conflicting values. Analysts may consider values and perceptions of citizens, but their own interpretations of what is important exercise more influence on the process of determining alternatives. Citizens' values and perceptions are not likely to be as uniform as rational analysts would like. Weighing qualitative factors, such as citizens' values, needs, opinions, and emotions calls for sensitivity in assessing their importance to rational choice. Facts and values are interrelated. To examine one without being conscious of the other is to deny a critical element in the design of policies that will affect citizens.

To conclude, rational design is basically normative in that it describes how decisions should be made according to a professional viewpoint, rather than describing what actually takes place—politically, economically, and socially—in the real world. As a result, conflict about goals and alternatives is inevitable and continuous. As a metaphor for part of the design process, administration as science offers much, but also leaves out much that is needed for fully effective public administration. As in the case of administration as art, the science metaphor puts blinders on both students and practitioners, limiting their vision and their use of much that is vitally needed in this field.

Incremental Design

Incremental design, a manifestation of administration as art, has to do with skill, creativity, performance, experience, imagination, aesthetics, and other matters of this nature. It includes, too, a historic reliance on such political skills as negotiation, bargaining, trade-offs, and co-optation. Although administrators of this persuasion give some credence to elements of twentieth-century positivism, including science, technology, and expert opinions, this is secondary to the artistic dimensions. These administrators perceive the faculty of mustering and controlling relevant resources to execute that which has been planned (and the planning stage itself) as more of an art than a science, so is doing a task that requires knowledge, craft, or skill. Administrative artistry can be seen as achieving their objectives symphonically, listening to sounds, sensing the feel of the situation, putting complex elements together in harmony, and playing the total product as a unity.

Although it may be argued that rational designers fail to weigh properly the values and power of political actors, incremental designers

do reconcile the diversity of values and power fields surrounding policy issues to develop a satisficing decision; but they, in turn, fail to weigh
fully the available facts and technology pertaining to decisions. The
pluralistic nature of the U.S. government results from the variety of
beliefs and interests in this country. In such a context, the role of public administrators and other policy makers is perceived to include
extensive interactions with groups and individuals, working toward
consensus through bargaining and negotiation.

Among those who perceive public administration as art, there are
many who are simply not interested in the theoretical or scientific task
of discovering knowledge through experimentation and observation
and who have little patience for the scientific method or even administrative theory. They are usually persons who are action oriented and
skillful in their managerial roles. Incremental designers on the artistic
side, however, are critical of rational applications, feeling that in much
of what they do they must depend on nonrational qualities in themselves: intuition, interpersonal skills, charisma, imagination and creativity, timing, negotiation, and other forms of political behavior. Thus,
a rational designer as an administrative rationalist is more concerned
with discovery of facts, laws, and principles; administration as art
addresses differences among individuals, the context of administrative
situations, special interests, power, and perceptual variations among
actors in the decision arena. In this process, artistry arises from the very
challenges created by activities in which the artist-administrator is
engaged while working to solve conflicts and problems. The process
involves effective leadership, political skills, and the artistic design; the
organizational processes include those of coordination, compromise,
exchange, and paying attention to a range of organizational needs and
strategies for survival.

In coping with changes, incremental designers believe that it is
unwise to change too rapidly, because the effects of swift change may
prove to be largely unintended. Thus short-term changes and problem
solving are perceived as desirable, but long-term changes are considered to be fruitless and even hazardous (Lindblom, 1968, p. 109; 1965).
In such a context, expert roles are minimized. The important part of
incremental (or pluralistic) design is not so much who makes the decisions but that participants are engaged in continually persuading other
actors, so that "mutual adjustments" evolve and that people realize the
diversity of perspectives regarding issues and develop workable accom-

modations within this diversity. This is the "art of the possible" at work in administrative behavior. Incremental design is most common in the policy-making process, which involves a diversity of beliefs, values, attitudes, and politics. In the political process, a problem is not readily identifiable. Instead, policy makers must seek a consensus, formulating the problem through bargaining and negotiation. Political consensus occurs through values identification rather than through a rational approach.[6]

Many policies in the United States are considered to be outcomes of incremental decisions. Such outcomes are not unusual but are, in fact, the normal results of pluralism and democracy. Pluralism lends itself to incremental decision making; thus incrementalism has become part of the policy system. In China, where the government is largely autocratic and bureaucratic, policies are often comprehensive and promote drastic change by extreme means. For example, although the population policy has undergone some changes recently, the old policy that mandates one-child families in urban areas in order to control the population growth has resulted in many forced abortions and cases of female infants being murdered by their parents. Such a categorical policy could hardly develop in a pluralistic political system.

As a strategy for conflict resolution, problem solving, and change, incremental design is reactive, focusing as it does on change by degree within a context of agreement. The format offers satisficing rather than maximizing decisions, often drawing support from articulate interests that are only marginally affiliated with the issue at hand but participate in bargaining to pay off old debts or gain future favors. This implies that incremental design rests precariously on ad hoc support structures, further jeopardizing continuity of policy, expert opinion, experimentation, and other values. The incremental decision process, a strategy of focusing on only small changes, has certain advantages. Lindblom proposes that in all policy making, "whatever policies are decided on will ordinarily suit some group's ends or goals. But it will also be true that they will not suit another's goals and can always therefore be condemned as irrational" (1968, p. 109). What is an incrementalist response to this situation? In any policy examination, the inadequacies of the previous decision must be examined. Making small changes in policy and hence occasional small dislocations in implementation makes the process of remediation that much simpler. One of the main features of the incremental approach is that it makes changes not by

TABLE 4.3
Comparing Aspects of Design

	Crisis Design	Rational Design	Incremental Design	Social Design
Actors/designer	Policymakers/ managers	Experts/ analysts	Influential actors	Multiple actors
Citizen involvement	Exclusion closedness	Exclusion closedness	Limited inclusion	Inclusion openness
Goals	Immediate goals	Long-terms perspective	Short-term perspective	Short-term/ Long-term
Bases of power	Formal authority	Technical knowledge	Political consensus	Sharing responsibility

giant leaps, but by small adaptations. The process of change, then, does not take place occasionally, but continually.

The incremental design format offers a means for achieving a modicum of agreement among actors in policy sets. It does not, however, feature innovation or creative policy building, nor does it reflect broader public interests. The current critique of pluralism includes the argument that meeting the needs of articulate interests does not necessarily resolve the more general problems that confront society or promote the public good. Meeting the needs of the more powerful voices in an agency's power field risks stinting on appropriate services to other clientele of the agency as well as to the public at large.

The incremental design approach clearly offers a means for making changes and solving problems in the very complex environments of contemporary public administration. What this approach lacks, however, is sufficient attention to alternatives implied by analysis, expert opinion, experience, and scientific exploration, and it lacks sufficient sensitivity to the less powerful and less articulate voices in the power field. As a metaphor for public administration, incremental design as administrative art invites receptive attention to one category of relevant matters while rejecting consideration of many other possibilities that could improve the plan, decision, or program. As with the science metaphor, perceiving public administration as art puts blinders on both students and practitioners as they study and work in public policy formulation and implementation.

Many critics of incremental policy making view that it is inherently conservative and reactive. Indeed, it does presume to conserve and use wisdom that is inherent in the political process. Lindblom concedes that it is possible to use rational design to make changes as large and significant as the actors' knowledge will permit. Given the limited knowledge of policy analysts, however, he suggests that it is normally a more reasonable strategy to make changes in small, and therefore more manageable, increments. If more rapid change is desired, he notes, the time between serial decisions may be reduced. Thus swift policy innovation and adaptation may be achieved by using an incremental design.

Social Design

A critical synthesis of the rational and incremental design frames (science and art) offers a conceptual lens that leavens interactive processes with political and social skills. Some argue simply that public administration should be seen as science but more than science, more than art—a constructive synthesis—with skillful administrators drawing from either or both perspectives to understand the complex dimensions and move their facilitative and deliberative process forward, anticipating contestation among the stakeholders and any actors who might be affected by the outcome of a decision. The design category on the far right of table 4.3—social design—offers a broader range of relevant meanings and activities than do the other two concepts, either alone or in tandem. I suggest social design as a conceptual metaphor for this field because it goes beyond the range of the other approaches to include philosophical and social considerations that better represent the real world of public administration.

Social design combines a high appreciation of the values of relevant actors by focusing on interpretation, understanding, sharing, and learning in organizational and social relationships (and action situations) and by taking a proactive stance regarding conflict resolution, learning, problem solving, and change. Meetings and forums facilitated by public administrators with a social design orientation invite the expression of the values held by incremental and rational design actors; this may result in agreement, or it may result in disagreement in the form of contestation. Social design adds multiple values, thus offering a much more comprehensive metaphor. My argument, again, is that the metaphors we employ to conceptualize public administration establish parameters, processes, beliefs, and behaviors for our field. A metaphor with large meanings and implications offers a way to broaden and enrich theory and practice in governmental administration. Crisis, rational, and incremental designs have shortcomings that make them inappropriate to use when creatively considering broadly shared choice and policy alternatives. None of these designs attracts a broad mix of citizen groups, expertise, individual citizens, and group interests in the development of public policy and, in particular, community problem solving. And none of these designs reflects the totality of what we should be teaching and doing in the field of public administration today. Because these designs are at the low end of the value appreciation dimension and the conflict resolution dimension (table 4.3), solutions to problems that they proffer often cannot stimulate effective collective action to implement the objectives. To the degree that crisis and rational designs do not reflect the values of organizational members and clients, and to the degree that crisis and incremental designs are unable to relate properly to technical-rational possibilities for coping with future problems, these design processes are inadequate for understanding and responding to complex social realities. Both value-based incremental politics and technical-knowledge-based rational choice need to be critically evaluated by the administrator and the stakeholders involved in the situation; here, the use of critical theory and public deliberation is an important conceptual base for social design.

The development of a process that facilitates interaction and participation is the essence of social design. A process is created as viable alternatives are formulated through social interaction and networking among administrators, experts, politicians, social groups, clients, and citizens associated with specific issues and problems. The process of social design assumes that design participants work to create solutions that are relevant to the problem and the means for implementing these solutions. Purposes and goals are socially constructed, developing out of human interaction, dialogue, and mutual learning. Political consensus is not the ultimate goal of social design. The focus, instead, is on understanding different ideas, experiences, and technical and social knowledge and on developing shared responsibility through decentralization. Expert knowledge is valued and put to use, but it, along with the experiential knowledge and intuitive feelings of other participants, is subjected to scrutiny and discussion. The social design process particularly stresses citizen participation.

Implications

The state of public administration today in both Western and non-Western countries may be best described in terms of crisis and transformation rather than stability and order. We are racked by continual organizational crises and chaos, most of which stem from an organizational incapacity to solve problems politically, financially, and humanely. Accordingly, crisis design is likely to continue for some time unless public organizations at all levels develop remedies that are creative, participatory, effective, and efficient. An environment of crisis inevitably affects the quality of an organization's internal management. More than ever, important decisions are unilaterally made by top-level managers. Employees are not involved in the decision-making process, even though these decisions will affect their working (and often their private) lives. This means that employees have less of a sense of psychological ownership of what they do and therefore are less committed to the implementation of organizational goals and tasks.

Although a crisis may be unavoidable because of the unintended consequences of past policies and actions, a crisis is also an invitation to new action. The challenge that a crisis provokes can bring new coping mechanisms to bear on a situation, ones that serve to strengthen an individual's adaptive capacity, thereby perhaps raising his or her level of mental health. In the same way, an organization can also learn new ways of coping in order to deal with a crisis, such as designing alternative ways of generating revenues and providing services to the public. Like individuals, different organizations react to a crisis in different ways. Every organization strives to maintain a sense of balance or adequacy, perhaps through a variety of reactive problem-solving and conflict resolution strategies or perhaps by developing innovative solutions after a critical and reflexive analysis of the crisis.

What is still lacking in incrementalism, however, is broader participation; characteristically participation is accomplished through the existing pluralistic framework, which is not, as we have noted, representative of the real needs of society. Indeed, one of the more substantial indictments of pluralism is its easy assumption that if the policy system meets the needs of each interest represented in it, then it will have met the needs of society as a whole. In most postindustrial countries, many public interest organizations and media play a significant role in voicing the problems and needs of ordinary citizens. In industrializing and non-

Western countries, however, it is only recently that nongovernmental organizations (NGOs) or nonprofit organizations (NPOs) have begun to exert some influence over the policy-making process.

Although rational policy analysts face inherent problems in their task of developing policy alternatives, the value of their professional knowledge should not be underestimated. To deny the legitimacy of the use of the rational approach in bureaucracy would be to reject the opportunity for professionals to apply technical knowledge and experience. Public bureaucracies are, more than ever, being forced to anticipate and learn to plan for the future. The unintended problems that plague policy implementation devolve not only from rational policy designs but also from incrementally developed designs. Designing important policies without professional assistance is, in a technological and postmodern society, hazardous. If policies are to be effective, the policy process should not confine itself to either the rational design or the incremental design approach. It should instead show the interdependence of the two perspectives. This may involve long public deliberation and contestation. For example, public administrators at the local level (counties, and cities) are forced to be reactive because of declining revenues and budget cuts in federally funded and state-funded programs. At the same time, they must be proactive in terms of planning ahead in order to reprioritize their goals, explore alternatives for generating new revenue sources, and maintain an adequate level of public services. Given this, social policy design emerges as a third perspective in dealing with conflicts, problems, and change.

Social design is a normative, descriptive, and critical strategy. It is normative because it prescribes the consideration of both rational-analytical strategy and incremental-political strategy. Policy should be based on the shared values of participants in a problem situation in which the knowledge of experts and administrators is related to that of outside groups and clients who will be affected by a particular policy decision. In this process, the debate includes not only economic and political considerations but also the feasibility of the policy obtaining social acceptance (the cooperation of organizations and clients during the implementation process).

Finally, social design is a critical approach, emphasizing the consciousness of the administrators, who are responsible for developing processes and interaction, for facilitating dialogue among participants, and for learning from unintended consequences. They must take a sharply critical stance in evaluating alternatives recommended by experts or demanded by interest groups and citizens.

CONCLUSION

Each of the three perspectives on public administration discussed in this chapter—administration as science, as art, and as social design—leads to a distinctly different pattern of administrative thought and action. Although these perspectives overlap to some degree, as dimensions of a larger design concept, they differ markedly in premise and in product. Public administrators committed to the science or to the art metaphor may expect to think and act in ways that fall short of what is needed—and what is possible—in many areas of concern in public policy making and administration. To continue to teach and train students of public administration in those terms is to narrow their perspectives and to stunt their professional growth, thereby limiting their potential contribution to public administration.

The image of public administration implied by the social design metaphor suggests what is actually happening in many organizations and communities at this time; it also suggests what many scholars and practitioners believe should be happening in the field. It is time for us to choose our metaphors accordingly. The major advantage of the social design approach is that it focuses attention on participation, relationship, dialogue, contestation, and the everyday lived experience of multiple actors with different backgrounds, while remaining open to developing critical strategies to the actors in their analysis and critique.

One of the keys to the social design approach is to create forums for all stakeholders and critical citizens to become involved. Several considerations need to be taken into account, such as how to generate and sustain interest so that administrators have a representative dialogue of the community at large. Is the dialogue taken seriously, or is it simply a formality? How do we educate public administrators about the importance of obtaining a genuine interest in understanding different ideas and experience? What if citizens do not respond to the opportunities provided? How can we avoid the problem of misinterpretation and misunderstanding of ideas and experiences of others? These are important matters that need to be considered when applying the social design approach, bringing it from its concept to practice and from social practice to theorizing.

CHAPTER 5

Social Design in Practice

Developments in public administration that broaden approaches to problem solving, take greater account of relevant variables in policy making, and challenge public administrators and citizens in positive ways offer many possibilities for strengthening both theory and practice in this field. Social design strategies have been widely practiced by administrators at the local level in their efforts to develop innovative and community-based projects and actions.

This chapter illustrates some of the values of and implications for the use of the social design concept as a guideline and as a metaphor for public administration by applying it to a few social policy issues. The social design approach is generally practiced in the following way:

1. The process begins with consideration of the diversity of values of the participants as well as the people who will be affected by the outcome of deliberation or problem solving. The ideas of different actors must be discussed, argued, and evaluated.

2. Participation must go beyond interest-group politics. Powerful groups are generally concerned with their own interests rather than the interest of the public.

3. The responsibility of administrators or policy makers is to design processes and facilitate interaction whereby multiple actors function together effectively. It is quite possible that the existing structure does not promote the participation of less-powerful groups or citizens.

4. Alternatives must be critically examined in terms of their political, economic, and social feasibility.

5. Policy design or decisions for the future require both analytical and social knowledge, but application of each must be critically examined through dialogue and discourse.

6. The voices of minority groups must be integrated into community problem solving.

The social design framework may be used as a cooperative approach to community problem solving. This democratic framework brings participating actors together, often voluntarily. These actors include a city administrator with managerial resources and authority, professionals with specialized skills and knowledge, and citizens with special concerns and ideas about problems in their community. In this context, formal authority and power are not the basis for developing problem-solving relationships among participants. The public administrator's responsibility is to facilitate various interactions and support the problem-solving effort.

COPRODUCTION AND COMMUNITY POLICING

Perhaps one of the most interesting developments in the area of community problem solving is a movement toward "coproduction" between public administrators and citizens. Traditionally, public managers have been either crisis oriented, incrementally oriented, or rationally oriented in performing their everyday activities and have viewed citizen participation as an obstacle to the "craft" of management and the "art" of government (Gawthrop, 1984, p. 105). They have seen their program objectives as the efficient operation and delivery of a public service. This narrow view of administrative responsibility has given way to the broader notion of coproduction, which is based on the "recognition that public services are the joint product of the activities of both citizens and government officials" (Sharp, 1980, p.110). Coproduction may be defined as "those actions by which citizens are intended to augment or contribute to the actions of public agencies and involve conjoint behavior" (Warren et al., 1982, p. 43). It is citizens' efforts that actually bring about the desired societal changes; the public administrator only assists or advises citizens in these productive efforts. Because citizens can act as critical evaluators of public services and can also create "service conditions," they should be viewed as "coproducers in the sense that their behaviors change the environment (social and physical) in which service delivery takes place" (Sharp, 1980, p. 112). Thus public policy and administration in recent years have brought an interest in participatory democracy to the fore, with a refocusing on citizen participation (and voluntarism); citizen participation has become an energizing force in the governance process (Box, 1998).

An interesting application of social design in community problem solving is the development of community-based policing in many city neighborhoods (Thurman, Zhao, and Giacomazzi, 2001; Peak and Glensor, 1996; Goldstein, 1990). This value-driven approach to providing police services functions at the neighborhood level, and its success is tied to changes in police organizational culture. The programs offer unique interactions between the police department and neighborhood organizations seeking to manage the future of their community through a "coproductive" effort. Neighborhood activities are consciously designed to improve individual safety and involve citizens and public agencies in interaction.

For many years, most especially from the 1940s to the 1970s, police administrators focused on developing different techniques to increase the control and efficiency of their agencies (Goldstein, 1990, p. 7). Somewhere along the way, police administrators lost sight of the people and the communities whom they served. The civil rights demonstrations, racial conflicts, riots, and political protests of the 1960s and 1970s made for strained relationships between citizens and the police. Moreover, beginning in the early 1980s, the public's growing concern about crime only increased this alienation. From 1967 to 1973, five national studies were conducted to assess police practices and fundamental social problems (Goldstein, 1990, p. 9). These studies indicated that the way to improve policing was to continue to emphasize professionalization, focusing on efficiency, control, the use of scientific techniques, and the social work role of the police officer.

As crime, civil unrest, neighborhood decay, community disorder, and citizens' dissatisfaction with policing began to rise, however, this professional orientation came under fire. In 1979, Herman Goldstein developed problem-oriented policing (POP), which addressed how a police agency as a whole could analyze a given citywide problem and its response to it (1979). Goldstein asserted the following: "[P]roblem resolution constituted the true, substantive work of policing and advocated that police identify and address root causes of problems that led to repeat calls for service. POP required a move from a reactive, incident-driven stance to one that actively addressed the problems that continually drained police resources" (1979, pp. 241). Goldstein considers POP to be "a better balance between the reactive and proactive aspects of policing." He says that POP makes "more effective use of the community and rank-and-file officers in getting the police job done"

(1990, pp. 3, 32). Beginning in the early 1980s, many police chiefs and administrators began to base their agency's goals on a philosophy known as community oriented policing (COP). This proactive approach focuses on developing problem-solving strategies and decentralizing police authority. The emphasis of COP is to improve the relationship between the police and the public, in which the police work with the people in the community that they serve.[1] Community policing is now practiced in many countries, particularly in the United States. Many different forms of community policing have been developed by police agencies in the United States and abroad. The programs take into account "the community needs, politics, and resources available" (Peak and Glensor, 1996, p. 71).

By 2000, more than 50 percent of cities in the United States, with a population greater than fifty thousand have established community-oriented policing programs. The effectiveness of the programs varies from city to city. On the whole, police chiefs think that community policing is important in that it helps citizens to feel connected to the police. Citizens work with the police on issues facing the community, including crime prevention, the detection and arrest of offenders, the preservation of the peace, law enforcement, the protection of life and property, community safety, and reducing the fear of crime. When police departments develop their mission statements, they include these elements, emphasizing their partnership with the community in resolving these issues.

One popular program is Neighborhood Watch. This program focuses on establishing a positive working relationship between police and the community through mechanisms both formal (advisory board meetings and monthly community meetings) and informal (storefront headquarters, an emphasis on service to the community, and a nonaggressive patrol stance). With technical assistance and leadership from the police department, a group of citizens can start their own Neighborhood Watch. The objectives of most programs are (1) to protect their local neighborhood through cooperation and participation and (2) to be observant of any suspicious acts in the neighborhood and report them to the police. The efforts of a small band of neighbors can be very successful in reducing crime in a neighborhood.

For example, through the proactive efforts of police departments and citizens' crime prevention committees in many cities in the San Francisco–San Jose–Oakland Bay Area, today there are hundreds of

Home Alert and Neighborhood Watch groups. These programs, which are implemented by police departments and built on citizen involvement, work to identify crime problems and develop preventive strategies. Although the crime rate in large metropolitan cities such as San Francisco, San Jose, and Oakland is still relatively high compared with smaller cities in the Bay Area, the police departments firmly believe that citizen involvement in crime prevention programs has been a major factor in combating and reducing various types of crime. Community-oriented policing alone cannot solve the problem of crime, but it is one facet of a multifaceted approach to law enforcement. The need for cooperation between police officers and citizens is documented by studies of many U.S. cities.

Social design is the foundation of community-oriented policing. It takes a broad approach to law enforcement and decentralizes the hierarchy that once held police organizations so tightly together and so distant from citizens. Police officers learn through their community interactions that citizens have valuable knowledge because they live in the areas where crimes are being committed. When law enforcement administrators and police officers acknowledge that they are not the sole experts and that citizens have expertise also, they find better ways of serving the community. Whether community policing actually reduces the rate of crime is still open to debate. However, in order to make the collaborative process between citizens and the police workable, police officers need to be less concerned with their power, tough professional image, and secrets and move toward the "service style of policing," which emphasizes providing services to residents, meeting citizens' needs, and conforming to the public's idea of how the police should operate (Wilson, 1968).

BRIDGING THE DIGITAL DIVIDE IN SILICON VALLEY

The digital divide is a global phenomenon that reflects many aspects of digital technology and the economy. Today, society and organizations increasingly rely on computers and the Internet to obtain, transfer, and communicate information. This new technology has made significant inroads into everyday life: many rely on it for shopping, banking, obtaining information, conducting research, and even enrolling in educational programs. Society and the organizations within society would find it difficult to function without telecommunication tools. Citizens of industrialized countries have more access to information technology, and most homes in these countries are wired. The digital divide between poor and rich countries continues to widen. Pippa Norris illustrates three distinct divides: "The *global divide* refers to the divergence of Internet access between industrialized and developing societies. The *social divide* concerns the gap between information rich and poor in each nation. And finally, within the online community, the *democratic divide* signifies the difference between those who do, and do not, use the panoply of digital resources to engage, mobilize, and participate in public life" (2001, p. 3).

A digital divide in Silicon Valley largely stems from socioeconomic differences among the races and geographical areas within that region. Silicon Valley, located in the southern part of the San Francisco-Oakland Bay Area, is faced with serious problems stemming from rapid growth in the past ten years. The area is internationally known as the center of technological development. Its success and growth have also generated a number of unintended consequences, such as a severe housing shortage, traffic congestion, environmental degradation, a soaring cost of living, and widening socioeconomic disparities. Perplexing issues for the region center around whether the bourgeoning regional economy is sustainable, what the regional economy's impact is on the quality of life, and how locals can obtain technological skills to be successful. Another serious issue is the widening academic achievement gap in schools, which prevents many students—especially Latinos, African Americans, and students from low-income households—from acquiring high-demand, high-paying, and high-tech jobs. In addition, Silicon Valley has a technology access gap: this means that many Silicon Valley residents do not know how to work with technology applications such as the Internet and have not acquired other skills essential for a career in the new economy. Thousands of Silicon Valley residents feel the effects of this digital divide in, ironically enough, the world's technological center. Minorities, low-income persons, the less educated, and children of single-parent households are among the groups that lack access to information resources.

Joint Venture is a Silicon Valley network led by a board of twenty-five to thirty business, government, education, and community leaders. The board, which consists of a wide range of people, such as business personnel, politicians, educators, city and county officials, and representatives of nonprofit organizations meets five times each year. It is a nonprofit organization funded by large and small businesses; local, state, and federal government; professional associations; labor organizations; foundations; and individuals. Today Joint Venture includes a "core" and eleven action-oriented initiatives. The core supports development of the initiatives, benchmarks their progress, facilitates internal and external communication, tracks changes in the economy of and quality of life in Silicon Valley, and serves as a forum for addressing new regional issues.

With support from the David and Lucile Packard Foundation and the James Irvine Foundation, both of them nongovernmental organizations, Joint Venture established the Silicon Valley Civic Action Network (SV CAN), involving thousands of residents and workers. On April 8, 2000, SV CAN hosted a community forum on two important issues—bridging the digital divide and promoting livable communities—at the Mexican Heritage Plaza in San Jose. The community forum broadened Joint Venture's focus on community outreach and civic engagement.

About two hundred people attended the forum and expressed diverse views on the digital divide. This enabled a large group of people to collectively assist Joint Venture in planning goals regarding this issue of concern to the community. Each participant joined a small-group discussion and spent three hours preparing ideas and materials for plenary discussion before the lunch break. The group reports were submitted to the planning committee. During lunch, people divided into different groups, continuing to discuss community issues and ways of improving them. After lunch, at a plenary session where all of the participants were together in one room, a summary was presented that categorized participants' concerns and suggestions for reducing the digital divide. Some of the major ideas developed in the forum included mentor programs, training workshops for children, use of technology in classrooms, training well-qualified teachers, promoting citizen awareness of the digital divide, and recruiting volunteers who can provide technical assistance to children and schools.

This one-day forum was a future search (a search conference) and included concerned citizens in the process of organizational and community planning.[2] The meeting stressed the importance of exploring ideas, talking over issues, sharing experiences, learning common concerns, and taking responsibility for what happened. Attendees seemed to be educated people who understood community issues. Participants were a cross-section of different ethnic groups; about 50 percent were Latino. Most future search conferences run for two and one-half days so that participants can develop a vision of the future. Although this particular forum was only one day, it created a valuable arena for dialogue in the civic space. At the plenary session, supporting comments were made by the mayor of San Jose, a California state senator, and the executive director of Joint Venture. They particularly emphasized the shared responsibility of state and city governments, businesses, and nongovernmental organizations. Discussion focused on collaboration, networking relationships, and community support. Since this event, the planning staff of Joint Venture has initiated some concrete change activity and structured a follow-up process for sharing achievements and learning. Because of the noncontroversial nature of the digital divide issue, there was no apparent disagreement during the meetings. Implicit in attending community meetings was participants' willingness to understand the issue and seek ways of resolving the gap by developing programs to help those without access to the Internet.

HELPING HOMELESSNESS

Homeless has become a significant social problem only within the last twenty years. More than a decade of research and program and policy development have identified the causes and effects of homelessness. People who are involved in homeless research and services now have proven approaches that can prevent homelessness before it starts and end homelessness where it now exists. Philip Mangano, executive director of the U.S. Interagency Council on Homelessness based in Washington, has boldly asserted that this is a "complex but solvable problem." The consensus on solving the problem is based on current approaches, funding, innovation, and leadership that require the coordination of all possible solutions. People should work toward the "community impact agenda"—where all programs fit into a comprehensive continuum of services provided consistently and designed for the long term (*San Francisco Chronicle*, December 24, 2003). The most important lesson learned from the past is that ending homelessness requires the partnership of many sectors. No one entity acting alone can make an impact on such a complex social issue. Government, the business community, and the philanthropic and nonprofit sectors must work together, not at odds, to implement the approaches that will eliminate homelessness. For example, the Housing for Emancipated Youth (HEY) program in the San Jose/San Francisco/Oakland region is a collaboration of thirty-six public, private and nonprofit agencies designed and funded by United Way of the Bay Area to assist foster youth to successfully transition to adult independence. HEY's partner agencies provide housing and social services for young people "aging out" of the foster care system at age eighteen, the emancipated foster youth. Because 50 percent of former foster youths become homeless within two to four years of exiting foster care, the need for housing and services for these youths is tremendous (*San Francisco Chronicle*, December 24, 2003)

Homelessness is a widespread and complex human problem in many countries. In the United States, although reliable statistics are hard to collect, *The Economist* reports that "between 700,000 and 800,000 people are homeless in the United States on any given night, and between 2.5 million and 3.5 million people will experience homelessness [in 2003]. By most measures, the figure is rising, made worse by a bleak economy" (*The Economist*, August 23, 2003, p. 19).[3] According to various research, homeless people are mostly single adults who are alcoholics, drug addicts, mentally ill, or simply unemployed. The U.S. Conference of Mayors estimated, in a survey of thirty major cities, that families with children made up about 38 percent of the homeless population in 1998, compared with about 27 percent in 1985.[4] Moreover, the needs and assistance that they require differ greatly. Although homelessness is an episodic event for many people, who rely temporarily on emergency shelters to help them get through a difficult situation, it is a chronic condition for others, particularly for those who have a serious substance abuse disorder or a serious physical or mental disability. Consequently, in addition to housing, these individuals may require intensive and ongoing supportive services, such as mental health care or substance abuse treatment, so that they do not slide into homelessness again.

In 1987, U.S. Congress enacted the Stewart B. McKinney Homeless Assistance Act, recognizing that state, local, and private efforts alone were not adequate to address the growing problem of homelessness in this country. Since the McKinney Act passed, federal resources for alleviating homelessness have increased significantly, and a number of new federal programs have been created specifically to serve homeless people. At the federal level, fifty programs, administered by eight federal agencies, provide services to the homeless, including the departments of Agriculture; Health and Human Services; Education; Labor and Veterans Affairs; and two independent agencies, the Federal Emergency Management Agency and the Social Security Administration. The federal government spent $2.2 billion in fiscal year 2002–2003 on homeless programs, and in the same period, many cities, such as San Francisco, Los Angeles, Chicago, Philadelphia, Atlanta, and Miami, each spent millions of dollars on programs for the homeless.

The most significant barrier that homeless people face in getting off the street is a dire lack of housing. Single-parent families and single adults cannot find affordable enough housing. Although the responsibility for providing housing for people across the country is shared by city, state, and federal governments, the problem has grown to such proportions that only with a massive infusion of federal housing dollars can the crisis be meaningfully addressed. When the federal budget for permanent affordable housing was cut, the problem of homelessness across the nation grew, and once the cuts reached $29 billion, the problem became one of epidemic proportions. The last significant attempt to build low-income housing was made in the mid 1970s, during the Ford administration. In 2003, a diverse national coalition that includes Religious Leaders' National Call for Action on Housing, the Religious Witness with Homeless People, and various coalitions on homelessness (for example, the San Francisco Coalition on Homelessness) emerged to campaign for passage of the National Affordable Housing Trust Fund, which is currently making its way through Congress. Such legislation would restore the capacity of the U.S. Department of Housing and Urban Development to build permanent, affordable housing, finally addressing the nation's housing crisis.

Designing and implementing programs to help the homeless, such as soup kitchens, shelters, job training, health services, and job referrals, requires the coordination and contributions of government agencies, volunteers, charity organizations, religious organizations, and businesses. Government alone cannot possibly solve the complex issues of the homelessness problem. Likewise, neither rational-economic analysis nor incremental politics can solve the problem of homelessness. The only meaningful solution to this lingering social problem depends on the collaboration and networking of multiple organizations and actors. A strongly hierarchical governing of such programs, which is often imposed by government agencies, would be counterproductive. Even if a program required intercity coordination, a hierarchical approach would not be possible. Furthermore, understanding the problems of chronically homeless people requires a broad knowledge and the contributions of many fields, including psychiatry, sociology, psychology, and anthropology. The analysis and interpretation of the problems of homeless people that scholars in relevant fields offer are invaluable to the design of programs that reflect homeless people's everyday experiences. In addition, the facilitative role of public administrators is to identify resources and activities that can assist the homeless and inform them about service-providing organizations. Unfortunately, people who provide direct services to the homeless people are often not well informed about the resources available. One resource is the Department of Energy, which provides insulation to qualifying homeless shelters. Other resources are the Veterans Administration and the Rural Housing Services in the Department of Agriculture, which make foreclosed properties available to nonprofit organizations for housing the homeless.

DESIGNING THE PUBLIC TRANSIT SYSTEM

The public transit problem in the metropolitan areas of the United States provides an excellent example of how social design could be put into practice.[5] Creating an effective transit system in the diverse environment of a U.S. metropolitan area is difficult indeed. In every metropolitan area in the United States, there are scores of population concentrations, but few dominate. There are several county governments and many city governments, thousands of business and manufacturing firms, many powerful interests, multiple domains, extraordinary real estate requirements and costs, demanding and changing technologies, insufficient funds, and other problems. In this environment, those committed to the model of administration as science (rational design) would approach the problem from its technical and engineering aspects. Guidelines would include reliability, safety, appropriate technical applications (conservatively viewed), and service to major centers. Traffic volume, speed, the location and cost of rights-of-way, and other matters of this nature would also be pertinent.

Incremental designers, the administrative artists, would focus more on the users of the facilities. They would be more interested in the political (and societal) dimensions of the project, and their product would be somewhat less abusive of the people and the area affected. These administrators would pay careful attention to political consider-ations, accommodate more variations among client needs, and treat the public interest more insightfully. They would be more sensitive to the consequences of all of the alternatives. Negative unintended outcomes would be less likely.

The social design approach to the transit problem, by contrast, would draw on experts of all sorts, as well as interest groups, politicians, and members of the public, to put together a creative amalgam that took account into technical, political, social, and people's needs. Both short-term and long-term goals and possible consequences would be consid-ered. A social designer would treat elemental functions of the system fully (collection, rapid transit, and distribution), but he or she would also reach for larger, more elegant solutions in metropolitan terms. Some of the social designer's considerations would include the following:

- inner city transportation for the poor; commuter transportation for the middle class
- conservation of energy and resources; protection of the environment
- transit services seen in broad terms, rather than as just physical facilities
- public transit perceived as connecting people, rather than simply areas
- maximizing benefit, rather than minimizing investment
- cherishing the integrity of neighborhoods and serving their needs
- public access to work, shops, and recreation; improving the quality of life
- relating all transit to metropolitan problems, including congestion, land use, quality of the environment, resource use, private trans-portation, costs, recreation, pollution, growth, economic health, minorities, and so on
- access to the "goods" of society by everyone; the "right of mobility" for those without cars, the disabled, the aged, children, stay-at-home spouses in single-car households, tourists, transients, the underprivileged, and so on

- system costs realistically appraised in comparison with the true personal and social costs that automobiles impose on a metropolitan area
- involvement of clientele, interests, neighborhoods, individuals, experts, and other interested parties in the decision process
- imaginative consideration of cost, comfort, safety, aesthetics, and state-of-the-art technology as these and other matters arise
- improved quality of working life for transit system employees.

One of the successful transit programs using the social design approach is the development of a transit system for disabled people that includes all elements of a democratic process. The local governments in the United States have been developing the transportation facilities for handicapped people better than most countries. Paratransit is a program that offers persons with disabilities an opportunity to connect to places within a community through nontypical public transportation options. Public transportation services for the general public usually employ a fixed route service that travels along a predetermined route at established times. Persons with disabilities commonly have difficulty accessing fixed route systems due to travel distances to designated stops. The Paratransit program and the resulting benefits for this distinct population are direct results of the Americans with Disabilities Act (ADA) of 1990. Today there are over 54 million Americans with disabilities that qualify for considerations under ADA. The ADA was established to provide a clear and comprehensive prohibition of discrimination on the basis of disability (Urban Mass Transportation Administration, 1991). Title II of the ADA requires that local, state, and other nonfederal public government agencies make services, programs, and activities accessible to those covered under ADA. Title II also seeks to guarantee that people with disabilities will have reasonable access to modes of public transportation. Transit authorities and providers must provide a service that is supplementary to regular fixed-route services for persons with ADA. This type of service is called "paratransit" and usually includes a bus service or other special transportation services that provide door-to-door, or curb-to-curb service and assistance for ADA users. There is an exception to this rule if providing this service would place an undue burden on the government agency. Title II also addresses the necessary enhancements in equipment used for providing paratransit service.

Without this vital service many disabled persons could not get to doctor's appointments, supermarkets, social events, and so on.

The input from stakeholders, seniors and people with disabilities, helps to develop local policy. In many local cities, the result of satisfied constituents was realized by providing access to essential places to those persons requiring public transportation. The strength of the paratransit programs comes from strong policy support from the community. This is a direct result of a system designed from community involvement and supported by federal, state, and local mandates. The continuous improvement of paratransit programs requires the survey of stakeholders in order to receive feedback directly from the users of the system. The role of city administrators is to actively seek out the voices in the community.

THE CLINTON HEALTH CARE REFORM PLAN: FROM SOCIAL DESIGN TO INCREMENTALISM

President Bill Clinton's introduction of the 1993 Health Security Bill serves as an important example of a national debate on a health care reform. Five days after his inauguration, the President Clinton appointed First Lady Hillary Clinton as head of the Task Force on National Health Care Reform. The task force was given a clear mission: write legislation to be submitted to Congress. Ira Magaziner, a policy expert and friend of the president, was appointed coordinator of the twelve-member task force, which included Donna Shalala, secretary of Health and Human Services. Magaziner, who disliked politics and public relations, designed the structured policy-making process with particular attention to detail. More than five hundred people were under his supervision, and they were organized into fifteen cluster groups, studying such issues as cost controls, coverage, benefits, longterm care, and the ethical foundations of the new health care system. The task force spent nine months debating, drafting, and revising legislative language in order to create a blueprint for health care reorganization (Morton, 2001, p. 72; Birenbaum, 1997).

On September 22, 1993, President Clinton outlined his proposal to a joint session of Congress. The bill guaranteed coverage for preventive, primary, and acute health care and limited mental health care, and long-term care services to all U.S. residents. Employers would pay at least 80 percent of the insurance premiums for their employees, and universal coverage would be achieved by 1999. The president submitted his Health Security Bill to Congress in November 1993. This bill was widely debated. In order to build support from the public, interest groups, professionals, politicians, labor unions, large and small businesses, and health related industries, the Clinton administration engaged in public debate through town hall meetings, conferences, focus group meetings, university forums, TV programs, and congressional subcommittee hearings. While the task force was formulating policy options, politics was left to the president, the first lady, and their political advisers. Hillary Clinton met with important health care constituencies and gave numerous speeches on behalf of national health insurance.

The Clinton plan, however, came under tremendous assault from various opponents, such as the Business Roundtable (representing about two hundred of the nation's largest companies), the National Federation of Independent Business, the U.S. Chamber of Commerce, the National Association of Manufacturers, and the Health Insurance Association of America. Lobbyists for every conceivable interest that could be affected by any version of the legislation swarmed over the capitol. According to the *New York Times* (August 29, 1994), opponents spent "more than $50 million in advertising and much of it simply false."[6] For example, negative commercials by the insurance industry led the public to believe that passage of the bill would mean the creation of a billion-dollar bureaucracy.

Between 1990 and early 1993, there was a vast grassroots interest in radical change in the nation's health care system. The White House assumed that a newly elected president had a mandate for reducing the federal deficit and reforming the health care system. However, the president and his task force misunderstood the mandate for a tremendously complicated overhaul of a system as sensitive as health care. When the task force produced a 1,342–page plan at the end of 1993, there were not many supporters of the president's proposal; political resistance began to emerge. The voters wanted reform, but they wanted something easy to understand, something that did not look as threatening as the Clinton plan. Sallayanne Payton, who was legal counsel to the Clinton White House for health care and a member of the task force, says that "the apparent public support for what was being described as 'health care reform' was a weak need. Middle-class dissatisfaction with the present state of affairs did not assure informed and vigorous support for universal coverage, come what may be" (Payton, 1998, p. 221).

There were other numerous mistakes, misjudgments, and unanticipated political barriers that surrounded the campaign to achieve universal health care coverage:

- The policy experts developing proposals for universal health care coverage, a comprehensive package of health benefits and federal subsidies for poor people, rarely spoke to the fiscal experts. Payton admits that "the Clinton Plan, as it was submitted to Congress, was a consequence of the Clinton planners' attempt to achieve comprehensive rationality within the logic of their goal of universal coverage" (Payton, 1998, p. 224).

- Many business executives rejected the complexity of the Clinton plan and the expansion of Federal authority that the president was proposing. They thought that they could control health care costs much better than the federal government could. They also feared that under the Clinton plan, they would lose the right to design health benefits to meet their employees' needs. The National Federation of Independent Business had strongly opposed the plan to require employers to help buy health insurance for their workers. According to these organizations, employers had to absorb added insurance costs, and then many of them would have to lay off their employees. Losing the support of big business was a significant setback for the president, because the administration had counted on such companies to offset the opposition of the small-business lobby. The National Federation of Independent Business argued that jobs would be lost if employers had to absorb added insurance costs. This tactic seemed to induce a fear in the minds of the public.

- Instead of analyzing the issues and educating the public about health care reform, newspapers and television largely increased public skepticism.

- Supporters of the Clinton health care reform plan, such as AFL-CIO, the American Academy of Pediatrics, the Catholic Health Association, the Health Care Reform Project, and the American Association of Retired Persons, proved no match for the groups opposing the president. Citizen Action, a consumer group, said that political action committees formed by insurance companies, doctors, hospitals, drug companies, and others in the health care industry contributed more than $26 million to members of Congress from January 1993 to May 1994.

- The president's allies continually qualified their support by expressing concern about specific parts of his plan. Labor unions worried that the plan was going to tax away some of the benefits that they had won in collective bargaining. Doctors specializing in internal medicine supported much of the plan but objected to the proposed cutbacks in Medicare and to the idea of federal limits on private health insurance premiums.

The Clinton administration handled the political process poorly. In order to share legislative responsibility, Congress created five committees. There were three in the House of Representatives: the Ways and Means Committee, the Energy and Commerce Committee, and the Education and Labor Committee. There were two in the Senate: the Labor and Human Resources Committee and the Finance Committee. These five committees, rather than a single, joint committee, dealt with health insurance reform. The struggle for universal coverage began to collapse in the committees because each committee worked independently. Separate committee deliberations opened up "greater opportunity for legislative disagreement" (Heirich, 1998, p. 120). Sallyanne Payton pointed out "a mismatch between the comprehensiveness of the president's proposal and the fragmented nature of Congressional considerations" (Payton, 1998, p. 211–12). The committees tried to reach consensus on how to cover everybody without antagonizing the small-business lobby, but they always ran up against the same insoluble issues. Without an employer mandate (putting the financial burden on employers) or a broad-based tax increase (putting the financial burden on taxpayers), how could they pay for it?

On August 2, 1994, Senator George Mitchell of Maine, the Senate majority leader, introduced an alternative health care reform bill, which would, through voluntary measures and subsidies, cover 95 percent of all Americans by the year 2000. The president said that the Mitchell bill met his requirements, but congressional leaders and White House officials all but conceded that there was no chance of passing universal health insurance legislation that year. On September 26, 1994, Mitchell announced that "there will be no major health insurance legislation this year." The Clinton administration showed a continuing uncertainty about how to deal with Republicans and other combative oppositions. Because of too many negative forces rising, the president had to withdraw the health care reform plan.

Implications

The Clinton plan opened up governmental processes, inviting participation. Citizens, powerful interest groups, nongovernmental organizations, politicians, professionals, and the media all became involved in the development of the health care reform plan. It was perhaps the most open process of public policy formulation to occur in this country, and it occupied from November 1993 and September 1994. The Clinton administration's appeal to the public is an example of the social design approach. The Clinton administration, however, demonstrated some major shortcomings in its pursuit of the social design approach. Moreover, the Clinton health care reform plan eventually became a victim of the incremental politics of Congress.

The demise of the Clinton plan was largely caused by poor political handling of the plan in Congress; in particular, Congress exhibited an unwillingness to compromise. The Republicans opted out of the consensus process, and the Democrats were doubtful about the future of the reform plan. There was a general agreement that the president would have gotten much closer to his reform goal if he had acted faster and compromised earlier, before the opposition had mobilized and his own standing had weakened. Some policy analysts thought that his delay was a fundamental error, the crucial stumbling block to the passing of the legislation.

The history of the Clinton health care legislation shows the complexity involved in attempting to legislate major change in an era of intense partisanship, with a public that does not trust the national government to manage big bureaucracy. The Clinton administration, particularly Hillary Clinton, had a strong conviction about its reform plan and was unwilling to compromise. For instance, Hillary Clinton and Ira Magaziner met with many outside groups but did not have confidence in them. They assumed that because the public favored fundamental change in health care, it was the kind of change the policy analysts (and the task force) wanted. Furthermore, the administration officials and Magaziner alienated potential allies in Congress by ignoring the politicians' points of view.

Perhaps the most important consequence of the failed reform plan was that it raised the consciousness of the nation about the fact that 45 million of its citizens are uninsured and that the rise in health care costs today is equivalent to nearly 14.5 percent of the Gross Domestic Product. Furthermore, through the widely publicized process of the health care debate, the public has gained some valuable insights into the complexity of the health care issue.

THE LIMITS OF SOCIAL DESIGN

The social design approach not only describes how problems can be solved through the collaboration of the stakeholders and the many people who will be affected by their decision, but it also stresses how they ought to be solved. It is descriptive in the sense that the work of many effective public organizations can be explained through the process of social construction, as presented in chapter 4. It is also a normative approach to problem solving, because an emphasis on process, values, learning, and change provides a direction for purposeful action in which humans interact with one another to create a shared reality. Through social design processes, actors can explore alternative possibilities, change traditional ways of solving problems, and develop new strategies for the effective implementation of shared goals.

Despite its conceptual advantage over other types of design and problem solving, social design is not widely practiced in rigid public organizations and inactive communities. If the concept of social design is to be related to administrative practice, then students of public administration need to examine critically constraints discussed in the rest of this section.

Policy design in government, particularly at the federal and state levels, is largely the outcome of incremental politics. This includes politics between and among government agencies, executive offices (e.g., the Office of Management and Budget and a state governor's office), the houses of Congress, experts, and special-interest groups. Citizens and interest groups with limited economic resources or political muscle are mostly unable to influence the decision-making process. The case of the Clinton health care reform plan demonstrates the difficulty of implementing the social design process at the national level. At the local level, however, the social design process has had numerous successes.

Because local governments are close to citizens and deal with community problems directly, various forms of civic engagement in the decision-making process can make for effective collaboration between public administrators and citizens.

Professionals in government agencies often view citizen participation as a hindrance to their comprehensive planning of long-term goals. They attempt to solve problems through technical means. Involving citizens and special-interest groups in policy design and community problem solving is time consuming and, at best, a slow process. Participation is often viewed as inefficient and, in the short run, unproductive.

Although the social design approach is more widely used at the local level, its effectiveness depends largely on the attitude and action orientation of city and county officials. Public administrators and elected officials often take a reactive approach to citizens' needs and community problem solving. However, when public administrators are reactive—indifferent to innovation, uninterested in changing the traditional way of governing—then citizens will eventually take on the advocacy role in order to change their behavior.

Finally, many public organizations are designed to be unproductive, unresponsive, bureaucratic, and resistant to innovation. Experimentation in social design requires proactive behavior on the part of administrators. These administrators need to be less conscious of their official status, willing to share their authority and power with less powerful individuals and change the centralized system to a decentralized, participatory process of management.

CONCLUSION

One positive attribute of social design is that multiple actors are involved. Additionally, administrative and policy-making formats are more democratic. Organizational change projects, such as organizational development, improving the quality of work life, organizational redesign, participatory management, creative problem solving, teamwork, action research, flextime, job rotation, networking, and career development, are natural outcomes of the enlarged perspective of social design. So are such social policy developments as AIDs education programs, long-range community planning, developing a mission statement and goals, building a sustainable (or conserving) society, and revising a city's general plan. These require the combined efforts of many people and groups, extensive interaction, and expenditures of resources of many kinds. Furthermore, social design and community planning involving politics and deliberation demand sharing information, clarifying the rules and language used, and developing trust between administrators and citizens through communicative action (Forester, 1985, pp. 202–27). In performing these problem-solving activities, public administrators may proactively facilitate citizen involvement in identifying problems as well as setting goals in order to guide the development of their communities. The most important implication is that government alone cannot solve many complex social problems, such as homelessness.

Currently, local public administrators are also finding it useful to work with citizens, interest groups, and advisory committees in designing alternative ways to deliver community services, such as community-based health care services. What is evolving is citizen participation in such activities as setting budget priorities, coproduction between citizens and government (as in crime prevention), social (community) networks among concerned individuals, neighborhood action groups for crime prevention, volunteer programs for the elderly, planning local transportation systems, and narrowing the digital divide. In all cases, the process requires citizen participation and a "future consciousness" on the part of many people.

CHAPTER 6

Understanding Action, Praxis, and Change

Changing an organization is one of the most difficult endeavors because not only does change require resources, but, most important, it requires that people share knowledge, learn, and make a commitment to their plans. When change results from the social construction process, as opposed to the application of theory to changing people's behavior, the participants develop a new understanding of what they have to achieve. As William James points out, the object (a change project in this case) itself is nonspiritual: what is spiritual is the subject's consciousness and existence, or, "what the world means to us" (Wilshire, 1968). In this chapter, I engage an essential and necessary aspect of changing organizations—understanding human action—and raise it to a level of special concern. Traditional organizational development (OD) methods for organizational change treat change as an object or an intended goal to be accomplished by following an established model. But these methods explain little about interpreting what the individual participants actually experience. When people are involved in changing organizations or creating projects through the action research process, they begin to appreciate and experience their contribution to the creation and accomplishment. Changing a person's behavior in organizations in the Eastern and the Western countries depends on how well an individual internalizes new ideas and makes them symbolically meaningful. Thus change results from a reflexive action that derives from his or her critical consciousness (praxis). Paulo Freire, a Brazilian education philosopher, points out, "Human beings are active beings, capable of reflection on themselves and on the activity in which they are engaged" (1973, p. 105). Because the process of changing organizations demands that participants in the process reflect critically upon themselves in relation to behavior, action, established culture, peers, and environment, the concept of 'praxis' is emphasized in order to distinguish a reflexive sense-making act of a public administrator from a less critical act of routine

123

practice. Other questions explored in this chapter are: How are actions of organizational members to be conceptualized? How is repetitive practice different from a critical, reflexive act (praxis)? What are its implications for changing organizations? These questions certainly apply to public administrators in both Eastern and Western countries.

THE DIALECTIC OF ORGANIZATIONAL ACTION

The concept of 'action' represents actual phenomena of human conduct in the everyday world of administration. No analysis of organizational change would be complete without a proper understanding of actions. Furthermore, a scholar's attempt to construct an administrative theory would be incomplete without an action frame of reference that incorporated the dimensions of the organization, the individuals in the organization, and the public. Although historically, action theory has been an important theoretical perspective in sociology and public administration (Parsons, 1937; 1968; 1978; Parsons and Shils, 1951; Silverman, 1970; Harmon, 1981; Denhardt, 1981), in recent years, it has received less attention from students of public administration. This shift in theoretical inquiry may be influenced by the currently strong management orientation toward controlling scarce resources and employee performance. Managers are more interested in modifying employees' behavior than in understanding the problems of actions.

In this chapter, I briefly discuss three perspectives on the explanation and understanding of action. I particularly emphasize my opinion that meanings of administrative action need to be dialectically constructed. The dialectical approach to the understanding of action proceeds from an examination of the assumptions and interpretations of acting individuals when they relate to other actors and external objects. When employees are pressured to conform to the rules of their organization, they do not have the power to disobey. They can, however, contrive ways to not cooperate with management's demand by being noncommittal and slow to do the work. But the latter choice may bring about undesirable consequences. Both managers and employees can impose limits upon each other that prevent effective collaboration. Thus the dialectical approach can help individuals to eschew a one-dimensional view of human action, one that is determined either by organizational requirements or by a voluntary (often selfish) choice on the part of the individual. The dialectical view of action provides a constructive ground for satisfying value judgments on the basis of organizational necessity (collective interest) as well as the individual's subjective intentionality. As long as administrative organizations aim to solve problems effectively to change, both internally and externally, then interdependence, interconnectedness, and a constructive synthesis between them are often inevitable and necessary, although there is no subtle way of achieving that synthesis (Bernstein, 1983; Schein, 1970).

The Functionalist Perspective: Objective Meaning-Context

The prevalent view of action in public administration literature is one that refers to the idea of administrative action, suggesting that an administrative agency enforces a particular decision or policy, targeting a particular client group in society. Administrative action also refers to a course of action taken by an organizational actor, such as an agency director. In this situation, action is largely interpreted as a system of action consisting of organizational relationships between actors and their environmental situations and interactions among the subsystems (subunits) of administrative action. This view of human action is common in functionalist explanations.

The functionalist view of administrative action is most forcefully illustrated by the complex work of Talcott Parsons, who was influenced by the positivistic and empirical epistemology of Kant and Durkheim, the interpretive and idealistic epistemology of Weber, and the psychoanalytic theory of Freud (Münch, 1987). Parsons's action theory was intended to go beyond the methodological dualism that was emphasized by his predecessors. He appreciated Weber's integration of positivism and idealism to his construction of an action theory and his development of ideal types. In his own action theory, Parsons integrates and explains interdependence and interpenetration among complex elements of a cultural system, a social system, and an individual's personality (Parsons, 1951, 1949, 1978; Parsons and Shils, 1951).[1]

For Parsons, social action is all human behavior that is motivated and directed by the meanings that actors perceive in the external world, meanings that they take into account and to which they respond. Parsons derives this idea from Weber's view of the subjective meanings of human action. He is concerned with the meanings of people and external objects. He calls his theory a "voluntaristic" theory of action, in which actors must choose among different goals (or ends) and the means to achieve them. Actors' choices, however, are influenced by a number of physical and social factors that limit the range of choices. Social norms and accepted values influence people's choices of goals and means. Parsons argues that the voluntary nature of action is limited by the systems of action, as an actor engages in interaction with other actors representing the social roles of the subsystems of the social system.

As we consider the functionalist view of human action in public administration, we cannot escape Parsons's analysis of social action, because the language and the normative requirement of expected roles used to describe administrative action are closely related to the concepts introduced in Parsonian action theory. As we apply his view of human action to the context of public administration, we may describe how the act of administrative organization (or reified administrative action) is made up of an agency actor, goals, means, and an administrative environment, which consists of norms, values, and organizational imperatives. An actor's choices and roles are largely determined by the existing organizational culture (accepted norms and values), economic and political environments, and rules and regulations. Conforming to these external elements is an ethical obligation of each actor, because the whole system must achieve collective goals, survive as an organization, and maintain organizational order if it is to promote stability and coordination among subsystems.

Functionalist explanations of action tend to focus on the power of the administrative state and the role of top executives and professional managers in guiding society and changing organizations. Consequently, having discovered the power of centralized administration, the administrative state believes that the only thing that is needed is to place competent people at the top of government bureaucracy. With this belief, government agencies devote more of their efforts to training managers for efficient leadership. Fewer of their efforts are devoted to train lower-level employees. Although in the guidance of a complex society government bureaucrats play a crucial role, the functionalist view is an amiable elitist and technocratic view of governing a democratic administration.

In the functionalist tradition, the integration of organizational action with that of individuals is taken for granted. It is the role of the proactive manager to motivate passive individuals so that they become efficient and productive. Thus the basic approach to the reality construction and explanation of individual actions is to largely reflect the values and perceptions of the manager, who tries to control and influence the reality of employees. In recent years, the popular rhetoric in management literature has been about "achieving excellence" with limited resources or "reinventing government" or "new public management," an idea that aims to justify the proactive role of entrepreneurial managers. This idea also implies that the organization should not just do something better but should achieve an optimal level of performance, which involves the positive commitment of employees. In achieving organizational excellence or better results, whether it involves the entrepreneurial activity of managers or the quality control of workers, managers are considered to be an active force in bringing about change and innovation. Although this argument has validity, given the conditions of institutional power and authority, employees are, unfortunately, largely viewed as passive individuals who must adapt to the needs of the organization and assume their organizational duty as a moral obligation. Furthermore, the problem of politics, social interaction, and participatory democracy is grossly underestimated. Administrative organizations in Asia are highly bureaucratic and depersonalizing. It has been the experience of government bureaucracies in Japan, South Korea, Taiwan, and Singapore that with the adoption of new information technology and computers, government services to citizens have become more efficient, transparent, and democratic to some extent.

The Interpretive View of Action: Subjective Meaning–Context

Interpretive theorists argue that functionalist explanations of human action fail to see the theoretical presuppositions and limitations of the positivistic and empirical epistemology. The basic failure lies in the functionalist assumptions about persons and actions. As we have seen, on the one hand, the functionalist concept of a person assumes that a person is mainly a passive and reactive object, subjected to environmental influences, such as organizational, economic, political, and social factors. Interpretive theorists' concept of the individual, on the other hand, is that he or she is an active, purposeful, and creative subject. The interpretive view stresses that what is lacking in the objective way of defining individual obligation and action is the problem of understanding the everyday world of an individual from the subject's own point of view.

The concept of social action, as introduced by Max Weber, must include the subjective meaning of the actor (Weber, 1947). For Weber, the individual and his or her action is the basic unit of organizational analysis. Weber emphasizes the interpretive understanding of meanings of action in order to develop a causal explanation of the cause and effect of human action. In order to understand an actor's reasons for acting, we must understand the symbols and language that the actor uses to describe his or her own behavior. Alfred Schutz further developed the major ideas of the interpretive view of human action (Schutz, 1962, p. 1967). He rejected Parsonian structural-functionalism, instead following Edmund Husserl's phenomenological method. Husserl was concerned with the problem of human consciousness and the individual's unique experiences of phenomena (Husserl, 1962; 1965; Macann, 1993). His method of understanding conscious experiences of the individual is called "phenomenological reduction." In this method, the individual is free from all theoretical and scientific preconceptions about objects and attempts to interpret the meaningfulness of phenomena as he or she experiences them. Husserl argues that conscious experience is intentional, because the individual is directing his or her attention toward the objects to be experienced. Intentionality in phenomenology refers not only to human action but refers also to the fact that all consciousness is consciousness of something (an object). Thus intentionality describes "some kind of relationship between a subject and object," such as a relationship between a manager and an employee (Phillipson, 1972, p. 124). As Sokolowski points out, phenomenology emphasizes that "the mind is a public thing, that it acts and manifests itself out in the open, not just inside its own confines" (2000, p. 12).

Schutz's analysis of action focuses on the subjective meaning-context, that is, the individual's subjective interpretation of the meanings of commonsense knowledge. For Schutz, actions are oriented to the completion of projects that people can visualize in the future perfect tense ("I will finish the budget preparation by next week"). In this regard, an action is the bringing about of something and always involves purposes, volitions, desires, and intentions. Actions are also related to two different motives: an "in-order-to" motive refers to a future state that an actor wishes to bring about by linking an activity to a project; a "because" motive links project to past experience (a prior causal condition).

Schutz sees a vital role for phenomenology in describing meanings of social action and the structures of everyday life from the actor's point of view. Schutz describes the social world as a complex of meanings of understanding that actors have constituted (subjective meaning-context). Actions are based on individual consciousness, and the self-conscious individual interprets the meanings of his or her acts. This interplay between consciousness and meanings, which is reflexive, is largely missed by the objective view of action as emphasized by functionalist theories such as the Parsonian action theory. Although he focuses on the phenomena of social experience in which the individual is a focus of social action, Schutz, like Weber, never denies the contributions of scientific and positivistic methods. In fact, he emphasizes that in order to relate subjective meaning-contexts to objective meaning-contexts, social scientists must construct models, or ideal types. He suggests that social scientists must consider three postulates (logical consistency, subjective interpretation, and adequacy) in constructing models that will enable them to deal objectively with human actions and their subjective meanings. Both Weber and Schutz are concerned with what meaning the action has for the actor, as opposed to his or her partner or a disinterested observer. Weber, however, is unable to explain how the subjective meanings of individual action can be shared with others in social situations. As I briefly mentioned in chapter 3, for Schutz, the notion of intersubjectivity opens the possibility of mutual interrelatedness between self and others in sharing experiences in the everyday world. His discussion of the "reciprocity of perspectives" describes the possibility of intersubjectivity.

How are meanings intersubjectively conveyed and understood? This question has been studied by ethnomethodologists as well as symbolic interactionists. Harold Garfinkel's work is widely known as ethnomethodology that focuses on the empirical study of everyday, commonplace activities and phenomena (Garfinkel, 1967). Garfinkel looks at (1) everyday conversations; (2) a common meaningful context of conversation; (3) the common understanding resulting from the conversation and intersubjective interpretation; and (4) daily exchanges and affairs. Garfinkel and his associates argue that the very heart of understanding social interaction is not in language in a linguistic sense but in the meaning context of ordinary conversation between actors.

Conversational interaction promotes interactional intimacy and an interchange of ideas and experiences (Atkinson and Heritage, 1984).

Ethnomethodology, like symbolic interactionism, attempts to interpret the dynamics of everyday life by closely examining experiences and the structure of action (Czarniawska-Joerges, 1992, pp. 117–38), but no framework has been developed for relating its methodology to the functionalist main concern of the social system. In other words, ethnomethodology concentrates on individual experiences, as opposed to an analysis of organizations (social systems). Actions must be understood in terms of the context of action (action in the particular situation), rather than in terms of a macro structural framework. Ethnomethodology focuses on the "context-bound" meaning of conversations; structural-functionalism, by contrast, is primarily concerned with the "structure-bound" meaning. For Garfinkel and other ethnomethodologists, when people adhere to rules and organizational demands, their responsive acts may be based on their anticipatory anxiety about meeting organizational obligations and accountability. Both ethnomethodologists and symbolic interactionists argue that the functionalist view of organizational order undermines the idea of the individual's willingness to conform to the patterns of organizational culture. Because individuals are not passive beings, they do not invariably comply with rules and regulations. They do not always make rational choices according to situational requirements. In fact, they often deliberately deviate from the existing norm.

Symbolic interactionists such as Herbert Blumer also focus on interpretations and definitions of others' actions (Blumer, 1969). Actors do not simply react to others but interact with others based on an assessment of the meanings of their acts. Blumer discusses three premises of symbolic interaction. The first premise is that human beings act toward things on the basis of the meanings that the things have for them. The second premise is that the meaning of such things is derived from, or arises out of, the social interaction that a person has with his or her fellows. The third premise is that these meanings are handled in, and modified through, an interpretive process used by the person in dealing with the things that he or she encounters (Blumer, 1969: 2).

Symbolic interactionism is concerned with the way that people construct the meaning of others' acts by incorporating the responses of others into their own acts (Becker and McCall, 1990, pp. 3–4). Human interaction can be understood as symbolic processes of the individual self. Blumer argues that people can think of themselves as the objects of their own actions or act toward themselves as they might act toward others (Blumer, 1969, p. 182). The object is not a simple response to a situation but is constituted by the individual's disposition to act. Thus people tend to construct and reconstruct their actions and, hence, their social world. Blumer opposes the notion of the mere response of individuals to external forces, such as organizational structure, rules, and functional requirements. Blumer is also opposed to functionalist explanations of reifying human actions. According to Blumer, organization is nothing more than a plurality of disembodied selves interacting in structureless situations. Individuals are the only ones who act: organizations do not. In other words, an organization is not a determinant of individual action.

The Dialectic of Action: Public Sphere as Meaning-Context

The discussion thus far suggests that the functionalist view of human action is based on an "oversocialized" view of people, which undermines the notion of people's ability to construct and reconstruct the meanings of their own actions (Wrong, 1961). Functionalists tend to be concerned mostly with those attributes of human nature that support consensus, conformity, loyalty, and role behavior. Individuals are seen as having undergone a process of socialization that renders them responsive to organizational demands. Functionalism tends to reduce the ethical responsibility of people into the necessity of organizational structure, purpose, and goals.

Moreover, the interpretive perspective focuses on the subjective meaning-context, thus tending to reduce objective aspects, such as organizational, political, economic, and cultural dimensions, into the consciousness and the interpretive capability of people in social situations. Its treatment of external forces (organizational, economic, and political) is inadequate and often even evaded. Therefore, both the functionalist and the interpretive perspectives tend to be reductionistic: a one-sided view of human action and social reality. What is needed in understanding human action in administration is an inclusive and critical perspective that dialectically encompasses both the objective meaning-context and the subjective meaning-context. Public administrators live in an organizational culture of positivism and functionalism that suggests that organizational norms, values, language, and tasks determine people's behavior. But in the real world of administration, the meanings of these objective requirements always rely upon interpersonally negotiated processes of interpretation and assumption. The actions of a public administrator always require reflexive judgments: What is "appropriate" action? What is my responsibility to management? What is my responsibility to myself? What are the implications of my actions for the public whom I serve?

The dialectical view of action attempts to connect human subjectivity with organizational objectivity. In fact, the social constructionist view assumes that as a result of the individual's continuous externalization and internalization, the phenomena of subjectivity and objectivity are in the state of dialectical transformation (Berger and Luckmann, 1967, chapter 3). In linking the subjectivity of human actions and the objectivity of institutions, individuals, and organizations, many social scientists begin from either the objective framework (i.e., structural-functionalism or the macro-micro integration) or the subjective elements (Parsons, 1949; 1951; Münch, 1987; Alexander, 1988). I argue that the dialectic must begin at the subjective level and move upward or else critically examine two approaches at the same time, because all actions, whether they are based on some objective obligation or on subjective experience, reflect certain reflexive judgments on the part of the individual actor. Actions reflect people's value judgments in relation to empirical (factual) knowledge or their personal desires.

A difficulty of dialectic is interpretation of the meanings of ethical action. Different actors have different and often opposing views. Functionalists tend to resolve this difficulty by holding that there are certain objective requirements (i.e., order, survival, efficiency, productivity, working procedures, and economic reward) for which organizational members strive and that therefore are collectively good. But some people may focus on the intrinsic elements of their work, such as effectiveness, quality, or psychological rewards, in preference to extrinsic elements. Therefore, certain objective conditions cannot be universally applied in order to determine what is good for all members. The functionalist approach is positivistic and theoretical; the interpretive approach is antipositivistic and atheoretical, because actions and the meanings of objects are contingent upon the interpretation of acting subjects. The interpretive view of action does not aim to improve the functionalist concept of action and organizational obligation but rather to understand the meaning of the objects, because the reified roles are continuously defined and redefined by acting subjects.

The dialectical reason for critically understanding the epistemological limits of the objective and the subjective views of human action is useful not only in a methodological way but also in a practical way. Dialogue and social interaction are used to examine constantly changing social phenomena, the ambiguity of these phenomena, and the whole variety of possible interpretations of the meanings of objects and human experiences. Thus the dialectic is a way of thinking about problems that emphasizes normative obligations imposed on the individuals and that takes human experiences. As Jürgen Habermas argues (Habermas, 1984; Ingram, 1987), if we try to understand action as a complementarity of attitudes, instead of as an either/or, then we may well reach a different level of understanding about objective knowledge and human experiences: we may achieve a better understanding of people's experiences and their obligatory relationships to an organization or how they reach a critical synthesis between these two (Cooper, 1990, pp. 223–32; Bosserman, 1968).

The dialectic is also a method for humanizing and democratizing organizational processes by recognizing the participation of individuals in interpreting the meaning of the content of organizational obligation. As long as the content and the process of participation in dialogue are recognized, we may say that actions in a public organization are dialectical. But if the managers are not willing to understand the subjective nature of employees' actions, insisting, instead, on their own definitions of expected roles and actions, then there can be no mutuality or reciprocity in sharing experiences. Burke Thomason says, "If one's opponents are dogmatically antidialectical in their attitudes toward social reality, it is justified to be dogmatically dialectical (in the ontological sense) so as to counter their influence" (Thomason, 1982, p. 160). Accordingly, managers may adopt "dogmatic countermeasures" to justify and maintain their personal perspectives and attitudes. Thus the antidialectical attitude may become a constraint to the process of making organizations more humanistic and effective in their governance.

When action is placed in the public sphere, a moral concern becomes the foundation of individual action or of administrative action representing an agency decision. In the dialectic of action, the interests of the public are often recognized as a legitimate justification for action. For example, when U.S. president George W. Bush justified his administration's action of invading Iraq in terms of protecting the country from "the axis of evil," the president's argument was "rational and highly principled" on the grounds of his reasoning (MacIntyre, 1984).[2] If Bush's rational decision to invade, reconstruct, and democratize Iraq after removing Saddam Hussein had succeeded as planned before the war, then his actions might have received little criticism. But because the reconstruction process has not been going well—mainly due to the resistance of the Iraqi people and the cost of rebuilding the country, creating a huge burden on the U.S. economy—President Bush has received a great deal of criticism. Critics say that his rational decision was based on unreliable information, that he misinformed the public, that he overstated the threat from Saddam Hussein, that there was a lack of transparency and a lack of public debate, and that he used the September 11 crisis as an excuse for the war on Iraq.

By treating action as a dialectical process, people may be able to change their ways of thinking about the processes of understanding organizational phenomena, interpreting intersubjectivity and mutuality, and linking the objective and the subjective meaning-contexts of human action. Because the dialectical view of action tends to rationalize individual or agency action, in order to avoid instrumental (or principled) judgment and make a socially acceptable argument, public discourse regarding policies and a course of action must be emphasized. Despite a possible political victory for those who hold power by persuading others, in a democracy, the contestation of opposing arguments is imperative. (This view is discussed further in later chapters.) To be effective in overcoming complex problems, action must be informed by the contestable viewpoints of objective and subjective contexts that influence our choices. Furthermore, action that occurs in public space appears to promote the process of people overcoming passivity and defensiveness, attitudes that are prevalent among employees of bureaucratic organizations. It is also a process of people learning to act collectively and to honor their own needs for self-expression, personal growth, and a reenriched culture, by integrating different experiences, knowledge, and cultures.

PRAXIS AND CHANGE

Many venerated philosophers and social theorists embrace the concept of 'praxis'[3] when they discuss human action. Because of its impact on the traditions of political and administrative thought, *praxis* has become an intrinsically important term in administrative theory.[4] Praxis is an elusive concept. To appreciate the concept fully, it must be approached in a number of different but compatible ways.

'Praxis' is often used interchangeably with *practice*, as both imply action. But 'practice' has a limited meaning in English that 'praxis' does not. Practice is habitual action repeatedly performed so that one may acquire skill. Praxis, like practice, concerns human activity that produces certain outcomes or objects. But, as Adolfo Sanchez Vazquez points out, "All praxis is activity, but all activity is not praxis" (1977, p. 149). 'Praxis' is an old term to which administrative action has given new life. The ancient Greeks define it as "practical activity," "action," or "doing." For Aristotle, 'praxis' meant a "special kind of human activity devoted to political life," as contrasted with contemplation or abstract reasoning *(theoria)*. In his analysis, theory implied "intellectual activities"—thinking, abstracting, and reflecting—whereas *political life* implied "practical activity." 'Praxis' implied the "performance of an activity that has moral significance" (Lobkowicz, 1967; Joachim, 1951). Whereas Aristotle related 'praxis' exclusively to politics, Karl Marx broadened the meaning to include "all activities that contribute to the humanization of the person" (Markovic, 1974). Marx was concerned with the consequences of action, "with altering the material conditions of life, with making the world a better place. That better place was for him one where human activity is at last everywhere fully human. To Marx, the goal of revolutionary praxis is to liberate human activity from the forces that debase it, to realize a condition wherein the life of noble action is available to each person because of the noble acts of every other person" (Allan, 1990, p. 4).

The praxis of human action is used exclusively in existentialism, phenomenology, critical theory, classic political theory, Marxist theory, and hermeneutics. Although praxis inquiry is emphasized differently by different philosophers and social theorists, there is a common concern with understanding human activity from the subject's point of view (in contrast to emphasizing activity that is a biological or natural act influenced by a passive, uncritical consciousness). Moreover, the functionalist or structuralist approach says that praxis provides "a powerful sense-making device" for organizational members in directing or influencing their actions, but it does not reflect how they interpret the meanings of functions and structure.[5]

Practice is different from praxis in that practice may take place without an individual employing any type of critical consciousness. Praxis is always an activity developed by an individual and directed at an object that is transformed through that activity. Thus, 'praxis' is defined as "human activity in which an individual uses a reflexive consciousness." As an individual engages in communicative action with others to transform his or her reality over time, the individual action becomes social praxis (Jun, 1994a, pp. 201–07).

Praxis can also arise out of social processes involving the sharing of mutual interests. As such, it is social activity in which individuals collaborate critically and reflexively with other actors in order to accomplish collective purposes. Thus social praxis involves an intersubjective praxis: a form of discourse embedded within a web of meanings that the actors experience personally in relationship with others. Jürgen Habermas's contribution to the understanding of the social concept of human action is most insightful in describing intersubjective action (1973; 1984). According to Habermas, practical interest is the foundation of social practice, which is communication and the establishment of mutual relationships among individuals. *Practical interest* refers to "those aspects of knowledge and action concerned with establishing a shared understanding in intersubjective situations in order to achieve community and mutuality." Thus dialogue and the use of language are the basic means of practical action.

Whereas social praxis is activity in which the subjects are engaged individually and collectively in changing social reality, an organizational praxis is action in which individuals attempt to transform organizational and individual reality and to create a new intersubjective reality, involving "the creation not only of new objects but also of new needs and potentialities" (Crocker, 1977, p. 18). Through the process of self-reflexivity and reasoning, the individual can evaluate knowledge and interest critically and can transform them through the exploration of meaningful alternatives. The act of reflexive self-inquiry can change the consciousness of the individual. In changing his or her own consciousness, the individual becomes involved in the process of reconstructing organizational reality.

THE PRAXIS-ORIENTED ADMINISTRATORS

Public managers are often viewed as people who are mostly concerned with "practical" results that satisfy basic organizational needs. The word *practical* implies a nonphilosophical and uncritical approach to activity; in other words, practical managers are generally committed to the sensible performance of their role as defined by the organization. They are less interested in philosophical and normative discourse that deals with purpose, conflicting interests, and ethical consequences of their action. Practical managers are interested in the efficient accomplishment of tangible results.

Many activities that employees perform are cumbersome and depersonalizing; but because these activities are also repetitive and do not require much thought, some people feel comfortable with their work routine. Much of the literature on organization theory emphasizes the necessity of improving the performance behavior of employees through having them master standardized procedures for conducting repetitive activities. Employees are expected to become efficient at applying procedures and rules through short-term training and the socialization process of working with others in the organizations. Many management-oriented theorists and practicing administrators assume that if organizations use new knowledge (or theories) in order to improve their organizations, then the organizations can achieve a high degree of objectivity, consequently increasing productivity and efficiency.

Other employees, by contrast, are critically aware of the inadequacies and undesirable consequences of their work routine, which is often imposed on them by their supervisors. In the latter case, a conscious administrator exercises a critical and reflexive consciousness, as opposed to habitually performing everyday activities. Praxis-oriented administrators are more sensitive to and aware of the moral consequences of their acts. They are more concerned with their clients' feelings and the public good. For example, a reflexive (praxis-oriented) manager evaluates his or her own acts, makes responsible decisions, questions administrative procedures, and corrects personal and organizational errors. His or her personal praxis is informed action resulting from self-reflexivity and self-determination.

In the context of a changing organization, the praxis-oriented administrator becomes a transformer of reality when he or she perceives the contradictions between individual freedom and organizational control and sets out to resolve these contradictions. In changing dehumanizing conditions, the individual exercises an emancipating praxis within the context of the organization. Through reflexivity and action, the individual has the possibility of transforming the organization, redesigning it in order to satisfy shared needs.

The praxis of the individual in the social (or organizational) context requires that the actor has the ability to share his or her interest and experience with other individuals in the same situation. Habermas supports the social nature of knowledge: a human activity is closely related to a person's practical interests, and knowledge is a social product of shared meanings and perceptions in intersubjective relationships (1986). Schutz has this to say: "[M]y experience of the world justifies and corrects itself by the experience of the others with whom I am interrelated by common knowledge, common work, and common suffering" (1967, p. 9). The views of Habermas and Schutz on knowledge and human action share some common concerns: they suggest the role of the subjects in changing the external world. Action is largely guided by perceived needs and the anticipated product (or practical interest); human knowledge (either concerned with practical outcome or theoretical activity) is linked to "the demands of practical needs" of the situation. I tend to concur with Karl Mannheim, who emphasizes that the construction of social knowledge—all knowledge in the human social sciences—is existentially determined in concrete historical situations (1940). In other words, ultimately, the individual has to determine the content of practicality, taking into consideration both objective and subjective contexts. As Mihailo Marković points out, a choice of action is an expression of certain individual needs as well as general social needs and interests: it cannot be made in a purely theoretical (objective) manner (1974, p. 76).

John Dewey, as a pragmatic philosopher, has a similar view about how people produce and justify knowledge. Knowledge is not based upon some antecedent reality: rather, it follows human activity. Dewey states, "[K]nowledge which is merely a reduplication in ideas of what exists already in the world may afford us the satisfaction of a photograph, but that is all" (1929, p. 137). He also argues that there is a natural relationship between knowledge and action: "If we see that knowing is not the act of an outside spectator but of a participator inside the natural and social scene, then the true object of knowledge resides in the consequences of directed action" (p. 196).

According to Habermas (1984), praxis expresses itself as a communicative action in which individuals interact with one another, relating themselves to the objective world (i.e., administrative organization). In order to transform the object, the individual engages in praxis to establish intersubjectivity through communicative action. Put another way, a meaningful construction of intersubjective understanding is possible only when managers and other organizational members engage in intersubjective praxis; that is, each subject tunes into the consciousness of another by trying to understand and share in the other's experiences and ideas through authentic and critical dialogue. This implies that when one party is not interested in engaging in open dialogue, is indifferent to the possibility of learning from another person, then intersubjective understanding is unlikely: the interconnectedness of intersubjective praxis does not occur as a result of people's defensiveness toward or difference to each other.

Furthermore, to be praxis oriented, the individual can begin by simply asking what is required for a relationship to persist. Each party to that relationship must have a continuing identity: that is, each party must perceive himself or herself as acting and engaging in dialogue with the other party. Praxis discourse allows administrators to understand the meanings of actions that are grounded in everyday experiences in the workplace, realizing the dialectical possibility of resolving various contradictions between two opposing intellectual traditions, the positivistic versus interpretive epistemology, and organizational goals versus individual needs.

CHANGING ORGANIZATIONS AND ACTION RESEARCH

To appreciate the relationship between change (or changing) and action, a conceptual distinction between *change* and *changing* is needed. The two words actually refer to fundamentally different ways of constructing social reality. 'Change' brings up an ex post facto frame of mind toward human events, a historical viewpoint. Change, as described in organization theory literature, is a linear process aimed at accomplishing of established change goals or successfully testing a change theory. The process of change is essentially deterministic in the sense that change theory predicts how to modify human behavior. When a change is proposed by adopting a government reorganization plan or other kinds of organizational change projects, the designers of change assume that people are likely to accept the proposed change if it can be rationally justified (Chin and Benne, 1984, p. 23). Systems engineers, managers, and consultants often tend to hypothesize a pre-determined reality within which the individual is merely a passive being whose behavior is largely shaped by the designs of their presup-posed change efforts.

Changing, on the other hand, is a dialectical process. It is a con-tinuously evolving creative process, a way of realizing new forms of complex human associations that constitute the construction of orga-nizational (social) reality. Changing is concerned with the shared and appreciative meaning of a project as the participants work together to accomplish their goal. The process of changing is based on the assump-tion that people are active and continuously interact with their envi-ronment and with one another. As people participate in designing and implementing change strategies, they are engaged in their own reedu-cation. Chin and Benne stress that "[r]e-education is a normative change as well as a cognitive and perceptual change" (p. 31). How can we incorporate the dialectical and interactive ways of transforming our thinking and being into the changing process? We may begin with a critical reflection on the existing composition of institutions and struc-tures. Changing begins with a struggle to new ways of constructing reality that reconceptualize existing modes of being and doing. As such, changing is an ongoing learning process that is deeply rooted in the present based upon the past and heading toward an imagined future. This imagined future consists of the reconceptualization of real-ity, or the opening of our minds to alternative ways of seeing and being.

High-level executives and managers can facilitate the participation of people in defining and exploring a problem in their own terms and also help them to develop a collective vision of their world. In his dis-cussion of action research, Earnst Stringer points out the following:

> [T]he taken-for-granted visions and versions of reality that make up people's day-to-day life-worlds, [bring] their unquestioned assump-tions, views, and beliefs out in the open and [display] them for inspection. As people struggle to realize a collective vision/version of their world, they will discover perspectives that reveal new possibili-ties for resolving their problems. These collective visions may involve minor adjustments to people's own perspectives or may result in transformations that dramatically alter their world-views. At best, this activity is liberating, enabling people to master their world as they see it in a different way—a tangible process of enlightenment. (Stringer, 1996, p. 59)

It is essential that the ordinary experiences of people be included as they are engaged in the process of changing their organizations. Although most management-driven change projects assume the deterministic and positivistic view of producing intended results, the implementation of the projects may remain incomplete. Throughout the world, there are numerous examples of the failure of top-down reform projects. For example, in 1998 a newly elected South Korean president, Kim Dae Jung, launched the first reorganization of his administration, spending $3.8 million for formulating a reform proposal by hiring several research and consulting firms. But because the plan was ill-conceived and hasty, its implementation lasted less than a year. In its second reform plan, failing to account for the shortcomings of the first plan, the national government continued its focus on the consolidation and streamlining of cabinet-level agencies. The failures of these reorganization plans were largely due to a misunderstanding of the fundamental problems of agencies. For example, the administrative cultures in different ministries were not taken into account; they did not participate in the design of reform strategies; and no incentives were provided for ministries to cooperate with the reforms. Many people predicted that the reorganization plan would not produce any substantive improvements in public services. This prediction came true. Instead, the plan only contributed to the power struggle between ministries because of new structural arrangements, which give more power to the office of prime minister. The incompleteness of organizational change projects is conspicuous at the national levels; it is also a common phenomenon in local public agencies, which attempt to design projects from the top down, not allowing broad participation. Thus the effective design and implementation of reform plans can produce a better outcome when executives and managers pay attention to the ordinary experiences of organizational members, facilitating these experiences in order to define problems and develop their own strategies for changing.

Action Research as a Framework for Learning and Changing

Although action research has been practiced by social scientists for more than a half-century, it is not well known among public administrators, perhaps because it lacks scientific rigor, structure, and a universal theoretical framework. Action research is, however, becoming an important subject among applied social scientists, people-oriented training consultants (not public management experts), interpretive theorists, and qualitative researchers (Greenwood and Levin, 1998; Stringer, 1996; Argyris, Putnam and Smith, 1985; Weisbord, 1992; Whyte, 1984). Action research is based on Kurt Lewin's 1940s work on group dynamics, which stresses group, rather than individual, actions (Lewin, 1947; 1951). Lewin emphasizes action research as a strategy of changing, and participation in groups as a medium of education and learning. Action research assumes that a group process provides opportunities for members to reflect on their experiences and thus gain insight into their own behavior and actions, analyze problems, design action steps to achieve established goals, and evaluate the consequences of their actions.

Action research is a practical framework for social design, teamwork, group problem solving, and changing strategies, a framework within which the various concepts that I discuss in the social constructionist and social design approaches can be synthesized and operationalized. First, as Eric Trist points out, action research aims to help us design the future, rather than adapt to it (1976). People involved in the problem-solving process are viewed as active agents with different ideas and experiences, rather than as reactive and passive. Next, action research is a way of facilitating "collaborative relationships in an area of conflict" (Foster, 1976). Different collaborators (top administrators, managers, professionals, employees, clients, and politicians, depending on the issue) join together to solve a problem. Dialogue and feedback are the mediums for sharing knowledge and resolving conflict.

Further, when action research is applied to planned organizational change, it can be a framework for integrating the "practical concerns of people in an immediate problematic situation" and the theoretical knowledge of change agents or outside consultants (Gardner, 1974). In addition, in the process of diagnosing what the problem is and what ought to be done, the analytical method may be used to gather relevant survey data concerning people's attitudes and perceptions, and the phenomenological method or qualitative research may be used to conduct open-ended interviews and elicit knowledge. The action research team can jointly evaluate the validity of factual information, reflecting upon its moral and value orientations. Finally, action research is a participatory framework for community problem solving. Anne Khademian's illustration of the East St. Louis Action Research Project (ESLARP) is a good case study of community-based problem solving. By the late

1980s, East St. Louis, Illinois, was a dilapidated city, having urban decay, environmental pollution, high unemployment, poverty, and crime. The implementation of numerous government programs, such as the War on Poverty, Model Cities, and the Community Development Block Programs, failed to stabilize the socioeconomic and environmental conditions. In the mid-1990s, the University of Illinois Champaign-Urban under the leadership of Kenneth Reardon initiated the ESLARP project through a productive partnership among residents, neighborhood organizations, and university students and faculty. The action research team shared the responsibility for defining neighborhood problems, setting an agenda, researching problems, and developing solutions (2002, pp. 1–14). The success of the project was attributed to not only the effective leadership of the project facilitators, but, more important, the inclusion of residents in dealing with urban renewal problems.

The process of designing action research and problem solving varies from situation to situation. The following list illustrates some basic steps that may be relevant to organizational and social problem solving:

1. Forming an action research group. This consists of the people who are interested in examining problems and taking action.
2. Diagnosing the problem. Action research group members must study significant problems analytically and phenomenologically.
3. Developing goals. Based on problem diagnosis, the action research group must define its collective goals.
4. Designing action steps. Group members assign shared responsibilities in relation to problems and goals.
5. Evaluation and feedback. Evaluation and feedback must be exercised in steps 1 to 4, analyzing both positive and negative consequences.

The process of action research is flexible and adaptive because it is supposed to evaluate human action based on continuous feedback during each one of the preceding steps. The success of action research and problem solving depends on the active participation of collaborators (action research group members) in order to assess whether problems were discussed openly, action purposes were accomplished, the process was participatory and open to organization and community, participants learned, and the degree to which the process contributed to the freedom and self-enhancement of the individuals involved (Gardner, 1974, p. 113).

When action research is used to solve organizational problems, it is necessary to anticipate some obstacles. The establishment of collaborative relationships and conflict resolution among group members is difficult because group members will necessarily differ in their interests and values. This implies that, as Chris Argyris has written, the effectiveness of problem solving invariably depends upon the degree of interpersonal competence and trust among members (1970). The process of action research may be impeded by unanticipated factors such as management's attempt to control the problem-solving agenda, the unethical conduct of some individual members, delays in implementation of assigned activities, or lack of management support.

CONCLUSION

I began this chapter by discussing how the omnipresent assumption of the functionalist perspective of human action in organizations has forced positivistic and deterministic approaches to behavior and action, treating organizational members as merely passive, reactive beings. The interpretive perspective argues that the objective requirement for action lacks an understanding of everyday experience of people from their subjective viewpoints. Both the functionalist and the interpretive approaches tend to be reductionistic in their methods of explaining and understanding actions. A one-sided approach to action may be justifiable from either the objective, management viewpoint or the subjective, individual's viewpoint, but its uncritical application to the activities of public administration could lead to an only partial understanding of social reality and action. It is a humanistic and practical matter to accept the limitations of a one-sided epistemology and try to find a critical, constructive way of realizing the dialectical possibility and the complex network of human relationships.

I also introduced the concept of praxis, emphasizing the responsibility of public administrators in changing organizations and constructing social reality through the exercise of critical and reflexive action. Unlike the concept of 'planned change' based on the application of change theory to the change target, changing an organization is an evolutionary (continuously emerging) process of understanding and transforming cultures, resources, people, and complex external environments. In this regard, action research is a framework that promotes dialogue, learning, sharing, and participation. Another similar approach is the "future search conference," which is used as a process approach to sharing knowledge, learning among participants, and building commitment.[6]

CHAPTER 7

The Self in Social Construction

The social construction of public administration must include a clear consideration of the nature of the individual within social and cultural contexts. From a positivist (functionalist) perspective, an organization is seen as an assembly of autonomous individuals working together for economic gain. Roles and tasks are assigned to ensure that individuals will meet organizational goals. Individuals are supposed to sacrifice their autonomy for organizational needs, and the self is reduced to the person's role in the organization structure. Alternatively, social constructionists see the self and identity being created and sustained through our social, historical, cultural, and temporal relationships. From this perspective individual identity is not determined by our role in society but is an ongoing process in which we shape ourselves and others within the various contexts and relations in which we find ourselves. While some argue that this conception of the self leads to ethical relativism, others, such as Max Weber, William James, George Herbert Mead, Alfred Schutz, and Jürgen Habermas, have formulated theories that attempt to balance these two opposing conceptions of the self.

The viable existence of organizational life presupposes that members make certain kinds of commitments and accept certain organizational norms but still have individual autonomy and freedom. In this chapter, I discuss how the individual constructs the concept of 'the self' in historical, cultural, and social contexts. The self as a human being is the most important intervening factor to come between phenomenal objects (other people, roles, and external things) and an individual's own behavior and action. During the 1960s and 1970s, there was a surge of interest in the changing consciousness of people in organization and in society (Reich, 1970; Bellah et al., 1985). Since the early 1980s, however, our attention has shifted to the macro concerns of managing a complex society, such as rising national debt and budget cuts, the costs of social programs, and the demand for better government performance. Where we put our attention has been influenced by the crisis in management and the dwindling economic resources to

147

meet this crisis. Also in this chapter, I ask questions about the nature of the individual and his or her role in the social construction process, by comparing Eastern and Western thought about the concept of self and discussing the dialectical relationships between and among self, culture, organization, and society.

SOCIAL CONSTRUCTION OF THE SELF: EASTERN AND WESTERN VIEWS

An exploration of Eastern and Western views is necessary for at least three significant epistemological and pragmatic reasons. First, the world is becoming increasingly borderless in terms of geographical and social space. Because of this growing network of interaction and interdependence among people, organizations, and nations, it is difficult for Western nations to sustain themselves without the cooperation of the East; conversely, Eastern countries cannot progress without working with the West. The "modern Western mind-set" is geared to control and change based on instrumental and rational individual achievement and on scientific principles. The Western view of identity also serves the dominant group interest because it establishes what are acceptable behavior, roles, and obligations. It also assumes that those who do not fit the norm (the underprivileged, diverse minorities) must be guided by leaders and professionals because they are unmotivated, or they act in less than rational ways. Any fundamental transformation in the organizations or society of the West would require that people change their minds about the way that they interpret the implications of science, health care, education, economics, the market, security, poverty, and the natural environment.[1] The Eastern mind-set tends to be more intuitive, less rational, and nonscientific in its orientation; it values personal connections. Although contemporary educated people who occupy professional and managerial jobs in the East have learned and often adopted a Western orientation, the majority of people in the East still think in a less rational and nonempirical manner. Even those professionals who adopt Western orientations still tend to retain aspects of their Eastern heritage.

Another justification for understanding the self from both the Eastern and the Western viewpoint is that this comparison allows us to go beyond the conventional idea that the organization and society have sole responsibility for governing, in order to protect people and help them grow. Those who design and implement this macro-oriented development and management philosophy justify it in terms of creating a prosperous future and material satisfaction by making rational choices on behalf of the people. This centralized policy making and hierarchical governing, however, ignores diverse group interests and local conditions and underestimates individual values, needs, feelings, and life experiences.

Finally, by understanding self as socially constructed in relation to others, we can overcome the problem of duality between the individual and the organization, between subjectivity and objectivity, and between administration and the public. These dualistic boundaries can be transcended only by thinking about self through the enlargement of the person's boundary into other spheres. People support change as a result of a change in consciousness; this transcendence in consciousness comes from viewing selfhood (both conscious and unconscious aspects of the self) as taking place in social and cultural contexts and, in particular, through communication with other humans.

Modern Western Concepts of Self

Although there is no one single concept of self in Western thought, the Cartesian view of the self has influenced the Western approach to economic, political, legal, cultural, and administrative systems. This concept depicts the highly atomistic, separate, I-me, autonomous individual or ego. Thus, most modern concepts of self have Cartesian epistemological roots, but anti-Cartesian views have also emerged with the development of post-Enlightenment philosophy, symbolic interactionism, ethnomethodology, humanistic psychology, and postmodernism.

René Descartes (1596–1650) is regarded as one of the founders of modern epistemology. In his method, the first reality discovered is the *thinking self*. His view of the thinking self ("thinking thing") is that of a separate and individual self with a rational mind. He argues that "an objective, ego-oriented world of meaning" allows the individual to be rational. His view on an atomistic view of the self does not include a person's social, or relational, nature. He assumes that "the real is the rational—so that the more rational we become, the more in touch with reality we are." Thus any rational person will accept "the existence of the self as an individual thinking thing" (Allen, 1997b, p. 7). This "thing" is not historically, relationally, and culturally constituted and is able to control society through practical reason and scientific means.

Thomas Hobbes (1588–1679) and John Locke (1632–1704) assert that atomistic individuals can come together to establish government by means of contract (Hobbes) or as affairs of fiduciary trust (Locke). Hobbes emphasizes the absolute power of the state over the individual, arguing that state power is essential because people are so possessed by the will to achieve power and security that they will wreak havoc on others, taking the property of others in order to make themselves more powerful. According to Hobbes, only a superior coercive power will prevent or punish the antisocial behavior of individuals. Locke opposes the idea that only government has full authority to secure public safety and to maintain order. He argues that citizens may dissolve the contract: "[People] may dissolve their government, but they may remain in society." Locke's liberal political theory is "less political—less about the state—and more social and individual. A free society, one free from governmental interference, is the refuge for free [people]" (Hacker, 1961, pp. 245–46).[2] Thus Locke sees the need for limiting the power of the state so that the individual may have more freedom.

The idea of atomistic selves is further reflected in the writings of many economists. Adam Smith (1723–1790), who established his reputation as not only a liberal economic theorist but also a distinguished lecturer on literature and moral philosophy, wrote two important books, *The Wealth of Nations* (1937/1776) and *The Theory of Moral Sentiments* (1966/1759). His work on economic theory became the foundation work of modern economic thought. His idea that every individual is motivated by prudent self-interest recalls Plato's concept of 'virtue': every member of the republic follows his or her own natural predisposition in developing his or her talents to perfection. Smith assumes that if people are allowed to follow their economic interests unrestrictedly (except for the control of criminal behavior and fraud), then a natural economic balance will evolve in which the state as a whole will profit from the integral interests and labors of the population. Smith recognizes that the wealth of a nation grows with the increased skill and efficiency of labor and with the greater involvement of the population in production and, eventually, in consumption (Smith, 1776/1937). Smith's unified theory of economic development, which is largely based on the promotion of the genuine self-interest of individuals, has influenced other theorists, such as David Ricardo, Jeremy Bentham, and

John Stuart Mill. Since the late nineteenth century, there have been numerous movements that critique this construction of the self that largely promote the interests of atomistic and self-centered individuals. These critiques have come from communists, pragmatists, feminists, communitarians, and contemporary virtue theorists.

Eastern Views of Self

When Western atomistic and self-interest-oriented concepts of self are applied to the complex and dynamic nature of Eastern countries, misunderstandings occur; a shallow understanding of people from other cultures produces not only distrust but also unintended consequences in working relationships. This misunderstanding often derives from our projection of known concepts and reasoning into the unknown culture. Gunnar Myrdal, in his insightful book *Asian Drama: An Inquiry into the Poverty of Nations* (1968), describes some of traditional Asian characteristics:

> A central claim is that people in Asia are more spiritual and less materialistic than Westerners. They are otherworldly, selfless, and disposed to disregard wealth or material comfort. They sustain poverty with equanimity and even see positive virtues in it. They have a special respect for learning and a capacity for contemplation and meditation. Their intellectual strength lies in intuition more than in reason and hard calculation. In current affairs, their main criterion is the moral worth of a person or a policy, and they are apt to censure expediency and opportunism in politics. With spiritual concerns and personal salvation paramount, the external world takes on an illusory and transient aspect. The attitude toward the environment tends to be timeless, formless, and therefore carefree and even fatalistic. The ideal is alleged to be detachment, withdrawal, if not renunciation and asceticism. This bent of mind gives Asians serenity and the capacity to endure extreme physical suffering. They are pictured as tolerant, non-aggressive, and non-militant in their social relations and their international politics. They are said to dislike definitive legal principles and to prefer to settle conflicts by mutual agreement rather than by formal procedures; to regard status as more important than contracts; and to desire peace with their neighbors and the world, and peace in their souls. (pp. 23–24)

Myrdal implies that the above illustration is a biased, generalized image of the characteristics of Asians. Although many Asians

still possess those traits today, because of the influence of modernization and industrialization, these traditional values and consciousness have been changing rapidly, becoming more like those of
Western countries; that is, many people have become materialistic,
egoistic, individualistic, and self-centered, paying little heed to the
interests and rights of others and the community in which they live.
Young people in particular do seem to be becoming more Western.
This changing phenomenon does not mean that Asian values and
concepts of self are becoming more like the self-concepts of the people in the West. Of course, mutual influences continue to occur, but
some basic cultural norms and people's values, based on their historical, cultural, and religious roots, will remain in people's minds for a
long time; some may never want to change their traditional beliefs.
Today we witness this tendency among people in Middle Eastern
countries when they resist the U.S.-imposed movement toward
democratization.[3]

Because the social construction of self in Asian countries has a
wide range of interpretations, in this section I briefly describe some
major Asian schools of thought—Confucianism, Buddhism, and
Hinduism—to illustrate the contrasting views of self.[4] Furthermore, an
understanding (or blending) of Western and Eastern conceptions can
lead to more humanistic and ethical ways of organizational governance
and human relationships. In many ways, Confucian principles for living a virtuous and ethical life complement the Western understanding
of the individual. Born in 551 B.C., Confucius became a cabinet-level
official of the state of Lu at fifty-one. After he resigned his government
job, he traveled through many of the feudal states of China accompanied by his disciples; he spent the rest of his life in literary studies. His
work helps to form the basis of Chinese culture, and his philosophy
continues to influence many Asian societies, particularly East Asian
countries. He preached an exclusively ethical doctrine, with an emphasis on the practical side of human conduct. According to Confucius,
"[T]he best individual morality in the world could fail collectively if
there were not good government as well" (Feibleman, 1976, p. 91). To
Confucius, becoming a moral person is an ongoing and lifelong
process, and this learning process must take place within one's particular moral community.

Confucius explained that there are six virtues and six accompany-
ing failures:

First, there is the mere love of morality: that alone, without culture, degenerates into fatuity. Secondly, there is the mere love of knowledge: that alone, without culture, tends to dilettantism. Thirdly, there is the mere love of honesty: that alone, without culture, produces heartlessness. Fourthly, there is the mere love of uprightness: that alone, without culture, leads to tyranny. Fifthly, there is the mere love of courage: that alone, without culture, produces recklessness. Sixthly, there is the mere love of strength of character: that alone, without culture, produces eccentricity. (Confucius Analects, XVII, 8)

According to Confucian ethics, a superior person (a sage) behaves morally; such a person is what Alasdair MacIntyre terms a "character," not necessarily a "superior" individual. According to MacIntyre, such people are "the moral representatives of their culture and they are so because of the way in which moral and metaphysical ideas and theories assume through them an embodied existence in the social world. Characters are the masks worn by moral philosophers" (1981, p. 28). One can take the role of a character without believing in its values—for example, managers justify their role through this "character" as moral and rational agents of the organization. MacIntyre says the problem with these characters is that they do not engage in reflexivity or moral debate. They accept their right to make decisions for others based on objective and rational criteria. Most modern managers are morally neutral technicians. For a superior person according to Confucius, living as the "character" within the moral community means above all else a commitment to the process of moral self-cultivation and constructing personal identity through the virtue of *jen* (benevolence) and *li* (propriety) (Tu, 1985; Chong, Tan, and Ten, 2003).[5]

In contrast to the Cartesian view of the atomistic self, the Confucian self is relational and interdependent. East Asian countries influenced by Confucian practice believe that certain sets of human relationships are the basis of the moral community. Traditionally, these relationships are described hierarchically in five pairs, namely, (1) ruler and ministers; (2) father and son; (3) husband and wife; (4) elder and younger brother; and (5) friend and friend (i.e., considering age difference). In these hierarchical relationships, loyalty and obedience are critical to the maintenance of trusting relationships, and the sovereign and his ministers share a common moral purpose of righteousness or justice. Thus vertical relationships are fundamental to the Confucian philosophy, and this hierarchical bent is reflected in the sociopolitical, administrative, and business aspects of East Asian countries. Many economists and social scientists believe that the successes of economic development in South Korea, Japan, Hong Kong, Singapore, and Taiwan can be attributed to a great extent, to these relationships of duty and service to one's country and to society. Loyalty is particularly important to Japanese social, political, and business relationships. In social interactions, Koreans try to establish their relative status in terms of age, family background, education, and job before they form a close relationship with a stranger. In Asian countries, close friendship entails a degree of loyalty toward one another, but when a difference in age and social status exists, the relationship becomes more paternalistic. In contrast to Confucian thought, Buddhism has no discussion of the hierarchical nature of human relationships. Thus, Buddhism helps us think in a nonhierarchical way by focusing on our being in connection to other things around us.

Buddhism is the dominant religious, philosophical, cultural, social, and spiritual force in most of Asia, especially in China, Japan, Korea, Vietnam, Cambodia, Nepal, and Thailand. Buddha, whose real name was Siddhartha Gautama, was born about 563 B.C. in southern Nepal, near the Indian border. Buddha means "enlightened one" or "awakened one." Gautama the Buddha was a member of a rich and powerful royal family. At the age of about twenty-nine, he became overwhelmed with the conviction that life is filled with suffering and unhappiness. After traveling throughout northeast India for about six years, he experienced enlightenment. He had, he believed, discovered why life is filled with suffering and how humanity can escape from this unhappy existence. Buddha's doctrine is derived from "experience in the transformations of consciousness and the stages of meditation," not from sense perception or logical operations. The core of the Buddha's knowledge is perceived only through meditation: rational thinking is not adequate to the task of understanding human existence (Jaspers, 1957). Through meditation, yoga, and prayer, an individual can become enlightened, liberated, and aware of his or her unity with the universe. A person becomes aware of the Middle Way, the way between the "extremes of asceticism, on the one hand, and indulgence, on the other. It is the concept of the rationed life, in which the body is given what it needs to function optimally, but no more" (Smith and Novak, 2003, p. 8).

Buddha denies the self: there is no self ("not self"), no individual, in his doctrine. Being and nonbeing in the universe is a reflection of one's own self. No-self is the nature of an intuitive and subjective perception toward oneself beyond the ordinary range of human experience that is full of the anxieties and defensiveness. According to Zen Buddhism, "to study the self is to forget the self." When the self becomes anxiety-free, one can act spontaneously. Suler points out, "In the spontaneity of no-self one acts without thinking, even though the plan and precision of 'thoughtfulness' remains. There are no boundaries, lines of pressure, traces, or intermediaries. When you first learn to play the piano, you have to think your fingers into position. But when this skill is mastered, the fingers play themselves, and, in fact, allow deeper layers of self-expression to emerge spontaneously" (Suler, 1993, p. 54). We humans often live in suffering, craving, hatred, and delusion because we lose sight of the real self and attach ourselves to our smaller self. Buddha emphasizes that "our concepts of the self or ego are illusory, that an ego-constructed world is essential to our ignorance and suffering, and that freedom or liberation entails self-transcendence—or, since there is no substantial self, transcendence of the illusion of the self" (Allen, 1997b, pp. 10–11). Karl Jaspers illustrates this concept further: "There is no true self. In sensory existence the body is the self. In the first stage of meditation, the spiritual self of the ethereal body becomes real; the former self vanishes into nothingness. But in higher stages the spiritual self is itself annulled. Thus even in meditation the self is not denied, but is shown to be relative. The true self is attained only at the highest stage which coincides with Nirvana" (Jaspers, 1957, pp. 30–31). Buddha rejects the notion that anything, such as a self or soul, is permanent and unchanging. "[E]verything is impermanent in the continuous becoming of lived experience," according to Buddha. He also says that "[a] false belief in an independent separate self is essential to the generation of our selfish desires, greed, craving, hatred, and ego-attachments" (Allen, 1997b, p. 11). The implications of Buddhism are to have compassion for others, act in an ethically disciplined manner, and conduct ourselves with restraint out of a sense of responsibility. (His Holiness the Dalai Lama, 1999, pp. 81–131). Like other religious teachings, Buddhism facilitates us to see human qualities of compassion, love, patience, tolerance, humility, forgiveness, mutual respect and understanding, harmony, and so forth. These would have a special role to play in our contemporary world.

Hinduism is the most important influence on the culture of India. A basic tenet of Hinduism is the caste system, which determines the way of life of most Indian Hindus. Like most religions, Hinduism has beliefs about the Divine, life after death, and how its followers should conduct their lives. Hindus believe that an individual's actions (Karma)—the bad or good actions that the individual performed in a previous life—determine his or her caste. Hinduism is concerned with the spiritual essence of the self. The religion is heavily mystical and deals with many supernatural ideas and forces (Feibleman, 1976, p. 74). The Bhagavad-Gita, a philosophical work and one of Hinduism's sacred writings, emphasizes selfless action, that is, "renunciation of any ego-attachment to the fruit of one's action" (Allen, 1997b, p. 9). The Gita suggests means for transcending a false, or illusory, self, that is, the ego-oriented self. This transcendence of self is seen as essential to spiritual liberation.

Although Confucius is more widely known to the West, the book of *Tao Te Ching*, the teachings of Lao-tze, is the most widely translated Chinese text, the text that establishes Taoism and offers a different view of the relationship between self and society. There are more than fifteen translations in English alone and other translations in Japanese, Korean, and German. Although the exact translation in English is difficult, *Tao* means "the way" or "the path," *Te* means "virtue"; and *Ching* means "book." Almost every chapter of the *Tao Te Ching* describes "this way of living." "The secret of living, according to the *Tao Te Ching*, is to open within ourselves to the great flow of fundamental forces that constitute the ultimate nature of the universe—both the movement that descends from the source and the movement of return" (Lao Zsu, tran., by Feng and English, 1989, xiv).

Lao-tze was born around 571 B.C. and was a keeper of the imperial archives at the capital before retiring and in middle life disappearing. Confucian philosophy is a philosophy of social order, and order by maintaining hierarchical relationships is seldom exciting. Lao-tze's proverbs convey an excitement and a poetry that Confucian commonsensical proverbs cannot. Confucians respect culture and reason, but Taoists reject these things in favor of nature and intuition. Lao-tze, because he discusses the mystery and beauty of the universe, the meaning of life and death, the shaking of the inner self, the realm of the obvious and the hidden, and action and nonaction, is a mystic. I believe Taoism (along with Chuang-tze's philosophy, which further developed Lao-tze's philosophy) will be widely appreciated by people in the East and the West in the twenty-first century because the teachings are naturalistic, free flowing, dialectic, paradoxical, and democratic because of the emphasis on horizontal and collaborative relationships with others.

Lao-tze's paradoxical expressions arise from his view of the relationship of opposites: all things merge in harmony. Allen Watts points out that "the relativity of one's perspective is a fundamental principle that everyone must understand in order to know the meaning of the Tao, which is the Chinese sense of the course of nature" (1997, p. 52). The following expression of Lao-tze is an example of what it means to be in a relationship of opposites:

> In this universe, we can see beauty as beauty,
> Because of the contrast of ugliness.
> And recognize virtue as virtue,
> Because of the contrast of evil.
> Have and have-not arise together.
> Difficult and easy harmonize with one another.
> Long and short oppose each other.
> High and low balance one another.
> Music and sound harmonize with each other.
> Front and back follow one after another.
> So, the sage is working by non-action,
> Teaching by not speaking.
> Ten thousand things evolve ceaselessly.
> Create, yet do not possess.
> Work, yet do not take credit.
> Accomplishment, then forgotten;
> Therefore, it is eternal.
> *(Tao Te Ching)*

In Taoism, the relativity of opposites is present in other aspects of the universe, such as yin and yang: yin is all that is feminine, gentle, dark, and meek; yang is all that is masculine, forceful, light, and active. Yin and yang exist in a mutual relationship and reinforce each other. Life arises from death, and vice versa; possibility arises from impossibility, and vice versa; affirmation is based upon denial, and vice versa. These opposites are very different, but they are inseparable; they are not in conflict with each other but instead embrace the possibility of unity. Opposites therefore do not have the same meaning as they do in the

West, with its strong sense of dualism; rather, opposites are an "explic-it duality expressing an implicit unity" (Watts, 1997).

In Taoism, self does not exist without the existence of the other; self as a separate identity is supported by the "equal and opposite sen-sation of otherness" such as the dialectical relationship between yin and yang (Watts, 1997, p. 68). Thus, the development of self-knowl-edge is recognition of the mutual relations between self and others. In Taoism, all changes in nature stem from "the dynamic interplay between the polar opposites" where each influences the other in the process of transmuting into other things. In the East, the emphasis is on going beyond extreme opposites, but "for the Western mind, this idea of the implicit unity of all opposites is extremely difficult to accept" (Capra, 1975, 114).

Transcendence beyond Self-boundary

This brief investigation of Asian philosophy, particularly Buddhism and Hinduism, reveals a shared belief that through spiritual liberation, the individual can transcend his or her immediate illusion, overcoming the self-restricting boundary that stems from selfish interest. Christianity, Islam, Judaism, and Taoism also teach individuals how to transcend the self-boundary line and to be aware that there is no boundary between self and no-self or no dividing line between the self and external things (Wilber, 1979).

Religions are a spiritual force that is intrinsically personal and help us understand human experience and conditions of society (Smith, 2001; Lynch and Lynch, 1999). Thomas Jefferson points out that religious beliefs and practices originate from the "liberty of the individual's intellect and conscience, and [therefore] religion is a strictly private matter" (Johnson, 1997, p. 25). It is difficult indeed to assign a role to spirituality in public organizations. I like to think, however, that the personal experience of spirituality can help individ-uals to be better aware of the self by having the will to negate and transcend self, to live harmoniously with others by prompting them to go beyond selfishness and greed, and to care for people in need. Furthermore, the spiritual aspects of individual lives could enable people to transcend the intolerable nature of human reality through the enhancement of human consciousness (Smith, 2001, pp. 79–102).

The transcendence of self to no-self and in relation to the other arises from one's willingness to change the primary boundary of the self. Ken Wilber calls this awareness that all life is one, "unity consciousness." Further, he says,

> [This awareness] cannot occur as long as the primary boundary, which *separates* the self from the universe, is mistaken as real. But once the primary boundary is understood to be illusory, one's sense of self envelops the All—there is then no longer anything outside of oneself, and so nowhere to draw any sort of boundary. Thus, if we can at all begin to see through the primary boundary, the sense of unity consciousness will not be far from us. (1979, p. 47)

In sum, Taoism has a slightly different approach to the problem of self and other, placing them in a nondualistic relationship. Although it does not address the transcendental aspects of boundaries, boundaries are never seriously considered because reality is seen as nondualistic: all boundaries are illusory. Thus, a nondualistic relationship between two opposites implies that we are a self only in relation to others.

THE SELF AND SOCIALITY: WESTERN VIEWS

Although both Eastern and Western views of the self stress the individual as moral agent, most Asian religious and philosophical concepts assert the inseparable relationship between the self and the entire moral universe, denying any duality between the self and objects. Eastern views oppose excessive individualism, which, it is believed, leads to egoistic and selfish behavior and limits the individual's spiritual growth or the development of a virtuous character.[6] Another commonality between Eastern and Western views of self is the idea of relationship with other people. Yet in the Eastern view, the transcendence of self is largely possible as the individual experiences the existence of others and realizes the limits of the egoistic self. Either at the spiritual level or in relationship with opposites, the person realizes that there is no separation: all of life contributes to the creation of unity. Eastern thoughts in general do not address the importance of discursive and rational processes for establishing relationships and how the individual, through relating with other people, can become an agent of reality construction. In this section, I discuss

Western views of how the individual experiences the meaning of relationship with others, that is, the "sociality" that emerges between and
among selves (Natanson, 1970, p. 47).

The self is the core of developing a we-relationship with other
organizational members that constructs intersubjective reality. The
idea of a we-relationship with intersubjective reality is a constructive
approach that promotes an appreciative and reciprocal relationship of
the self with others. When the we-relationship develops in an organization, the individual shares his or her experiences with others and
engages in learning, moving toward a "domain of 'betweenness' which
characterizes social action" (Natanson, 1970, p. 48). The quality of
"betweenness" in the we-relationship depends on various elements,
such as face-to-face interaction; dialogue; the commonality of work;
the strength of mutuality; sharing of past, present, and future interests;
and the willingness to participate in the relationship. Other approaches, introduced by such theorists as George Herbert Mead, Chris
Argyris, and Carl Rogers, also deal with the possibility of transcending
the self through relationships with others.

In his influential book *Mind, Self, and Society* (1934), Mead
describes how, through the use of significant gestures, the self and the
consciousness become individualized (and internalized), evolving out
of an intersubjectivity or sociality. Although Mead is often seen as a
social behavioralist, his explanation and interpretation of the self
demonstrates a phenomenological and interpretive orientation. Mead
attempts "to explore and describe experience within society, treating
consciousness, language, communication, and meaning as emergents
from the social process" (Natanson, 1973, p. 5). The self is constituted
through communicative practice, not necessarily through the influence
of the social environment, although the self may be influenced by a certain environment.

According to Mead, the evolution of the self is a process of interaction between an "I" and a "me"; the I and the me constitute the totality of the self. The me is all those perspectives on the self that the individual has learned from others: the attitudes that the I assumes toward
his or her own person when taking the role of the other. In a self, there
is also something that responds to his or her own behavior. The *me* is
the representative of the attitude of the other or others: it is the objectification of gestural behavior. That which responds to this objectification is the I. The I and me relationship is the "inner forum," the silent

internal conversation that is continually going on inside the human organism; it is an ongoing dialectical process (1934, pp. 173–78, 192–200, 209–13, 273–81). In internal dialogue, the I is thought of as an "audience." The I responds to the me, and the me reflects the I. The I is the actual process of thinking and acting, and the me is the reflective process. Because the self engages in social activity in the relationship of I and me as a communicating process, the self emerges in a form of dialogue.

Mead provides a dialectical framework for relating the self to the role of the other. He emphasizes the process of "reflexive role-taking": seeing oneself from the perspective of the other (1934, pp. 15–56, 254, 360–62, 364–67). An interaction between the self and the other makes it possible for the individual to improve his or her self-knowledge in relationship to others through human collaboration. In his discussion of a mutual relationship between the individual and the community in which he or she lives, he argues that "people have to adjust themselves to him [or her] as much as he [or she] adjusts himself [herself] to them." Through this process, "the change may be desirable or it may be undesirable, but it inevitably takes place" (p. 216). According to Mead, this illustration of a process of "mutual adjustment" is sociality. The Habermasian view of rational communicative action between people in the social process is also a view of sociality that emerges as intersubjective reality (1984). Thus both Habermas and Mead argue that the self is constituted socially, and the human self is a product of sociality that emerges between and among people.

One theoretical perspective that seems particularly helpful in enabling students of public administration to understand relating the self (or the individual) to the organization and its members is the approach that deals with interpersonal relationships and interpersonal competence: the self in relationship with other members of the organization. Although symbolic interactionism provides an important theoretical framework in sociology and social psychology, the concepts developed by Chris Argyris and Carl Rogers during the 1960s and 1970s, concerning the problem of interpersonal relationships in organizations, have had a profound influence on the study of participatory, effective, and humanistic organizations. How well the individual relates to other members of the organization is an important factor in the social construction process. Argyris has had extensive experience with research, consulting, therapy, and training people to become effective individuals in relating to organizations, community, and family.[7] During his lifetime, Rogers had similar extensive experience.

According to Argyris, interpersonal competence is the ability of the individual to cope effectively with interpersonal relationships. He stresses three criteria for such effective interpersonal coping: (1) the individual perceives the interpersonal situation accurately; (2) the individual is able to solve a problem in such a way that it remains solved; and (3) the solution is achieved in such a way that the people involved are able to continue to work with each other at least as effectively as when they began to look at the problem (1968, p. 147). An important aspect of interpersonal competence is the "changingness" of the person, the individual's capacity for change. It is a latent capacity in the individual and a latent function in organizations. Rogers argues that change capability is inhibited in many organizations by pessimistic attitudes among people, particularly administrators, toward many long-range policies (1968). He illustrates this with the example of administrative refusal to face up to many urban problems and insists that in the future, highly functional interpersonal relationships will be the natural built-in motivation for individual growth and change, rather than change that is introduced by top management and submissively accepted by those in the ranks below. But Roger's prediction for building interpersonal relationships has not taken place over the last thirty-five years since he first articulated it, and administrative organizations continue to underestimate the importance of developing interpersonal change capability.

POSTMODERN VIEWS OF THE SELF

Beginning in the 1960s, the Western view of self, particularly on ideas concerning the experience of communicating and relating to others, was questioned by poststructuralist and postmodernists, such as Jacques Derrida and Michel Foucault. In classical phenomenology, the subject of experience, "the transcendental ego,"[8] is necessary to objectivity or the objectification of subjectivity. The denial of self in relation to organization and others by postmodernists, however, is tantamount to a rejection of "the notion of a stable, coherent self" and an insistence that "the self consists of nothing more than superficial, disjointed fragments" (Goldman and Papson, 1994). This philosophical perspective within late modernism not only recognizes the limitations of a subject-centered approach within a philosophy of consciousness but also rejects a concomitant abandonment of subjectivity. Postmodernists replace the *person* as a thinking, experiencing, and conscious self with the idea of a *subject*, because people are not autonomous and free-thinking individuals but products of language and discursive practices. The role of the subject in institutions, culture, and society is minimized. To postmodernists, the subject is "a mask, a role, a victim, at worst an ideological construct, at best nostalgic effigy" (Carravetta, 1988, p. 395). Because postmodern views of the subject are diverse and disjointed, it is not possible to represent them as a cohesive unit. Therefore, I discuss here the thoughts of only a few key thinkers—Michel Foucault, Jacques Derrida, and Jacques Lacan—in order to give some flavor for a postmodern approach to the self.

• Michel Foucault (1926–1984), who was very much a part of poststructuralist thinking, argues that the subject no longer has the power to control the self and disputes the liberal humanist ideology of enlightening the individual self. He treats the subject as simply a victim of power relationships, describing the "death of the subject." In a system in which the power structure is rigid and authoritative, the individual subject is incapable of resisting institutional power and cannot control his or her actions. Foucault, however, sees power residing in any relationship, hierarchical or otherwise. He suggests that to obtain productive services from people "power had to be able to gain access to the bodies of individuals, to their acts, attitudes, and modes of everyday behavior" (Foucault, 1980, p. 97). So the subject is constituted through different forces, discursive and nondiscursive practices (language, ways of talking, rules, experts, and so forth), desires, and materials.

• Jacques Derrida (1932–2004) is concerned with the issue of the origin of meaning. To existential phenomenologists and symbolic interactionists, the individual is conscious of and able to express meanings; meanings also have relationships with other meanings. Derrida denies that the self as an active, transcendental ego is the underlying basis of meaning (Surber, 1998, p. 203). For Derrida, there is no perception, and there is no consciousness before any text. Derrida stresses the decentering of the text, which means that texts have plural meanings. He rejects the idea of having a single, unified meaning: meaning is in the text. All different interpretations of the meaning of a text are equally interesting (Derrida, 1978). In order to discover hidden assumptions and different meanings, a text must be demystified. To demystify a text is "to tear it apart to reveal its internal, arbitrary hierarchies, and its presuppositions" (Rosenau, 1992, p. 122). Derrida advocates the need for decentering our thoughts so that we can understand how it was centered in the first place. This is the idea of deconstruction, which Derrida emphasizes in most of his arguments. Derrida critiques the assumptions of both phenomenology and structuralism by denying "transparent expressions of some subject or author or as mere instances of a unified and overarching system" (Surber, 1998, p. 203) Although these assumptions are necessary to these schools of thought, their hope of finding a correct interpretation or a truth where interpretation itself can come to rest is mislead by our habit of mind and language (Derrida, 1970, pp. 247–65).

• Jacques Lacan (1901–1981) was a practicing psychoanalyst as well as a theorist who carefully reviewed Sigmund Freud's work (1982; Bowie, 1991; Sarup, 1992). Surber says, "The heart of Lacan's critical project was to recover in Freud's writings a notion of 'subject of psychoanalysis' as irreducibly multivalent, dynamic, open, and decentered" (1998, p. 195). To public administration students, Lacan is more interesting than Derrida, because his theory offers "a way of thinking about the social and the linguistic construction of the self, of thinking through the problem of the individual and society" (Sarup, 1988, p. 6). McSwite argues that the development of public administration theory has been seriously impeded by the promotion of utility maximizing behavior (the rational ego) of the economic rationalism, and believes that Lacanian theory of the self would make an important contribution to public administration because his theory allows for the "existence of an unconscious dimension of mind, at least an unconscious dimension that is independent of the control and apprehension of the conscious mind" (1997a, p. 57). Lacan tries to integrate phenomenology and structuralism in relating the self to the linguistic construction; phenomenology stresses the free self (subjectivity); structuralism emphasizes language determinism. Lacan uses structuralism but never rejects the subject (ibid.). He encourages the process of decentering the subject to discover multiple meanings. His theory is also dialectical: an I-thou relationship mutually defines subjectivity; society and individual inhibit each other; the subject changes the world; and the subject overcomes the master-and-the slave relationship (in the Hegelian sense). The slave changes and frees himself by working. Lacan provides numerous examples to illustrate the subject's experience: for example, he considers the Oedipus complex to be a linguistic transaction describing the set of relationships involving the Phallus as a signifier, the Other in the Name-of-the Father, and M with the Mother-signifier (Surber, p. 199; Sarup, pp. 10–14).

Although Lacan recognizes the dialectical relationships, he argues that full recognition by the subject and the object (the signifiers) is not possible because we cannot share another person's consciousness fully. Accordingly, he believes that "the subject and the object are irreconcilably divided" (Sarup, p. 13). Furthermore, as we try to learn from others, because of the possibility of misinterpretation and misunderstanding, intersubjectivity can never be sufficiently achieved.

I tend to concur with other social science critics that a "subjectless" inquiry by Derrida and Foucault leading to a textual analysis or a power/knowledge relationship just is not persuasive and unclear where the arguments take us (Goldman and Papson, 1994; Taylor, 1995; O'Neill, 1995; Callinicos, 1990; Haber, 1994). As applied to public administration, an analysis of text has its role in understanding politics, power relationships, and symbols and may help us understand multiple meanings of text and also find out who or what is left out of a text. But it is hard to believe that text-centered inquiry could become the main thrust in critiquing complex social and administrative phenomena. To understand the problem of power relationships, we need to pay attention to the experiences of people by listening to their viewpoints. Foucault's analysis does add new insight to an analysis of power relationships. His argument, however, is critical and negative without providing any positive suggestions as to how the subject can cope with the alienating environment of institutions. Many postmodernists (Lacan being a notable exception) tend to be antisubject (i.e., they see the death of the subject). By emphasizing the fuction of language, Lacan never rejects the subject, but he still does not offer constructive ways of dealing with the problem of intersubjectivity in organizational and social contexts. It is hard to imagine studying public administration without promoting the ideals of individual realization, participatory democracy, humanistic organizations, and moral community; indeed, how could we pay less attention to the problems of people at the organizational, societal, and global levels?

Among the various theories and approaches that are currently in vogue, each has advantages and disadvantages, but the postmodernists' views of the subject in general seem to add little that is useful for understanding the ontological problem of public administration except Lacan. By exploring postmodern views of self, however, we may realize that modern views of self as interpreted in the East and the West have been under radical criticism in recent years. Postmodern thinkers, however, help us understand changes taking place at the global, societal, institutional, and individual levels by questioning the traditional assumptions of modern organizations and human nature (Turner, 1994).

IMPLICATIONS OF EASTERN AND WESTERN VIEWS

The concept of the self provides an important linkage between East and West in studying problems of people in society and administration. Through understanding of the differences, we may be able to learn what is inadequate in having meaningful life, acting ethically, or working as a compassionate administrator in the workplace. By understanding the similarities between East and West, we can explore their complementary approaches to the improvement of people's responsibility to others as well as the development of organizational ability to achieve a "higher-order concept that integrates the two" and generate a synergistic alternative (Suler, 1993, pp. 134–14).

The concept of the self in Eastern philosophy is difficult—perhaps impossible—to grasp, as depicted in the Buddhist teaching of the self/no-self and the Hindu philosophy of egolessness. The self is considered an illusion. To be free from the burden of suffering, we must not be bounded by a focus on the self. Whereas Eastern thought tends to negate the importance of the individual, Western thought emphasizes "the self-conscious, self-indulgent, self-aggrandizing forms of spiritual pursuit" (Suler, 1993, p. 11). Western ideas strongly emphasize the active nature of the individual in constructing his or her own identity and vision. This concept is reflected in the theories and methods of changing organizations, which are propounded by Western scholars today, such as introduced in voluminous books and articles on organization development (OD) and corporate organizational change.

Perhaps the most important commonality between Eastern and Western thought is an emphasis on constructing the self in relationship with others. Among Eastern philosophers, this idea is discussed by Confucius, Lao Tze, and their disciples. The importance of human relationships is also developed by Buddhism, phenomenology, and humanistic psychology. The spiritual ideas of Buddhism, such as mutual respect, harmony, compassion, and love, are similar to Husserl's transcendental phenomenological reduction (1966), Schutz's "we-relations" (1967), Habermasian intersubjective ethics (1984 and 1990), and Mead's self in sociality.

Perhaps the most important idea from the East is an understanding of the human mind and the interconnectivity of everything. In order to resolve social and organizational problems, we have to start within the human mind; Buddhist mental training is useful here. We must look at the violence within ourselves, control it, and then transcend it before we look at the violence outside. Thus the social construction of possibilities begins with the self in relationship with others. This idea is stressed by scholars from both the East and the West.

It is not my intention to simply integrate Eastern and Western ideas into an understanding of organizational phenomena. As Suler points out, the integration of ideas could degenerate into a form of "Eurocentrism" or "Orientcentrism": one ideology could be touted as better at explaining human phenomena. It could be assumed that Western concepts could cover all the bases (Suler, 1993, p. 13). Suler points out, "[T]he most ideal form of integration encompasses a drawing together from both sides simultaneously. It involves a fluid shifting back and forth between interpretations from the East and interpretations from the West" (p. 183). In this process of exploring social, cultural, and human contexts, we need to amplify the similarities as well as understand the differences.

The postmodern view of the self is remarkably different from the transcendental and transformative emphasis of the self as discussed in this chapter. Although the critical analysis of text and power relationships in organizations suggests some important insights into the process of decentering the self from modern bureaucracy, the role of the self, however, is grossly underestimated by French postmodernists. In changing organizations, relating the individuals to the change process is imperative because the individual members must learn the meaning of change and be the participants, not necessarily through the centralizing and converging of individual functions to meet organizational demands, but rather through the voluntary and participatory means. This also implies that meaningful organizational change does not occur without active involvement and contribution by organizational members.

THE SELF-REFLEXIVE INDIVIDUAL
IN A SOCIAL CONTEXT

According to existential phenomenology and existential psychology, the self is constructed in part by self-reflexivity; that is, one's own self is viewed as an object of reflection and knowledge. Human beings have a reflexive quality of examining our selves in relation to others. The self is able to engage in the practice of reflexivity because an individual is a self-conscious and self-questioning being who is "capable of formulating and reflecting on his or her means and ends of action" (Lash, 1993, p. 202). In the everyday life of the self, an individual turns his or her attention inward, reflecting on personal thoughts and experiences. In turning inward, the individual questions his or her ways of being in the world and is critically conscious of acting in a reflexive manner. A reflexive act in this sense involves "psychological introspection" in which "the self becomes object to itself, [and] consciousness is aware of consciousness" (Carr, 1999, p. 85).

Reflexivity is a necessary practice for examining the everyday activities of public administrators in light of social context (including administrative situations), human interaction, criticism, and dialectic. When public administrators reflect on their role in relationship to the situation, the culture, and the public, they seek to define the meaning of their role performance contextually. They also interpret their responsibility and construct the meaning of action in relation to significant others, such as members of the organization, the public, and citizens. Their act is critical in the sense of revealing negative and undesirable consequences of enforcing particular policy or administrative procedures. Thus reflexivity calls us to examine critically our own practices as researchers, educators, and practitioners. Because public organizations thrive on stability, it is interesting to see how deliberate destabilization through incorporation of a reflexive process affects an organization and the individuals trying to implement practical reflexivity.

As public administrators engage in social interactions, they may be able to construct dialectical possibilities by placing their responsibility into the larger contexts of society, citizens, and ethics. Reflexivity is dialectical in the sense that it entails the exploration of alternatives through understanding and overcoming the limits of institutional inadequacies as individuals engage in discourse with others intersubjectively. If public administrators understand the limits of their theoretical stance, politics, managerial approaches, or administrative practice, then they can change those limits by considering the implications of using new ways to change organizations. As administrators actively engage in a reflexive process through dialogue with others in an organization, they open up possibilities for emancipating themselves from their own assumptions, biases, and procedures with regard to administrative practice. Reflexivity, although an important faculty of the individual actor, is not easily practiced in an organization where distrust and fear are common.

Reflexivity helps an individual to see beyond presuppositions and frameworks. In *Being and Time*, Heidegger sees reflexivity as "a positive means of showing the limitations of our previous outlook and of moving beyond that outlook" (1962; Lawson, 1985, pp. 58–89; Macann, 1993, pp. 56–109). In the same book, Heidegger discusses the reflexive character of "Dasein" (the Being of man). He considers Dasein to be different from the Being of all others, such as animals or physical objects, in that reflexivity is the center of Dasein. Heidegger argues that "existence is not an unquestioned simplicity but is an existence which owes the character of its existence to its own concern with that existence" (Lawson, 1985, p. 71). As an existential phenomenologist, Heidegger considers the basic task of phenomenology to be understanding, through reflexive engagement, the hidden aspects of Being and the meaning of Being. Through a reflexive understanding of Being, an individual can explore relationships and possibilities.

Because self-reflexivity requires critical thinking, it is a difficult and demanding task. In an organization, people are accustomed to performing routine activities, which do not require a critical assessment of what they do. They find themselves subject to both conscious and unconscious pressures to act within and conform to the status quo. If one's continued employment, promotion, and pay raises depend upon meeting existing system requirements and rules, then to question existing ways of doing things can be an isolating activity. One can be accused of "not being a team player," or of "stirring up trouble." Becoming self-reflexive and being critical of organizational goals and practices—even the mere idea of changing the bureaucracy—can cause anxiety and stress.

Given these drawbacks, what motivates people to be reflexive? When an administrator wishes to be ethically responsible, to improve his or her sense of self-worth, or to change the work environment, he or she is likely to first engage in an activity of self-realization. This means that the person attempts to understand himself or herself in relationship to others and the organizational context through critical self-reflexivity. Thus self-reflexivity is the acquired ability to question one's connection to oneself and to others. As people deeply engage in the act of reflexivity, they begin to understand and to appreciate complex relationships. In doing so, they recognize that they are active subjects and begin to critically take circumstances into consideration rather than merely react to them, to shape activities in a self-confirming manner in relationship to significant others.

Why is reflexivity crucial to social and administrative practice? How does an individual practice reflexivity in the organization and the community? This question grounds reflexivity in the everyday world of administration. The social construction of self accepts the organizational phenomena that we are self in relation to others and emphasizes ou[...]cting realities and the need to involve others in its c[...]lexivity should not be practiced exclusively on an i[...] individual basis: it consists of more than an individu[...]s or her existence in the organizational world or crit[...]ge and methods. Rather, reflexivity should be embed[...]rience and embrace the recognition that we construct [...] as we interact with those around us. We draw on the [...]e live, work, and make sense of our world, we do so in [...]others and the otherness of our surroundings (Shotter [...]002). Therefore, in order to act in more responsive ways [...]r intersubjective understandings, we need to engage in [...]s critical, open, and self-reflexive. We also need to pay [...]lifferences of ideas and experiences (Habermas, 1984; [...]70; Bourdieu, 1990; Bourdieu and Wacquant, 1992).

THE SELF IN BUREAUCRACY

A bureaucracy is a rational construction of a structure of relationships arranged hierarchically for the purpose of organizing human activity so that it meets established goals. The fact that it is a rationalized and instrumental construction, however, does not necessarily mean that an organization performs rationally. What is rational is itself a construction that can be used by those in authority to determine the actions of others. Nor does it mean that all activity within it yields rational consequences or people behave in a rational manner. Bureaucratic actions, like thoughts, do not derive their substance from some ultimate truth or accomplishment: administrators' claims to organizational legitimacy are based solely on how well they represent the organization's construction of reality. People inside and outside of bureaucracy lend legitimacy to a bureaucracy. Therefore bureaucratic actions may be considered rational insofar as such actions are consistent with the expectations of those in authority. In many non-Western countries, for example, government bureaucracies with rampant corruption certainly do not receive the support of citizens. People continue to accept these depersonalizing institutions, however; this is largely because of the power that government officials have over their lives. In this case, people's submission to authority is virtually inevitable, because from birth they experience no alternative to hierarchy.

The relationship between the self and rigid bureaucracy is reinforcing in mutually destructive ways. It is destructive to the individual because the bureaucratic functionary must deny the feelings of powerlessness and helplessness that are inherent consequences of bureaucratic practice. The psychological tension that is subsequently created from continuous denial and repression of those feelings will seek relief. The individual, marking the real world with mental constructs through which the person can justify the commitment that was made to remain in the bureaucracy, expresses such relief most commonly as unconscious projections. In-as-much as the commitment was made in order to avoid a crisis that would force the person either to leave the bureaucracy or to confront it (risking the fear and anxiety that either choice would create), the projections are real to the person. Consequently, those projections are integrated into the person's belief system, thereby rationalizing the values that justify bureaucratic tasks as important to the organization, the self, and society. But the belief in the significance of bureaucratic tasks can only be viewed as delusional, because the newly organized belief system is entrenched in denial and was, in fact, created to deflect from the self the crisis of the aforementioned responsibility.

The bureaucracy is also, in the very process of consolidation or expansion, destructive of itself. Consolidation is meant here as the process of centralizing power within the bureaucracy; expansion means the bureaucracy's tendency to enlarge its scope and influence over the social landscape. In time of economic prosperity, bureaucracy expands its structure by introducing additional agencies and functions. As economy declines and government faces budget cuts, bureaucracy tends to shrink its operations by consolidating structure and functions. Although these processes are necessarily in reforming government organizations, what is destructive about them is that they exist in contradiction to each other, producing tensions that bureaucracies have traditionally responded to with an almost instinctive surrender. Thus resolution is not sought in a purging of the emotions but in terms of greater repressive measures against the very subordinates on which it must depend for its survival and in the maintenance of its goals. That is why management must so often confront such issues as low worker morale, layoffs, the need for service improvement, performance evaluation, and disenchanted citizens who must face unhappy and disgruntled public employees. If management were aware of the reciprocal relationship between its repressive measures and the resultant consequences (i.e., low morale and low productivity), then its actions would perhaps be more constructive. Management might consider various organizational changes, including participation and openness of dialogue, to remedy these problems.

Bureaucracy is premised on the belief that organizational members will carry out their assigned tasks and functions and implement rules and regulations properly. There is, however, no ontological basis for bureaucracy's exclusive existence. There is no ontological reason why people's activities must be arranged hierarchically and why, therein, they must suffer the indignity of having to acquiesce their identity in favor of an organizational identity (Hummel, 1994, p. 11). Yet bureaucracies continue to exist, and people enter them, becoming unreflexive and uncritical beings and prisoners of their own reifications. Thus not only do those people connected with a bureaucracy perceive it as a monolith; but those same people have lost an awareness of themselves as motivated, creative beings capable of dereifying or redesigning or even dismantling organizations. Bureaucracies are creations of human interactions and assumptions: they do not exist independent of the self. Max Weber describes only what people have created in their need for social organization.

Novels portray unreflexive (and unreflective) individuals and organizations. One of the most famous novels of this sort is *The Trial* by

Franz Kafka (1948), which depicts human life deteriorating into a mere performance of organizational tasks that are devoid of justice, humanness, or compassion. In *The Trial*, the arrest of Joseph K. is sudden and seems to him to be unjustified. Joseph K. believes that the court is an utterly aimless, absurd institution, interested in condemning innocent victims while keeping them in ignorance of what action is being brought against them. The novel is a satirical description of a dehumanizing bureaucracy in which the hierarchical order is corrupt. Bureaucrats have a very narrow concept of their work but insist upon the importance of this work. It is, they believe, their duty to provide efficient services: their technical rationality and accurate measurements show their dedication to their profession. In *The Trial*, a lack of reflexivity turns individuals into uncritical functionaries in a rigid bureaucracy. Obedient functionaries carry out the routine work of a bureaucracy. An extreme example of this lack of reflexivity is seen in the activities of Nazi bureaucrats, who were technically efficient, blindly loyal, and uncritical human beings (Arendt, 1964; Adams and Balfour, 1998). Today most organizations in democratic societies are not like the one described by Kafka. Members, clients, and customers of large organizations, however, are made to feel marginalized and possibly dehumanized from time to time.

The following case of a Japanese bureaucrat who was blindly committed to rules of a bureaucracy illustrates how one can lose a sense of compassion and caring for citizens. The case involves the death of a seventy-nine-year-old widow who suffered from hypertension. The summer of 1994 was unusually hot in the central part of Japan. According to the *Asahi-Shimbun* (a major newspaper), the woman was living in a tiny house that had a tin roof and faced the southeast. She was living alone on her late husband's small pension and on government assistance. On July 9, 1994, a government employee from the local social welfare agency in Okegawa paid a routine visit to her house and discovered that she owned an air conditioner. The public servant ordered her to remove the air conditioner immediately, because it was considered a luxury item according to the welfare guidelines established by the central government. To make sure that they were acting correctly, the government employee's office called the central government in Tokyo and received the order to follow the rules specified in the administrative guidance established by the Central Social Welfare Department. Despite her pleas to the city social welfare office to be allowed to keep the air conditioner, officials there ordered her to remove it, advising her to exchange it for some other household appliance. Fearful of losing her welfare assistance, she went to the nearby electrical appliance shop and exchanged it for a rice cooker. When, on July 18, 1994, the temperature inside her house reached over 104 degrees, she tried to cool off by opening the refrigerator door. She was, however, unable to cope with the heat wave and finally was hospitalized for six weeks to recover from dehydration and malnourishment. When she was discharged from the hospital, the kind electrical appliance shop owner loaned her an air conditioner. Despite the compassion shown by her neighbors, she died shortly afterward.

This kind of bureaucratic behavior is not unique to Japan; rather, it occurs in many countries. Frequently, bureaucrats must obey the orders and rules established by the central authorities, because they do not have the autonomy to exercise their own discretion. The case of Okegawa did much to convince policymakers in Japan to revise the implementation of social welfare policy by transferring some central government functions to the local level. However, neither the local nor the central government public servants showed compassion for the old woman. They were blindly interpreting the regulations, even though the guidelines did not specify that an air conditioner was a luxury item. When the death of the woman became public news, no one in the social welfare agency took responsibility. Instead, government employees blamed the ambiguous rules and guidelines. Clearly, they did not exercise autonomy and critical reflexivity: they did not examine the established rules in the context of the needs of another human being.

It is my contention that if people wish to change such dehumanizing activities, then they need to engage in reflexive practice, questioning how they relate to their surroundings, to others, and to their knowledge of the world. A reflexive person in a bureaucracy is existentially serious in the sense that he or she tries to understand the limitations and depersonalizing aspects of bureaucracy and to overcome them. As Kiros points out, "[T] he existentially serious individual is painfully aware of the existential fact and comports his or her entire desire toward the realization of [a] self-imposed goal" (1998, p. 185). The self-reflexive individual does not simply work in the organization: routine work is not enough. Instead, this person is existentially serious about his or her life in a bureaucracy and explores ways of understanding and interpreting paradoxical aspects of the bureaucracy, such as stability and flexibility, control and autonomy, power and powerlessness, voice and silence, conformity and caring, and domination and empowerment.

Bureaucratic culture encourages unreflexive action, and its focus on rationality, efficiency, and the administrator (and manager) as authoritative expert can lead to the justification of inhumane action. Managers and administrators become "morally-neutral technicians" (MacIntyre, 1981) in which the goal is often to protect the interests of the self and the institution rather than to serve the public first. Employees are "normalized" into acceptable practice, the "right way of doing things" (even though they may personally disagree), and rational criteria for making decisions. Unreflexive actions, especially when grounded in a techno-rational culture, objectify people as costs and benefits and allow us to justify our decisions as experts who serve the interests of the organization. Socio-ontological resources are ignored in the drive to ensure that rules are followed; officials do not use their discretion to make a humane choice. Self-reflexivity calls upon us to challenge these taken-for-granted practices and think about morally responsible choices.

CONCLUSION

Undertaking a cross-cultural dialogue on concepts of the self may help one clarify social and cultural difficulties in one's own tradition, while at the same time broadening one's understanding of a different tradition. For example, when one learns a foreign language, takes a class on foreign history and culture, or lives in another culture, one's perspective on one's own native language, culture, and life experience is deepened and expanded. In the same way, comparing Eastern and Western views of self enhances one's self-reflexivity, helping one to examine how one's own activities are socially constructed.

For those who believe in a clear separation between the self and external things, such as between the self and citizens, the community, institutions, society, nature, or the world, problematic boundaries can be ignored or controlled. But those who do not believe in a rigid separation—as established in Taoism—work hard to transcend boundary restrictions. Accordingly, public administrators who do not see an intersubjective relationship between the administration and the public, between objectivity and subjectivity, or between management and employees maintain a separation between themselves and external things, working only within their primary boundary. Others try to go beyond their immediate psychological and administrative spheres, moving into the social and public spheres. As Lao Tze suggests, they raise the practical question of how to search for possible unity and how to live.

Only consciously aware individuals who are reflexive and willing to experiment with different means for transcending the self, as suggested by Confucian teaching and Western virtue theorists, can practice the virtuous character of the individual. It is not enough to have virtues as individual moral ideals: we must facilitate the process of turning these ideals into responsible conduct, not just for the individual moral agent but also for the whole organization. In contemporary public administration, the dimensions of bureaucracy have become more important than the concerns of individuals. A missing element or a weak link is a focus on the importance of the self in relationship to others and the community. Administrative organizations tend to isolate individuals by treating them as passive, reactive humans. But when we perceive people as self-transcending or self-actualizing social beings who are capable of exercising self-reflexivity and interpretation, and who have the potential to learn and to change, we see that the self is a most important agent for changing relationships and for overcoming the tendency of bureaucracy to depersonalize its actions and for people to be narrow-minded.

The social construction of organizational reality rejects the duality of administrative phenomena. Instead, it considers both sides of a problem, such as the objective view and the subjective view. Shunning duality, it embraces relationships, interdependence, reciprocity, and dialectic. These ideas can be seen in both the Eastern view and the Western view of social reality. Moreover, both Eastern and Western public administration must find ways to improve organizational governance without sacrificing the unique individuality or autonomy of each person. Public administrators must facilitate the process of changing organizations by relating the organization and the individual, the administration and citizens, and objectivity and subjectivity, rather than separating them. They must learn the problems and learn the values of organizational members and citizens if they are to comprehend their responses to changes that originate with the administration.

CHAPTER 8

The Social Construction
of Ethical Responsibility

Many administrative responsibilities with which the public administrator is charged are fundamentally ethical in context. In public administration, however, there is an increasing tendency to assume that the
"reality" of the administrative context renders ethical and moral considerations old-fashioned, even ludicrous. Time pressures, political
considerations, tight deadlines, complexity, harassment from supervisors, demands from clients and the public, and scrutiny by the media
are explanations cited to justify behavior that is merely expedient or as
Herbert Simon describes it "satisficing." The consideration of the
ethics of everyday administrative decision making is sometimes made
to seem pathetic or softheaded.

Public administrators frequently emphasize their administrative
functions too much as they work to meet their organizational obligations and perform their assigned tasks. Ethical questions often
interfere with their commitment to efficiency and productivity. In all
problem-solving situations in which administrators are involved,
however, ethical judgments are inherent. The ethical side of public
administration demands responsible performance, both individually
and collectively, of all aspects of the administrative role. This must
become an immutable professional commitment that goes far beyond
simply applying established rules or a prescribed code of ethics. Terry
Cooper points out that "responsibility is the key concept in developing an ethic for the administrative role" (1998, p. 65). And yet paradoxically, a public administrator often faces situations that require a
personal decision about what is right and wrong, obligation to the
organization as opposed to responsibility to the self, good and evil,
and justice and injustice (Harmon, 1995). Despite the complex
nature of ethics in the public service, public administrators can never
escape the ethics of administration because of their responsibility to
the public that they serve.

This chapter emphasizes that the social construction of ethics is important for public administrators because in the pluralistic work environment, people must come up with the appropriate actions to take, concerning problematic issues. Alan Wolfe points out in his discussion of the social construction of morality that "individuals create their own moral rules through the social interactions they experience with others" (1989, p. 212). Thus the meaning of ethical responsibility is shaped either through the individual formulating the right thing to do in a conflict-ridden situation or through the individual interacting and communicating his or her view with others, who may or may not share the same view. Ethical choice is socially constructed by reflecting on an ongoing process of individual self-cultivation and self-constitution. My premise in this chapter is based on the belief that no society (or community) can flourish without civic virtue. A public conception of autonomy is not only political, in the Rawlsian sense, but also social. John Rawls points out,

> [Citizens] are prepared to offer one another fair terms of social cooperation (defined by principles and ideals) and they agree to act on those terms, even at the cost of their own interests in particular situations, provided that others also accept those terms. (1993, p. xliv)

The need for a public conception of autonomy goes beyond the liberal view of private interests and is related to the role of citizens in a civil society. Policy makers and managers have the responsibility to empower organizational members to develop a sense of autonomy (or self-rule) as well as to facilitate a shared understanding of values.

THE ETHICAL DILEMMA OF THE RESPONSIBLE ADMINISTRATOR

The problems posed by the "organization ethic," political pressures, political favors, and whistle-blowing present a dilemma for public employees as they are concerned with organizational obligation, political influence from the external environment, and responsibility for the public.

The Organization Ethic

The prime tenet of traditional organizational life is to put loyalty and team play above personal conscience. William H. Whyte calls this "the organization ethic," and it normally has a strong effect on organization members (1965). The organization ethic demands loyalty and acceptance of institutional tactics and policies in return for companionship, security, advancement, and the shared adventure of the common enterprise. This ethic is dominant in most organizations. As a result, individuals may come to believe that not only do they merely work for or with the organization but also that they belong to it and depend on it for meaning and identity. The longer a person is employed by an organization, the harder it becomes for her to jeopardize her job or leave her job. If she did, she might have to give up her income, status, retirement plan, and fringe benefits.

Leaders sometimes demand loyalty that is blind and unquestioning: conformity in every detail. The "loyal" member becomes the "yes person," the sycophant who is more determined to display his personal loyalty than to deal critically with difficult issues. A member may conform because he is truly loyal or because he fears for his job or reputation if he does not conform. But whatever his motivation, the organization ethic demands an outward show of loyalty, which is manifested in conformity. In his study of executive task forces, Irving Janis concludes, "In a sense, members consider loyalty to the group the highest form of morality" (1972, p. 12). Edward Weisband and Thomas Franck note, "Being right is no excuse for disloyalty to the team." They give the example of the member of the tribal council who insists on shouting, "The dam is out," when the chief has said that the dam is safe. The member is in trouble either way. If the dam is safe, he will look ridiculous and be chased into the desert. If it is crumbling, he will probably drown with everyone else—unless he has already been stoned to death for confronting the chief, who is the embodiment of the tribe's collective wisdom. This is truly a "no win" situation (1975, pp. 3, 6).

The kind of loyalty demanded of team players does not allow much constructive dissent—only a little from within. Organizational leaders often demand full suppression of public signs of disenchantment and view with disfavor anyone who is almost totally loyal. They demand total loyalty. (The blind loyalists to Richard Nixon during the Watergate scandal displayed such a behavior.) A few public officials have resigned as a form of mild protest, hoping to inform the public without offending the organization. They have generally ended up accomplishing neither, and they usually have not been called back into public service.

The Connection between Politics and Business

Unethical behavior by public officials is often a product of our plural-istic political system; in the private sector, such behavior stems from greed generated by entrepreneurial opportunities. The problem is espe-cially prevalent in the business world, where competitive pressure and desire for profit make bribery, payoffs, misrepresentation, short-cuts, and other questionable behaviors more likely; but it is increasingly evi-dent in the public sector as well. Far more than business executives, public officials have felt the sting of such labels as "unrealistic," "starry-eyed," or "idealistic" for insisting on equity or morality in critical situ-ations. In a world where most power is held by elected representatives, and where such representatives must secure reaffirmation from their constituents every two, four, or six years, there is much pressure for conspicuous effectiveness and short-term achievement in administra-tive agencies. Thus public officials are pressured into implementing "quick and dirty" solutions and extending favors to business leaders, often at the price of bypassing ethical norms and forfeiting professional standards.

Big corporations have great wealth and power, and they strongly influence the policies that shape American society. Often this influence is contrary to the public interest. Some years ago, Neil Jacoby made five allegations against big business that continue to be relevant (1973, pp. 10–15). First, corporations exercise economic control over the private sector by shaping economic policies to suit their own needs. Second, corporations exert political control by buying into political campaigns; by controlling the judicial system, which exonerates corporate crimes; and by gaining privileged access to the democratic process. Third, big business policies are controlled by a power elite: the role of the share-holders is largely ceremonial. Fourth, corporations dehumanize their employees by stifling their individuality and ignoring their civil rights. Fifth, corporations degrade the environment and our quality of life by polluting, exhausting natural resources, and focusing on profitability without examining the side effects of these profits on the public. All of these concerns suggest the need for a broader, clearer statement on the matter of ethics in official behavior, in both the private and public sec-tors. The recent cases of corporate corruption, involving such U.S. cor-porations as Enron, MCI, and Tyco demonstrate the unethical and greedy motives of executives in those companies, who disregard the public interest. In most Asian countries, business leaders have always influenced government officials; they are allowed to quietly pull strings because of their financial contributions to politicians and parties. The uncovering of corruption in South Korea in 2003 resulted in the indictment of high-level politicians—of both the ruling and the opposite parties—who received large cash contributions from business. Some significant results of this scandal were that the corrupt politicians were not reelected in the 2004 national election and that the consciousness of voters was raised regarding democratic government.

Political Machines and Dirty Hands

Many large cities in the Eastern United States were, by the end of the nineteenth century, governed by an organizational phenomenon known as the political machine. Used by Democrats and Republicans alike, the political machine was generally found under a strong-elected-mayor type of municipal government and featured city hall to precinct organization and communication, down to the block and even tenement level. Through district, precinct, and block leaders, the political party in power saw to it that the needs of constituents were readily met. Whether people needed a job, a loan, a place to live after a fire, or help with the courts, the machine accommodated them (Riordan, 1963, pp. xi–xvi). In addition, newly arrived immigrants, reaching American cities in great numbers during this period, were aided and, to some extent, enculturated more rapidly through political machines. All of this was given with only one thing asked in return: that the beneficiaries give their votes to candidates of the political machine.

One of the most effective political machines of this era was New York City's Tammany Hall, headquarters of the Democratic Party and the seat of almost continuous political power from 1854 until 1934 (Riordan, 1963, p. x). Like other political organizations of its type and time, Tammany Hall dispensed favors and made loans to constituents; sent representatives to weddings, christenings, and funerals; nominated candidates for city officers (including the mayor); and presided over patronage for political jobs. Political machines administered the "spoils system" on the local level, presided over an early welfare system, and helped to educate many citizens about the intricacies of representative government (ibid., p. xix). Despite these quasihumanitarian activities, the political machines' negative activities were often excessive and brought about their eventual demise. When George Washington Plunkitt, New York state senator and longtime Tammany Hall political leader, died in 1924, *Nation* magazine summed up his political credo by stating that he understood that in politics, honesty does not matter, efficiency does not matter, and progressive vision does not matter. What matters is the chance to get a better job, a better price for wheat, or better business conditions (Ibid., p. xx). Because of their excesses, the political machines of Tammany Hall and other American cities eventually gave way to reform governments. With the demise of Mayor Richard Daley's machine in Chicago in the 1970s, there appears to be no large U.S. city with such an organization still intact. However, ethics violations can and still do take place, although in a reduced and less organized fashion.

A similar evaluation might be made of politicians in less industrialized and industrialized countries in Asia. The abilities that enabled the politicians of ruling parties in particular to curry favors, win elections, and dispense patronage did not lend themselves readily to social vision; like Tammany Hall, ruling political parties in Asian countries abuse the tremendous power at their disposal because they have no goal for justice, social change, or serving the public good. Particularly in developing countries, authoritarian governments have a tendency to create their own ethics. Justifying whatever they do with self-serving rationales is a regular feature of both government bureaucrats and politicians. Too often political leaders everywhere display an "ends justify the means" philosophy that marks them as inadvertent disciples of Machiavelli. Michael Walzer notes that not many politicians are successful in politics "without getting [their] hands dirty" (1973). In fact, public officials often commit crimes deliberately and systematically.

The Problem of Whistle-blowing

Public employees who discover that the agency they work for is violating the trust of the people it is supposed to serve face an ethical dilemma. Do they go public and blow the whistle, offering information to the media? Do they attempt to correct the agency's unethical conduct internally? Or do they remain quiet out of loyalty to the group and to protect their jobs? Over the years, public employees in both Eastern and Western countries have not tended to express publicly their misgivings about public policies and public agency conduct. Why is this so? Largely because political and administrative systems have tradi-tionally fostered "conformity rather than conviction." In particular, bureaucratic organizations emphasize group loyalty rather than indi-vidual accountability; they reward people for their willingness to play the organizational game (Weisband and Franck, 1975).

Deena Weinstein describes whistle-blowing as a form of "bureau-cratic opposition" exercised by those who do not have any authority to change bureaucratic policy. She assumes that not all individuals work-ing in the bureaucracy are blindly loyal to management, that some have not lost sight of who they are. According to her description of these individuals, whistle-blowers tend to "act on motives that are not rooted in fear, resentment, or selfish enjoyment. [They are] able to question the prevailing 'definition of the situation' and to act on their critical insight" (1979).

There are, of course, strategies for whistle-blowing (Hirshman, 1970; Nader, 1972). The whistle-blower can be overt or covert. Advan-tages of the latter course include protection from arbitrary dismissal, reassignment, or loss of income while the matter is investigated and resolved. Or the whistle-blower may instead choose to resign and make the case from the outside. He or she may hold a press conference, mak-ing a public statement about the basis for the resignation or launching an attack on the perceived wrongdoing. In the film *China Syndrome*, Jack Lemmon portrays the ethical dilemma of an engineer who rejects blind loyalty to management and coworkers; instead, he establishes an alliance with a TV reporter and a camera operator. In U.S. public administration, there have been numerous whistle-blowing cases, con-cerning cost overruns of defense contracts, the violation of environmen-tal regulations by industries, and the mismanagement of public funds.

Whistle-blowers may work through outside contacts, leaking charges to the public. This is less popular, as a rule, than more overt expression, preferably within the organization. To bring an allegation to the attention of top management is considered the most honorable approach, if such a channel can be opened. The creation of an atmos-phere of ethical responsibility implies exhausting potential solutions within the organization before going public or seeking outside aid. This fits within the "exhaustion of remedies" rules in the codes of many gov-ernment agencies. It helps avoid the multidimensional costs of public hearings, litigation, and scandal. Ordinarily, individual employees who have evidence of unethical conduct by their superiors or peers do not have to go to the press or other external channels. In the United States, the protection of legitimate whistle-blowers in the federal government began during the Carter administration. For example, after passage of the Civil Service Reform Act of 1979, an Office of Inspector General was established in each cabinet-level agency. This office investigates charges without revealing the identity of the whistle-blower and reports results of the investigation to the whistle-blower. Furthermore, federal agencies may be required to conduct investigations and prepare reports on the substance of complaints made by whistle-blowers.

Whistle-blowing is rare in Asian countries. Additionally, there are no strong forces, either inside or outside the public bureaucracy, that act as a vigilant and countervailing force to the excesses of corporations or politicians. Furthermore, the media and civil society organizations in all Asian countries are relatively weak, too weak to act as agents of social change by supporting whistle-blowers. The traditional organization ethic in those countries is such that employees remain silent when they perceive the organization to be involved in corruption, graft, mismanagement, or other harmful activities. Dissenters (or wave makers) are more likely to be ostracized than applauded; they are more likely to be thought quitters, betrayers, or heretics than people of principle. No laws protect whistle-blowers in Asian countries. Under the protection of the basic rights of citizens, people may go to the public to disclose an agency's unethical activity, but the burden of taking a course of legal action discourages people from whistle-blowing.

The *Economist* reported that during the first half of 2004, twenty-one thousand new corruption cases in China—an increase of nearly 7 percent over the previous year—were investigated. The Chinese officials fighting corruption have no protection from the government and even receive death threats from the targets of their investigations. A county-level Communist Party chief from Fujian province published an open letter of his agitating story on the website of the *People's Daily*, explaining a death threat faced as he deeply probed into a corrupt redevelopment project. As a result, not only was he confronted with the problem of getting cooperation from other officials, but also his superiors accused him of "making a grave political mistake by publishing his letter, violating party discipline and threatening social stability" (September 4–10, 2004, p. 43).

In Japan, whistle-blowing is very rare: the culture frowns upon anyone who reveals the unethical conduct of his or her colleagues, his or her superior, or a government agency or who exposes inefficient administrative services. The administrative culture of Japanese bureaucracy puts its emphasis on employee loyalty, obligation, and conformity. Group harmony is encouraged; individualism, diversity, and critical reflexivity are discouraged (Jun and Muto, 1995, p. 133): "The nail that sticks out must be pounded down." Masao Miyamoto, M.D., completed his postgraduate work in psychiatry in the United States and worked as the deputy director of the Mental Health Division of the Ministry of Health and Welfare, at a Japanese national government agency. He has been the most incisive critic of Japanese bureaucracy and has contributed numerous essays to a leading newspaper, *Asahi Shimbun*. In response to an article he wrote titled "The Nail That Sticks Too Far Out Can't Be Pounded Down," a concerned reader wrote to him: "[Y]ou should know that bureaucrats immersed in the philosophy of self-sacrifice for the organization look on criticism with a jaundiced eye. They are not to be trifled with. And they may well decide that a nail like you should be pulled out. Please, be careful" (Miyamoto, 1994, p. 190). Because he persistently hinders the behavioral norm (acceptable behavior) of a conservative bureaucracy, he was demoted to a dead-end job as quarantine director at the port of Kobe, which is far away from Tokyo; several years later, he was fired from his post for criticizing Japan's bureaucracy to an audience at the National Press Club in Washington, D.C. Until recently, the Japanese government has done nothing to protect whistle-blowers. In late 2003, Premier Koizumi's administration drafted a bill to protect whistle-blowers and invited public review to improve its content.

In public administration in both Eastern and Western countries, opposition to one's superior may result in the loss of one's career, plus a serious break in relationships with one's peers. When a public employee feels powerless against higher authority, he or she hesitates to speak up, even if the unethical behavior of a superior or peer may cause great harm to the public. Moving to a position of ethical responsibility requires a public administrator to speak out to the public and to organizational leadership. When an employee becomes a whistle-blower in defense of the public good, he or she does not act out of selfishness. Many Japanese think that Miyamoto is a brave man, a hero: he had the personal integrity to stand up to Japan's public bureaucracy.

CONSTRUCTING ETHICS IN ORGANIZATIONS

Ethics influence the purposive behavior of public administrators because their motivations and actions involve an interpretation and understanding of the situation that requires ethical judgment. For this reason, the ethical responsibility of public administrators cannot be value-free or positivistic. In a positivistic view, the ethical behavior of individuals is prescribed in terms of an organization's idea of ethics and language. Organizations (for example, government agencies) demand ethics from employees in terms of expected duties and obligations. What is required in situations involving ethical practice is prescribed in laws and ethical codes without considering the experiences or practices of individuals.

Although there is a substantial dichotomy between organizational obligation and individual responsibility, in the ethical life of public administrators, the dichotomy between objective responsibility and subjective responsibility is ambiguous because the conditions that are responsible for organizational obligation depend on the actions of individuals. The requirement that a public administrator should behave in accordance with established laws and a code of ethics is only one of the many elements that the administrator can consider. The administrator may see other elements, such as compassion, caring, communication, and integrity, as equally important in making an ethical judgment.

An Objective View of Ethical Responsibility

Objective responsibility imposed by the organization is one of the most common ways in which administrators experience problems in defining their responsibility. Objective responsibility arises from legal, organizational, and societal demands on the role performance of public administrators (Cooper, 1998, pp. 66–78). Expectations are imposed from the outside and encapsulate a dual dimension of accountability and organizational obligation. All objective responsibility involves responsibility to someone, such as superiors, elected officials, or citizens. Organizational obligations also include a responsibility to accomplish goals through assigned tasks and functions. A code of ethics is the major form of external control, as it represents values collectively imposed on individuals by organizations and professional associations. This approach attempts to project ideals, norms, and obligations for particular professional groups and is supposed to be customized to the particular situations of a profession. The limitations of a code of ethics are that it is vague and abstract and can be difficult to apply to specific situations where ethical guidance is needed (p. 152). Moreover, a code of ethics lacks incentives for adherence, so an administrator could still make unethical decisions. When a code is vague, interpretations can differ widely. Therefore, a code of ethics is harder to implement than a law because of a lack of enforcement mechanisms, sanctions, or adherence.[2]

External control establishes limits, requirements, boundaries, standards, and sanctions to govern the operation of organizations. Although external controls call for the enforcement of laws and codes of ethics, administrators will have a difficult time adhering to those laws and ethical guidelines without exercising a degree of internal controls that depends on subjective judgment. Objective responsibility through the use of external control assumes that once ethical demands are legislated and become laws, administrators can no longer exercise their personal discretion in applying their own values to situations. Instead, they are coerced by sanctions to engage in certain types of conduct (Cooper, 1998, p. 141). When people attempt to cling to the enforcement of external rules and regulations, they become increasingly bureaucratic and depersonalizing to their clients.

Laws and ethical codes are generally prescribed in "the language of universals" that assumes the universal quality of professional obligation (Rohr, 1998, pp. 9–15), and they must be viewed as instruments that complete the process of creating ethically responsible conduct. In order to make a law or code meaningful, however, the enforcement must depend upon an individual's ethical reflection and critical consciousness. Objective criteria are an abstraction of the presumed behavior of people in organizations, not the behavior itself. The implementation of a law or code of ethics is contingent upon the compliance of people who are expected to act morally in conducting organizational work. For example, most governments in Asia have laws that specify severe punishment of those who engage in corrupt behavior, but corruption in the public sector is still rampant, except in Japan, Hong Kong, Taiwan, and Singapore. Thus the eradication of corruption requires not only tough laws but, more important, depends upon changes in culture, behavior, transparency, and raising the level of the quality of life (Quah, 2003).

An emphasis on objective responsibility takes a macrolevel approach to ethics (see Table 8.1), which is generally based on an

TABLE 8.1
Perspectives on Ethical Responsibility

Responsibility	Level of emphasis	Constitution of ethics	Assumptions about human nature
Objective responsibility	Macro strategy: an emphasis on communitarianism; loyalty and obligation	Legalistic and institutional demands: laws, rules, ethical codes; role performance; accountability to authority	The situated self: passive being and malleable; acting on organizational interests; not challenging rules; self-aware of functional responsibility
Social construction of responsibility	Meso strategy: an emphasis on self-transcendence, virtues, and relationships	Social interaction: communicative action; dialogue, and discourse; working toward intersubjectivity; cultural influence on moral character; social experiences in cultural context	The social self: engaging in interpersonal relations; possibility of reshaping the future by moral concerns; a self through participation in the social process with others
Subjective responsibility	Micro strategy: an emphasis on individualism, the self, autonomy, and discretion	Interpretation and understanding of ethical issues: critical consciousness; individual praxis; integrity and self-cultivation; relativity of moral practice	The moral self; moral conscience: actively constructing self-identity; reflexive and interpretive capability; against the universalization of morality

assumption that human nature is passive, reactive, and malleable. People should be subordinate to universal rules and organizational goals. The behavior of people working in a large bureaucracy is conditioned by the organizational culture. It is the individual's responsibility to conform to established rules and regulations. The individual should follow a prescribed course of action rather than considering constructive alternatives to a problematic situation. William Whyte describes this type of individual as an "organization man" (1965). An organization man avoids conflicts and does not challenge procedures or programs. He seeks constancy and predictability, enforces poor procedures as well as good ones, is not interested in innovation or creativity, and is good at maintaining the status quo and order in the workplace. This type of manager exhibits loyalty to the organization and, in turn, demands loyalty from subordinates.

The limitations of objective responsibility and external controls are uncovered in order to demonstrate the ways in which they lack an ethical basis and how, ultimately, an individual's reflexive and subjective judgment is needed.

The Ethical Self and Subjective Responsibility

Administrative activities and decisions that affect citizens may be reduced to a situation of individual ethical choice. Because ethics cannot be separated from the function of the individual self, such as consciousness, values, cultural experiences, and motivation, ethical responsibility is incomprehensible to a public administrator who considers only objective requirements. A public administrator develops a professional ethic through personal experience, organizational role, and the socialization process inside and outside the organization. Subjective responsibility is the building block of an ethical disposition, as an individual is compelled by his or her conscience to act in a particular way. Although objectivity informs a person that he or she must meet legal and organizational demands, it is a person's inner drive—composed of beliefs, values, and character—that compels him or her to act in certain ways (Cooper, 1998, pp. 78–84). When an individual works in an organization, he or she learns a sense of ethical behavior. An individual's ethics are therefore always tinged with his or her subjective judgment. For this reason, an administrator's actions in an organization may be enigmatic when she or he is faced with a choice between objective responsibility to the organization and her or his subjective interpretation of how to act. Thus the question of ethics is often reduced to a question that only the individual or the organization can answer. According to Hans Jonas, the main obstacle to an adequate theory of ethical responsibility is scientific materialism (material prosperity in the technological age) that denies the reality of actors, subjects, or minds (1984). In order to construct a new ethics of responsibility, we must pay attention to the very ontological possibility of subjectivity or mind: that is to return to the immediate experience of our selves and our world.

The subjective perspective with regard to the interpretive view of action, which is discussed in chapter 6, primarily emphasizes the experiences and perceptions of the individual. Ethics must be subjectively made meaningful by "creating sense-making" (Allan, 1998). Weber insists that social reality depends upon the actions of individual actors, that is, the subjective meaning of the actor in bureaucracy. When we apply Schutz's phenomenological view of the life-world to the administrative context, we see that what is important in making an ethical choice is subjective meanings of ethical concerns (Schutz, 1967). The problem of subjective responsibility and action can be illustrated in terms of the 2004 episode involving the U.S. treatment of prisoners of War in Iraq. The violation of human rights involving the inhumane treatment of Iraqi prisoners by some U.S. soldiers, as disclosed in despicable photographs, demonstrates that despite the treaty signed at the Geneva Convention to protect the rights of prisoners, soldiers ignored the law and deliberately committed atrocities, even deriving some satisfaction out of their inhumane acts. It is not acceptable to say that the soldiers were just following the orders of higher authority or acting according to established procedures. In recent years, we have witnessed numerous atrocities involving wars and ethnic conflicts.

Hannah Arendt succinctly summarizes the moral conscience of the individual during the Nazi Holocaust, resisting social solidarity and believing in personal integrity, as follows:

> [H]uman beings may be capable of telling right from wrong even when all they have to guide them is their own judgment, which, moreover, happens to be completely at odds with what they must regard as the unanimous opinion of all those around them. Those few who were still able to tell right from wrong went really only by

their own judgments, and they did so freely; there were no rules to be abided by . . . because no rules existed for the unprecedented. (1964, pp. 294–95; also cited in Bauman, 1993, p. 249)

Zygmunt Bauman, in his book *Postmodern Ethics*, stresses that because "moral responsibility is precisely the act of self-constitution," any attempt to move from the moral self to the social self (or the situated self) would diminish the individual's sense of moral responsibility (1993, p. 14).

The micro approach to subjective responsibility assumes that human nature is reflexive, critical, interpretive, and self-constituting (see Table 8.1). Contrary to the general observation of the macro view of responsibility, people do not always act according to the prescribed law, a code of ethics, or administrative procedures. Because an organization consists of individual members whose behavior is unpredictable because of their interpretation of a situation and because of personal judgment, ethical judgment derives from individual interpretation and action first. The ethically responsible administrator is concerned with arriving at a justifiable course of action; thus the individual struggles with problems, rather than merely memorizing rules or a code of ethics dictated by the organization. The administrator may discover that a good judgment requires not only critical self-reflection, but also personal instinct (Harmon, 1995, pp. 79–96).[3] And although ethics are important guidelines for administrative action, an administrator's personal sentiment, consideration of others, integrity, and reflexive ability to make judgments are also important.

The internal necessity that is required for us to arrive at more conscious and critical ways of thinking occurs through the process of self-reflexivity (Harmon, 1995, 79–88; Cunliffe and Jun, 2005). Self-reflexivity can lead administrators to more critical, responsible, and ethical actions. Administrators need to practice reflexivity in order to adequately assess the moral possibilities of a course of action and also to think more systematically about the values that are embedded in the choices that we would otherwise make on practical or political grounds alone. Self-reflexivity requires individuals to think critically as they draw from their own experiences; they must begin with the self in order to arrive at sound, objective decisions. Through this process, they critically examine how they relate to others and negotiate on an external level, and they consciously examine the limitations of their ethical choice.

From the Ethical Self to Social Construction

The social construction of ethical responsibility realizes that there are reciprocal interactions among the administrator, society, culture, organization, and citizens. Learning ethical responsibility is dialectical in the sense that the organization and society can influence the individual through accepted cultural norms and expectations, just as the individual can influence the organization and society through his or her self-constitution and changing relationships. Learning ethical responsibility is an ongoing process of interaction among people through externalization, objectification, and internalization (Berger and Luckmann, 1966) within the cultural context (Allan, 1998, pp. 37–59).

To a large extent, ethical behavior is different from moral character, although this phenomenon varies from culture to culture. In Eastern countries in particular, where traditional values influence many aspects of a person's moral life, individuals learn how to behave appropriately in different social contexts. Public administrators in Asian countries tend to behave differently from administrators in the United States because of what is socially acceptable behavior in those countries. Language is used differently in organizational relationships to distinguish a person's relationship to another party; the ways in which individuals in Japan, South Korea, and China interact and communicate are distinctly different from the ways in which people in the United States conduct their affairs. To get along in organizational and social life, the individual learns perceptual orientations, cognitive biases, cultural norms and beliefs, family values, symbols, and habits. Through an ongoing socialization process, these elements become the attributes of a person's moral character.

Public administrators need to be conscious of their subjective and objective responsibility to serve the public, but when they face difficult issues and are no longer clear about the right thing to do, their concern can be discussed with others "to make the moral order possible" (Wolfe, 1989, p. 213). Equally important, their decision sometimes needs to be socially limited in situations involving unethical behavior, such as corruption, discrimination, or unfair and uncaring services rendered to citizens. Furthermore, by gaining support from the organization, an employee can use his or her voice to ward off the influence of powerful interest groups. When an employee, for example, has information about hazardous wastes being dumped in open public space by private companies, with agency support he or she can fight against polluting industries as well as pressure from any politicians or high-level officials.

Consulting others in an organization, however, does not mean that an administrator is free to make an unethical or inhumane judgment. For example, as discussed in chapter 7, when a Japanese social worker was faced with a difficult ethical choice, he consulted his immediate supervisor and an official at the central government. They all reached the same conclusion: to take away an elderly woman's air conditioner during a hot summer. They failed to discuss the humane thing to do to help the old woman without violating the established guidelines, which were ambiguous and open to interpretation. Their action may be viewed as functionally correct, but the outcome was, obviously, grossly flawed.

The social construction of ethics has negative consequences when group members reinforce one another's unexamined behavior. When reaching a positive and unopposed consensus only among group members closely involved in making a decision becomes the urgent task, group members (i.e., participants in the decision-making process) tend to ignore negative information that may contradict their preconceived course of action. Irving Janis calls this pathological behavior "groupthink": group members tend to support their leader's desires and discourage critical thinking (Janis, 1972). Particularly in a crisis, a cohesive group has a strong "we versus they" feeling toward an adversary group, a psychological symptom that exists alongside "shared stereotypes" about an enemy or competing party. The decision-making process on the Iraqi War clearly demonstrates uncritical thinking among the key players. On July 9, 2004, the seventeen-member U.S. Senate Intelligence Committee of nine Republicans and eight Democrats revealed the 511-page report on the investigation of the U.S. intelligence judgments about Iraq's weapons programs (*New York Times, Washington Post,* and *San Francisco Chronicle,* July 10, 2004). The committee members unanimously criticized that the flawed and exaggerated prewar intelligence by the CIA and other spy agencies fueled the Bush administration position that Saddam Hussein's regime posed a serious threat to the United States. They agreed that "groupthink" led to incorrect intelligence about Iraq's supposed chemical and biological weapons and its development of nuclear weapons and pushed aside the doubts of dissenting analysts. The intelligence officials did not communicate their uncertainties and had a collective presumption that Iraq possessed weapons of mass destruction.

The social construction of responsibility is considered the meso-level approach (see Table 8.1): ethical judgment begins with the individual's subjective understanding of an ethical situation and moves to interpersonal and group relationships. It is not a balancing approach—seeking to reconcile two opposing views of objective and subjective responsibility—rather it is a constructive and deliberative strategy. It employs dialogue and discourse between the self and others to arrive at an ethical decision. The individual takes an active role in constructing an ethical life in relationship with others. The social constructionist view of human nature assumes that people have the ability to act, interpret, and exercise reflexivity; this is reflected in the individual's ability to make an ethical choice. The social concept of the self here implies that the individual can engage in social practice through communicative action and cultivate his or her ethical judgment.

Because organizational regulations and policies can often be interpreted in different ways by different people, what is required is socialization that helps us actively construct choices in self-confirming ways in communicative relationships with others, by exploring organizational and public obligations. Contrary to the postmodern argument, such as Bauman's position, this transcendental learning process does not necessarily surrender to the communitarian emphasis of serving organizational interests. Instead of passively carrying out the requirements of organizational duties, an ethically conscious administrator can expose the contradictions that present themselves in organizational policies and practices and can exercise personal discretion in applying his or her own values to situations within the organization. Thus the ethical responsibility of a public administrator is to be grounded in the individual's understanding of self and self-realization; this, in turn, connects the individual with others through active participation in organizational activities and working with citizens in the public sphere.

The Problem of Social Construction of Ethics

There are three important points in the preceding discussion. First, the meaning of ethical responsibility can be shaped through the individual's sense of ethical responsibility. Second, the meaning of ethical responsibility can be shaped through the individual's process of interacting and communicating his or her viewpoint with others, who may or may not share the same meaning. Third, a dialectical and reflexive construction of ethics (or sharing of mutual interests) is possible when the actor moves from the micro level of understanding to the meso level, not from the macro level to the micro level. The macro-level strategy may influence the ethical behavior of the actor to some extent, as long as the actors are reactive and loyal to the organization and willingly comply with universal ethical standards, such as laws and codes of ethics. These ideas, however, present some limitations, as people behave and think differently involving ethical matters.

There are at least two limitations of the social construction of ethics: (1) the influence of cultural norms prevails over the individual's critical thinking; and (2) the individual's subjective judgment is crucial in making a choice. When a public administrator's moral life is constituted by the influence of culture, it inevitably comes in conflict with the individual's attempt to perform good work or to overcome the limitations of organizational demands. Public administrators in Asia, such as China, South Korea, Japan, and Singapore, who are strongly influenced by Confucian culture, may apply these cultural norms, values, and experiences to group decision making. Their instincts in judging others may reflect their own emotions and the expectations of accepted behavior in that particular cultural context. Because of their past experiences in handling similar situations, they may interpret a situation using reified categories and old principles to make a choice, thus underestimating the uniqueness of a local situation. So in making an ethical decision, external criteria, such as ethical codes, past administrative practices, or cultural norms, may dictate the act of an administrator. The individual may go along with the opinion of a majority or the guidance of other peers against his or her own moral belief, by sacrificing individual autonomy and his or her reflexive interpretation of cultural elements or external demands.

Another problem is the difficulty of avoiding ethical relativism, that is, to believe that one ethical judgment is just as good as any other. In general, this represents the postmodern perspective (Bauman, 1993). As Bauman implies, public administrators live through crisis, and there are no universal solutions to "the messiness of the human predicament" (p. 245). He also states, "[M]oral responsibility is precisely the act of self-constitution" (p. 14). The ethical life of a public administrator largely depends upon the individual realizing what an individual is supposed to do or ought to do. Because an individual's ethical life requires reflexive judgment in terms of values and moral beliefs, in this respect, an individual may become relativistic, insisting on his or her own judgment. This tendency makes sharing or shaping an ethical consensus with others difficult.

An important element of a bridge that spans the preceding limitations is personal integrity (and civic integrity). When it comes to subjective responsibility, integrity of the self endures the honesty and sincerity of the individual. "Loss of integrity is not a function of change of beliefs, but rather of unreflective change" (May, 1996, p. 24). When taking personal action, what a person does must coincide with what he or she holds to be true. This melding of integrity with action directs administrators on a path of growth.

Integrity has a great deal to do with the individual's commitment to organizational goals and to dedication to serving the public. Public administrators, however, often compromise their action, as they use their organizational skills to manipulate the public, break the rules, or promote their own self-interest. They may lose their integrity, all the while engendering trust in the public. Public administrators have an inherent desire to "do the right thing" because they have learned important virtues through their socialization from childhood to adulthood. Most people in public service want to see changes. They want change because change would directly help their own growth and sense of self-worth. Some administrators, of course, do not choose to change. Change must come from within; the motivation to change originates in the individual self.

A PUBLIC CONCEPTION OF AUTONOMY: CONFUCIAN AND WESTERN VIEWS

A public conception of autonomy embodies reflexive activity: individuals realize the constraints of individual autonomy and move toward a shared understanding of others by engaging in social relationships as well as questioning their own assumptions and values. Thus the social constructionist view of moral thinking regarding others is essential in the public conception of autonomy and the formation of a self-concept. Charles Taylor says, "[T]o understand our moral world, we have to see not only what ideas and pictures underlie our sense of respect for others, but also those which underpin our notions of a full life" (Taylor, 1989, p. 14). Taylor considers the autonomous self to be identified with others, and he describes the necessary relationship between autonomy and virtue, or goodness. To an extent, Western views of the self are similar to the Confucian view of the self.

The individual self, according to Confucianism, is not an object in the world, but rather a subject, capable of achieving an ideal of perfection independent of the contingencies and limitations of the empirical world. This philosophy results from a recognition of the intrinsic independence of subject-nature from object-nature, as well as a consciousness of inner freedom and the power of the self to realize complete freedom. The ontological justification of moral consciousness stemming from a sense of individual autonomy gives the ontological meaning of an individual's existence and his or her fundamental ability to transform constructively the self and the world, which consists of his or her society, living community, and institution. Self-realization and understanding develop as an individual opens to the views of others, deliberately relating to others in the public sphere.

The self in this context is regarded not only as autonomous but also as free from any limitations imposed by external requirements. This is the classic Confucian view of the ontological self-realization of the individual, that is, the discovery of the uniqueness of the individual self, the discovery of the universal in the individual, and the discovery of the individual in the universal. In this regard, Confucian moral philosophy is a dialectical view of how the individual recognizes his or her freedom, which is his or her power of self-determination and self-transformation (Cheng, 1991, pp. 280–84). The self is no longer bounded by a self-concept but relates to others and the world. Confucian morality emphasizes the moral autonomy of the individual, recognizing the meaningfulness of the moral behavior of individuals who make moral decisions and formulate moral reasons.

The argument for autonomy implies that it must provide an understanding of the human condition, which reveals the need for transformation. This means that community consciousness is derived, in part, from recognizing the negative aspects of the human condition, which generate all human problems. Although Confucian morality recognizes the negative aspects of the human existence, such as passivity, irrationality, doubts, fears, conflicts, and immoral acts, it also views the individual as a subject capable of controlling, disciplining, and perfecting the self.

Morality is not merely a matter of an individual observing moral principles, but of the individual creating moral principles in the light of self-understanding and of understanding the meaning of the total reality of a given situation. Kant's view of individuals is that they are autonomous persons who are rational in the sense that they are motivated by rational reasons and are able to seek means to satisfy their personal goals. If the observation of moral principles, as dictated by reason, is the predominant consideration of Kant (1963), then cultivation of the person as a creator of moral principles is the predominant consideration of Confucian theory. Thus for Confucian philosophers, morality is embedded in an ontological theory of the individual developing into a person who shows consideration for others in the community.

Confucian thought also provides a perspective for recognizing a conflict between obeying authority and fulfilling other principles. Further, it acknowledges the problem of conflicting authorities demanding obedience, and it recognizes that the individual may need to make agonizing decisions and carry out autonomous acts (Allen, 1997a, p. 154). According to Confucius, our most important relationships begin in the family, in which different members contribute to the well-being of the whole, "according to their role-specific obligations"; obligations to the family are considered "the source of our social obligations; our obligations to others were developed out of and modeled on the family" (Ivanhoe, 1990, pp. 1–2).⁴ The Confucian idea of the relational self is different from the Western liberal communitarian view of the autonomous self in that the self is constituted and defined by its social situatedness in relationship to loyalty, friendship, and obligations. In other words, for liberal communitarians, the self is largely a product of social factors (May, 1996, p. 3), whereas the Confucian self begins with the inner self, which guides proper human conduct, such as the virtues of "filial piety" *(xiao)* and "respect for an elder brother" *(ti)* (Roetz, 1993, pp. 53–66). In the Confucian *Analects*, the virtue of *yi* (righteousness) is fundamental to an understanding of the dynamics of person making, that is to say, a person making his or her own life (Hall and Ames, 1987, pp. 88–93).

A lack of autonomy as well as a lack of control over person making can lead the individual into becoming an uncritical human being in the bureaucratic institution. Hannah Arendt painstakingly illustrates the dehumanization of bureaucrats in terms of their loss of autonomy in Nazi Germany. Arendt argues that the dehumanization of the Nazi bureaucracy set the stage for great evil (Arendt, 1964; Canovan, 1992; Adams and Balfour, 1998; May, 1996, chapter 4). In dehumanizing institutions, loyalty is the most important virtue. As Nazi bureaucrats became socialized by Nazi organizations, these bureaucrats became willing to perform immoral acts. Arendt calls this "the banality of evil," referring to the fact that evil deeds, which were committed by the Nazis on a gigantic scale, could not be traced to any particularity of wickedness, pathology, or ideological conviction in the doer, whose only personal distinction was a perhaps extraordinary shallowness (Arendt, 1971, p. 417; 1958) as well as a lack of feeling toward another entire ethnic group as disclosed in the Abu Ghraib prison scandle.

In today's bureaucratic organizations, it is not outside the realm of possibility that administrators could lose their critical consciousness and sense of moral responsibility toward other human beings as they experience a loss of autonomy and self-identity. To the extent that public employees are concerned with job security and fear punishment, they will be inclined to show excessive loyalty and even perform dehumanizing acts. To recapitulate: in order to become a good administrator and a good citizen in a civil society, an individual needs to have a clear understanding of the self, which is gained by critically reflecting on his or her own rights, obligations, and moral responsibility.

CIVIC VIRTUE AND THE PUBLIC GOOD

Aristotle defines the ideal *polis* as the one most likely to promote virtue in its citizens, the exercise of which constitutes their good. Following his view, the ideal community (or good governance of local government) is the one that best promotes the interests of citizens as defined by the good. But it is difficult to realize this concept of 'the good' in a large, complex community because of the pluralistic and multicultural aspects of community. Community consists of different values and identities of individuals and groups. Citizens in a multicultural community value their association with a particular group as well as form a concept of the good in relationship to their own context (Kymlicka, 1995). This suggests that public administrators inevitably deal with the pluralistic nature of the good in the community. The perplexing questions are about how public administrators in a multicultural society can help citizens see diversity as a strength to be built upon and how public administrators can provide opportunities to develop intergroup and public discourse for dialogue and the sharing of mutual concerns in the community.

The query underlying these perplexing questions is how differences in concepts of the good can be resolved. If a person takes a relativistic view of the good, the differing views of different groups or individuals should be left alone, and the government should protect different cultural interests and group identities. Moral relativism emphasizes moral diversity among different cultures as well as moral disagreements within cultures (Bunting, 1996; Young, 1997). Critics of the relativistic view of the good argue that, among the different views that deal with community problems, it is quite possible that some ideas are better than others (Howard, 1992, p. 6).

Moving beyond a pluralistic and liberal view of the good, political liberalism, as presented by Rawls, approaches the concept of the good from the principle of justice (Rawls, 1971; 1993). Rawls argues that justice is the most fundamental virtue of the individual's moral life. It is the one that best expresses the individual's nature (Rawls, 1971, p. 491). The individual's true nature and true self require him or her to be just. Justice is the first virtue in an individual's character to hinder any inclination to oppress others. It is also the most important principle for preserving humanity.

According to Rawls, citizens are free, equal, and moral beings in that they possess two fundamental moral powers. The first is the capacity to form, revise, and pursue a conception of the good. The second is the capacity to propose, and to honor before others, fair terms of social cooperation. Citizens are politically equal in that they all possess these two capacities to a degree sufficient to support full membership within a fair system of social cooperation. Furthermore, they are politically free in that they retain their status as citizens regardless of their concept of the good. They are assumed to be capable of and responsible for honoring the demands of justice; ideally, they also affirm the basic social institutions, which fundamentally shape their individual characters and interests.

As mentioned earlier, in Confucian morality, good involves not only a self-consciousness of the subject-nature but also a sense of community in view of the fact that virtues are ways that the individual relates to others. Good is conceived as a direct presentation and manifestation of the reality of the self. This view contradicts Hegel's view of the individual in civil society. According to Hegel, in civil society, the individual constructs self-consciousness as he or she engages in communal life, such as property exchanges with others in the marketplace (Hegel, 1952, pp. 99–118). Through participation in communal life in civil society, the individual's wants and needs are met. The corporation acts both to achieve security and other benefits for its members through the promotion of group interests and to inculcate in its members a sense of belonging and membership in a body, a group beyond each particular individual. In this way, particularity, in Hegel's terms, is returned to itself through participation in the universal state (Seligman, 1992, p. 49). The paradox of Hegel's communal life is that the individuals in civil society disappear into the universal state. As Seligman points out, individual or group interests become transformed into the realm of the state proper (and, more concretely, the universal interests represented by the class of civil servants), which is the sole representative of the universal idea (pp. 50–51).

CONNECTING ADMINISTRATORS AND CITIZENS

How can citizens and administrators carry out virtuous responsibilities in order to improve their community? In an increasingly multicultural society, it is difficult to agree on a common definition of what it means to be virtuous. Throughout his or her life, a person may order and reorder the virtues while developing his or her character without thereby causing harm to others. A person may, for example, place the highest premium on love or on truthfulness. But even though justice is not the first virtue of that person's character, that person may not (should not) advocate injustice toward others in the community. It is an important responsibility of public administrators to facilitate and cultivate in all citizens a sense of civic responsibility toward their community. It is fair to say that not all citizens are motivated to contribute to their community because of an inherent social and voluntary nature, an idea espoused by liberal thinkers. I believe that it is important to provide a sense of individual autonomy and help people develop their selves. The individual who is unable to understand critically his or her moral thinking also needs to develop the capability of relating to others. This view is argued by those who attempt to disentangle republicanism from liberalism (Dagger, 1997; Gutmann, 1987; Galston, 1991; Macedo, 1990; Kymlicka, 1995). For example, many argue that Rawls's political liberalism has failed to connect autonomy and civic virtues (Dagger, 1997, p. 191). Rawls and other liberal communitarians depend too much on individual commitment to institutions and voluntary associations.

William Galston argues that liberal theorists in the past focused too much on the justification of rights and on the institutions that secured these rights, without paying attention to the responsibilities of citizens. This, he says, has greatly contributed to the decline of urban communities (Barber, 1984). According to Galston, the virtues required for responsible citizenship can be divided into four groups: (1) general virtues—courage, law-abidingness, and loyalty; (2) virtues of the liberal society—independence and tolerance; (3) virtues of the liberal economy—work ethic—the capacity to allow moderate delay of self-gratification, an adaptability to economic and technological changes; and (4) virtues of liberal politics—the capacity to discern, and the restraint to respect, the rights of others; the willingness to demand only what can be paid for; the ability to evaluate the performance of those in office; and the willingness to engage in public discourse (Galston, 1991, pp. 221–24). Of particular significance to the political virtues is the citizen's ability to question authority, listen to diverse views, and engage in public discourse.

In Table 8.2, which follows, I list a set of significant civic virtues of both administrators and citizens. This list is not intended to cover the entire range of civic responsibilities but to suggest the ideas that are useful to reconnect administrators and citizens in a civil society. Because administrators are also citizens in their community, the ideas listed are not mutually exclusive, but overlapping. This table also suggests the relationship between citizen and administrator by presenting a list of relevant character traits that underlie human and administrative praxis as administrators engage in participatory relationships with citizens. The complexity of human nature may require different orderings of the virtues without thereby implying that if the pursuit of, say, self-interest in a reflexive manner were to replace justice as the preeminent virtue of an individual's character, he or she would be prone to oppress other persons.

The list of virtues of the administrator may, at first blush, appear overly idealistic, focusing as it does on democratic qualities; but a measure of balance is achieved by organizational loyalty and commitment. If public administrators were expected just to implement established policies according to rules and regulations, they might need a different set of virtues. However, it could be argued that if the rules are followed

TABLE 8.2
Civic Virtues of the Administrator and the Citizen

Virtues of a civic-minded administrator	*Virtues of a good citizen*
• Is concerned with public good • Is fair in providing services • Engages in social interaction • Uses self-reflexivity • Participates in public discourse and dialogue • Is loyal and committed • Has a sense of autonomy • Is trustworthy • Engages in deliberation • Is caring and compassionate • Cultivates a context for development of citizen responsibility • Promotes citizen participation • Assesses citizen needs • Shares information	• Has a sense of justice • Has a sense of public good • Believes in equality • Values liberty • Advocates for others • Is concerned with community • The willingness to acknowledge the others (or opponents) • Has a sense of decency and compassion • Values civility • Associates with others and is involved with community • Values cultural diversity • Is self-aware • Engages in public discourse • Pursues self-interest in a reflexive manner

properly, then administrative behavior is virtuous. The effective implementation of the rules, however, depends on the ability of administrators to interpret the meaning of the rules and apply this meaning to the situation at hand. It is also important for administrators to listen to the claims of all citizens and treat them fairly as they consider the merits of their claims.

Connecting administrators and citizens is essential in gaining the support of citizens and their concern about the common good. A feeling of alienation on the part of citizens can lead them to feel a lack of responsibility to the community (May, 1996, p. 39). Furthermore, administrators in particular need to be reflexive; however, as Arendt points out, this quality can be obliterated by the urgent demands of living (Arendt, 1971, p. 421). Like Nazi Germany, bureaucratic institutions are especially good at instilling in people a sense of this urgency and at pressing it in such a way that otherwise conscience-driven individuals come to accept even a reversal of their previous values: what was once seen as wrong becomes right. In Arendt's view, socialization in institutions can have this negative effect. It is one of the most important things to be countered if evil is to be diminished in the world (May, 1996, p. 71; Arendt, 1964).

If an administrator is to be civic-minded, he or she must creatively balance his or her ethical responsibility with the virtues of good citizens, such as a sense of justice, active and sincere participation in public discourse, decency and compassion, and the willingness to acknowledge the others. These are the important elements of "civic integrity." To build meaningful and trusting relations, a public administrator must reduce bureaucratic values, such as authority consciousness, rule-abidingness, and other formalistic characteristics of administrative conduct, and work to develop the social capital of interconnectedness, open-mindedness, and gaining the public's confidence. In a multicultural community, it is difficult for people to develop trusting relationships with those from different backgrounds, interest, race, language, or gender. In this new century, this will be the most challenging responsibility of public administrators.

Collective action is often needed in order to accomplish projects in organizations and in the community. When an individual is able to transcend self-reflexivity, he or she becomes aware of his or her ethical responsibility toward other citizens, to make available communicative opportunities and "socio-ontological resources" (Shotter, 1993, p. 163). This means recognizing our place in creating ethical discourse, respecting the rights of those around us to speak, and understanding how our assumptions and use of words orients ways of relating as well as a sense of identity. Lyotard (1984, p.18) speaks of this type of understanding as "knowing how, knowing how to live, knowing how to listen." In this regard, reflexivity toward others is a civic virtue (Dagger, 1997): it is a basis for interactions and social practice. In order for an individual to become concerned with organizational or community interests, he or she must identify with others through a sense of justice, active participation in public discourse, care and compassion, and respect toward others (Jun, 1999 pp. 224–25).

The virtues of public administrators can include other characteristics that underlie broader responsibilities, such as concern for the public good, praxis-oriented action, searching for alternative solutions, facilitating interactions, listening, and dialogue. Unlike conventional politics and administration, the new virtues of public administrators are necessary in order to promote better connections between citizens and administrators. It is also the responsibility of public administrators to cultivate citizen virtues so that citizens exhibit a true concern for other people and for their community. Raising citizens' consciousness regarding sustainable development, world hunger, human rights, disadvantaged people, and community problem solving is particularly important.

CONCLUSION

As a result of the growth of strong government and the bureaucratization of institutions in the twentieth century, the sense of ethical responsibility on the part of individuals in organizations has greatly declined, as has their sense of the importance of caring about and compassion toward other human beings. Because of its emphasis on efficiency, costs, and performance measurement, the promotion of ethics and effectiveness has been replaced by more quantitative and results-oriented management and by an efficient enforcement of procedures. Despite the emphasis on economy and management in public administration, however, most public administrators have a deep sense of ethics about "what is right"; this sense of ethics is further shaped through their interactions. Individuals reflexively modify their sense of being in the world as they gain new knowledge and experience. Thus a transformation from the individual level to the group and organizational levels presents the most promising possibility of making public institutions ethically responsible.

The social constructionist view of ethical responsibility assumes that a dialectic of ethics is possible as individuals share their interests with and learn from others as well as debate the importance of established laws and regulations and the code of ethics (Wolfe, 1989; Winter, 1966; Allan, 1998; May, 1996). Understanding the ethical process from the micro level to the macro level is a more efficient way to enhance individual responsibility than the other way around. The macro level of ensuring responsibility by emphasizing people's compliance with laws and procedures may influence people's ethical behavior, but the process of carrying out responsible conduct presents a high degree of uncertainty. Because we are concerned with ambiguity in making ethical decisions, external criteria, such as ethical codes and laws, are ineffective. Good judgment may emerge only because of the "conscience of the moral self," which can enable the actor to construct an ethical view by critically reflecting on others' viewpoints.

The issue of individual autonomy and civic virtues has a long history in both Eastern and Western philosophy, and thus it has greatly influenced society and institutions as well as notions about the ethical responsibilities of citizens in a civil society. Eastern philosophy, particularly Confucianism and Taoism, has influenced the Far East Asian countries in terms of teaching the virtues of the good citizen. For the past several decades, Asian countries have been concerned with the development of the Platonic good society, with the elite and Western-trained technocrats playing the major role in directing citizens in accomplishing the developmental goals of the state. As these countries become economically affluent and experience many social problems, they become aware of the civic responsibilities of citizens in governing their own community. Civic responsibilities have also gained the attention of politicians, academics, and civic leaders in Western societies, particularly the United States (Seligman, 1992). Both liberals and communitarians are concerned with the different emphasis on the rights and responsibility of individuals and their community.

Unless public administrators continue to cultivate civic-minded virtues, they cannot be truly effective in establishing trusting and confident relationships with citizens in the community. The exercise of those virtues is simply part of what it means to be engaged in collaborative activities with citizens. Administrators should be willing to admit and confront social imperfections through a public appeal to collective convictions (Galston, 1991, p. 227). If they are to be effective administrators of civil society, they need to possess certain virtues or be forced to act as though they had the capability to work with citizens. It is ultimately the responsibility of the individual administrator to actively acquire civic-minded virtues. Further, an administrator who engages in meaningful administrative praxis while working with citizens finds that critical reflexivity is an important part of individual autonomy. Civic-minded administrators can facilitate public discourse; both personal wishes and the good of the community can be discussed.

CHAPTER 9

Civil Society, Governance, and Its Potential

Public administration exists in the context of the social world: it is not an isolated entity in society. Government develops policies and administration to meet the challenges of society, but its activities are also greatly influenced by global politics and issues. As new issues emerge in the societal and global environment, policy makers and administrators interpret them according to their perception, knowledge, and experience. By interacting with other actors, they construct the meaning of the social situation and develop a course of action. As Donald Kettl points out, a transformation of governance presents "substantial challenges for public institutions, how we manage them, how we study them, and how we prepare the nation's future public servants" (Kettl, 2002, p. 150).

In this chapter, I discuss the transformation of society and of public administration, particularly the transformation of the governing process in the broad contexts of globalization and civil society. I explore the current idea of civil society and the role of nongovernmental organizations (NGOs) as an important force for democratizing the relationships among government, business, and civil society. Several cases illustrate the problems and possibilities of improving the governance process in the local community as well as the fallacy of modern development projects that are the result of central planning or pluralistic politics.

THE CIVIL SOCIETY TRIANGLE: A NEW FORM OF GOVERNANCE

The revival of interest in civil society has profound implications for the transformation of the dominant mode of governing administration and society. Globalization has become a strong force in promoting the value of civil society internationally. Although this movement has emerged in various forms, perhaps the most significant change has been the transformation from vertical governing and managing the public to horizontal governance; this involves less hierarchical and more democratic relationships among the government, business, and civil society. Among the significant developments that are changing the nature of governing are self-governance processes that involve relationships among NGOs, various nonprofit associations, and voluntary organizations.

Civil society is as old as humankind itself. Society began when people started to live together by mutual consent in order to debate, determine, and act jointly to further some common purpose and a common political community. Civil society is "those human networks that exist independently of, if not anterior to, the political state" (Isaac, 1993, p. 356). Political parties, business associations, labor unions, cooperatives, women's groups, professional associations, religious organizations, membership-serving organizations, community groups, social clubs, and advocacy networks are all forms of civil society organizations. In recent years, the spread of nongovernmental, and, in particular, voluntary organizations has renewed people's interest in the concept of civil society, because civil society and the public sphere not only offer the potential for exploring new ideas and possibilities for social innovation through citizen empowerment but also can form a social force to oppose or support the policies of government and big corporations. An example of this is the recent protests by the farmers against agricultural policies in South Korea, Japan, France, and the United States.

When citizens are engaged, civil society is revitalized; through dialogue and discourse in the public sphere, community problems are discussed, and goals are formulated. Jürgen Habermas views the public sphere as "a network for communicating information and points of view (i.e., opinions expressing affirmative or negative attitudes); the streams of communication are, in the process, filtered and synthesized in such a way that they coalesce into bundles of topically specified public opinions." The public sphere is the social space in communicative action that involves interpersonal relationships among potential dialogue partners (Habermas, 1995, pp. 360–61). Civil society is of basic importance to the functioning of democracy. Both civil society and governance are unique to the West and to the Western route to modernity. However, these combined ideas provide a useful perspective in understanding social, administrative, and political relationships, particularly in a democratic society. We may call this a "civil society triangle" among government, business, and civil society. The interdependence and the continuously transforming relationships contribute to the development of a viable democratic society. When one of these sectors is too strong or too weak, a society is likely to experience serious problems with social injustice, economic inequality, corruption, and political turmoil. The Asian financial crisis in the late 1990s attests to a severe imbalance between the global economy and domestic governance. The banking crisis in Japan, South Korea, Thailand, Malaysia, and Indonesia has its origins in a poorly regulated banking system, a lack of responsibility among high-level business and government officials, and ineffective governing of public institutions in a pluralistic democracy.

In recent years, industrialized and industrializing countries in Asia have focused on the need for developing civic capacity. For example, after neglecting the importance of civic engagement at the expense of rapid economic development, the Japanese government has, since the early 1980s, begun to facilitate the development of civil society; South Korea began this process in the late 1990s. In 1998, the Japanese government passed the Law to Promote Specified Nonprofit Activities (the NPO Law), the first law to recognize the legal status of hundreds of nonprofit organizations (NPOs). In the same year, the South Korean government passed the law prescribing the guideline for providing government financial support to NGOs. Today a majority of NPOs and NGOs in both countries receive a great deal of government support.

Most Asian countries, including Japan, have inefficient and low-functioning democratic governance, although South Korea and Japan practice representative democracy. Local officials are unable to solve local problems without the support or the approval of the central government. They have never been given a real opportunity for local autonomy or self-governance because of the lack of financial independence and lack of taxing authority. Since the enactment of the Law for Promoting Decentralization of 1995 and the Omnibus Law of Decentralization of 1999, the relationship between the central and local governments in Japan has been incrementally improving, with more power being accorded to local governments (Shigeru, 2003, p.162).

Another interesting phenomenon in a civil society triangle is the decreasing role of government: as the influence of the business and the market economy expands, the role of government tends to decline. In the face of global trade agreements that supersede national and local laws, nation-states are no longer able to claim self-determination. Many contemporary problems, such as the environment, economy, and trade, are of a global nature, requiring both a global and a local approach. Policy makers in different countries, however, find that their ability to control such problems is limited by a more pervasive influence of international politics and policy, such as the rules of free trade imposed by the World Trade Organization (WTO) and the economic power of multinational corporations. In general, national governments today are incapable of dealing with unanticipated consequences of economic globalization. As David Korten (1995) states, "It is a crisis of governance born of a convergence of ideological, political, and technological forces behind a process of economic globalization that is shifting power away from governments responsible for the public good and toward a handful of corporations and financial institutions driven by a single imperative—the quest for short-term financial gain" (p. 12).

People who support the promotion of civil society and grassroots development tend to distrust and disparage the motives and the capabilities of governments and of profit-seeking private enterprise, which exploit people in similar ways. Instead, these people tout the potential of grassroots communities and voluntary associations to empower their members and solve their problems through their own collective initiative. The public sphere is an arena where people can debate myriad social problems as well as explore new alternatives and the relationships among them.

Another impetus for developing civil society and relationships in the public sphere is related to the ineffective governing of public organizations in a liberal democracy in solving complex social problems. First, as governmental interventions in managing public programs as well as regulating society become ever more complex, large bureaucracies become less efficient and less responsive to the needs of citizens and the community. These unwieldy bureaucracies are more concerned with legitimating a centralized and bureaucratic government at a time when the need for decentralization and devolution of authority is increasing. This phenomenon is particularly conspicuous in governmental efforts to achieve administrative reform. Another common

problem is that decision making in a liberal democracy is heavily influenced by the interest-group politics played by big corporations. Those
groups with few resources have little influence on the decisions that
affect their interests. Disadvantaged groups and citizens have few ways
to participate in the policy-making process, except in elections. Last,
the world is becoming more multicultural in terms of political, social,
economic, and cultural interactions among people, social groups, and
organizations. Because of fragmentation and localized growth in
diverse communities, government agencies are no longer the centers of
decision making.

The relationships among these three sectors can also explain the
effects of social networks, social capital, trust and mutuality, and the
participation of local citizens in the strengthening of democracy. The
argument for effective governance in civil society stems from the belief
that pluralistic politics largely involving the state-business relationship
limit the development of a strong democracy (Barber, 1984; Rawls,
1993; Sandel, 1996; Bohman and Rehg, 1997).

Thus the most important goal of a democratic society is to build a
participatory process in the public sphere, where citizens freely and
openly communicate values and goals, with a view to defining the public good. The term *the public* is not necessarily synonymous with the
term *the state*. What the state decides is for the public good differs from
the way that it is formulated through the participation of citizens and
civic organizations. A civil society triangle that includes the participation of NGOs, associations, and voluntary organizations provides an
opportunity for a creative partnership to respond to public needs, often
more efficiently and effectively than government agencies do. Governance involving civil society is a new form of cooperation between the
government and the public.

FROM HIERARCHICAL GOVERNING
TO DEMOCRATIC GOVERNANCE

In managing a complex society, the processes of both governing and
governance inevitably play a vital role. The instrumental and rationalistic emphasis of twentieth-century public administration legitimized
expanding administrative activities by establishing a hierarchical
structure, authority relationships, and rules and regulations and by

TABLE 9.1
A Comparison of Hierarchical Governing with Democratic Governance

Hierarchical Governing	Democratic Governance
Centralization: national government controls programs and funds	Decentralization: devolution of programs and authority to local governments
Uniformity and hierarchical autocracy	Fragmentation and autonomy in decision making
Implementing agency goals	Implementing shared goals
Vertical relationships	Horizontal relationships
Control and command	Networking and collaboration
Pluralistic and interestgroup politics	Negotiating through dialogue and discourse
Formal authority and policing power	Joint partnership and shared responsibility
Agency as the center of coordination	Multiple temporary arrangements regarding coordination
Enforcing laws and regulations	Local initiatives
Information control and secrecy	Information sharing and transparency
Limited participation and consultation	Open participation and public deliberation
Tendency toward antidemocratic and instrumental rationality	Discursive democracy and communicative rationality

professionalizing public services. Since the 1990s, however, we have seen that the administrative practice of the past is not adequate to meet the challenges of the present or the coming decades as we deal with the diverse and fragmented nature of politics and administration nationally and globally.

A comparison between governing and governance is briefly presented in table 9.1. The words *governing* and *governance* are often used interchangeably; many people use 'governance' to signify the changing characteristics of politics and institutional relationships, although their meaning is not much different from that of governing. The integration or coexistence of the governance processes into the traditional framework of governing, however, has become a global trend.

There are a number of reasons for transforming relationships in a civil society and the governing role of government into the governance process so that relationships are less hierarchical (or nonhierarchical) and collaborative. First, in the United States, the management and implementation of federal programs for such issues as welfare, health, and housing have become "neither hierarchical nor authority-driven" as federal officials and politicians realize the importance of local strategies for dealing with enduring social problems (Kettl, 2002, pp. 123–30). For example, with the passage of the Personal Responsibility and Work Opportunity Reconciliation Act of 1996, the management of welfare programs has shifted to the state and local levels.

Another trend is to understand the changing relationships among the three sectors—government, business, and civil society—in the public sphere; we need to transform the traditional, hierarchical mode of governing into participatory governance (Jun, 2002, pp. 289–92). The conventional way that government relates to business and civil society is vertical governing. Not only does the government control economic and political activities in society, but it also maintains functions, order, and tensions, imposing rules and obligations. Thus governing is based on formal authority and policing power in implementing legally established policies, even if the process emphasizes participatory and consultative interactions. In governing, public authorities exercise policing powers to overcome defiance and attain citizen compliance (Rosenau, 1992, p. 4). When the government is viewed as the center of coordination and governing of economic, political, regulatory, and organizational activities, the communicative and cultural influence of people in the public sphere is greatly underestimated (Peters, 1996; Kooiman, 1993; March and Olsen, 1995; Osborne and Gaebler, 1992). Public administration literature tends to emphasize the efficient role of public institutions in relation to business, the market economy, and pluralistic politics. Governing is necessary in order to oversee public services and equitable distribution of government resources, but it has its limits. Too great an emphasis on governing slows the possibility of social innovation and self-governance in localities.

As the capacity of civil society, networking, and communication structures has expanded, the hierarchical notion of governing has gradually changed into multiple interactions in the public sphere in which processes are nonhierarchical, horizontal, collaborative, and discourse oriented. When government works jointly with the private sector and nongovernmental organizations, public administrators can act as facilitators in fostering the development and renewal of civil society. Anthony Giddens points out the role of government in renewing civil society. This includes government and civil society in partnership, community renewal through harnessing local initiative, involvement of the third sector [the civil society], protection of the local public sphere, community-based crime prevention, and the democratic family (Giddens, 1998, pp. 69–98).

Governance in the context of civil society refers to activities backed by shared values and goals among citizens and organizations in which coordinating responsibilities may or may not be legally and formally based in order to foster cooperation and resolve disagreements among people and organizations (Rosenau, 1992). Governance promotes joint partnership among public, private, and nonprofit organizations in order to enhance the effectiveness of the implementation of public programs as well as to reflect the diverse values of citizens and groups in the process of policy making and problem solving.

As opposed to the hierarchical and autocratic nature of government, the concept of "governance" is grounded in the constructionist view that reality is socially constructed by citizens in the community and specifically by the stakeholders in the social situation. Thus the concept of local governance is an outgrowth of an increasing awareness on the part of citizens and NGOs that currently they have little to say about the political processes that determine the interests and shape the decisions that are a product of the community in which they live. Thus the governance approach essentially focuses on the process of concerned citizens, groups, and organizations constructing an intersubjective reality by sharing their experience and concerns. Government agency no longer plays the major role in coordinating their activities. The relationships among government, business, and civil society are temporary, because their interactions are largely based on each one's need to meet the challenges of the community and the market. As actors participate in the deliberative process involving dialogue and discourse, they may or should be able to form a sense of public reason for collective action toward the common good (Habermas, 1998; Dewey, 1963; Gouinlock, 1978; Bohman, 1996; Christiano, 1997).

Finally, public bureaucracies operate under the assumption of instrumental-technical rationality as depicted by Max Weber. As agencies engage in the enforcement of rules and procedures, the potential of individuals is not realized. Since they focus mainly on the economic needs and goal accomplishment of bureaucracy, instrumental rationality is essentially antidemocratic (Dryzek, 1990, pp. 1–7). Recognizing that Weber's idea of instrumental rationality is incomplete, Habermas emphasizes communicative rationality: the meaning of rationality can only be adequate when people understand how they construct institutional order through the social practice of communication (1984); through communicative action they form intersubjective meanings that provide the foundation for a sense of rationality and legitimacy.

I agree with Dryzek's position that instrumental rationality and communicative rationality are not "separate and incompatible" (1990, p. 20). Instead, they are dialectical: each can complement the other in order to facilitate the process of democratic governance. As democratic administration demands both efficiency and effectiveness, institutional solutions should not be rejected as long as they are intended to improve human processes and public interest. Structural and functional alternatives that are less hierarchical and help to facilitate interaction and collaboration cannot be ignored if they can help to improve organizational performance, individual happiness, and citizen appreciation; participants should critically examine whether alternatives reflect discursive and deliberative governance. Furthermore, reflexive knowledge is valuable only when democratic governance can deal with it productively.

NGOs AS A FORCE FOR SOCIAL CHANGE

In recent years, NGOs have become an active force in societies that seek democratization. They are crucial for effective citizen participation in civic and social life and make an important contribution to participatory democracy. They perform many services and provide public goods that government and business organizations either cannot or will not provide. The role of NGOs in successfully implementing development projects has been discussed in various studies (Carroll, 1992; Clark, 1991; Howell and Pearce, 2001; Korten, 1990; Livernash, 1992; de Oliveira and Tandon, 1994). Furthermore, many NGOs are also engaged in activities that force political change in many countries

(I cite only a few studies here: Ndegwa, 1996; Fisher, 1998; Foweraker and Craig, 1990; Schwedler, 1995; Kiss, 1992).

The question today is how do we foster NGOs in societies that have a short history of voluntary, participatory, and charitable activity, such as in the case of non-Western countries? How do we develop a civic capacity so that citizens take the responsibility of self-governance, free from government control and less dependent on large business organizations? How can we encourage people to become good citizens, that is, critical and civic-minded citizens? NGOs and nonprofit organizations around the world seek ways to address these questions. Although economic globalization has helped certain groups of people in many countries, market forces alone cannot deal with various social problems, such as poverty, social exclusion, unemployment, housing, and homelessness. Economic globalization and the market are about the exchange of goods and economic values, not ethics or social justice. One of the important tasks of NGOs in civil society is promoting the public good.

In a globalizing world, NGOs respond to both domestic and global issues because "many local problems have global origins and need solutions that are both local and global" (Krut, 1997, p. 3). When the state cannot take an active role in confronting social problems, due to, perhaps, lack of effective executive leadership or resources, these issues receive the attention of NGOs. Today, NGOs—because they are organized by citizen coalitions—are often seen as a panacea that will spread democracy around the world (Heyzer, 1995; Tandon, 1987; Boulding, 1990). Hazel Henderson speaks glowingly of NGOs "creating a new force in world affairs, the independent civil society, which challenges both nation states and global corporations" (1996, p. 30).

Worldwide, NGOs are proliferating at an unprecedented rate. In a broader context, the term *NGO* means all nongovernmental and nonprofit organizations throughout the world.

> In Western Europe, it generally means nonprofit organizations that are active internationally. In the transitional countries of Europe and the former Soviet Union, it tends to mean all charitable and nonprofit organizations. [In developing countries], the term NGO generally refers to organizations involved in development, broadly defined. Hospitals, charitable organizations, and universities are usually called voluntary or nonprofit organizations rather than NGOs. (Fisher, 1998, p. 5)

In the United States, the most common NGOs are grassroots, voluntary, and community-based organizations.

Although many NGOs attempt to secure legal status, they are also subject to compliance with domestic regulations. The activities of NGOs are numerous, and it is impossible to list them all here. NGOs have three broad areas of activities. Many NGOs focus on encouraging government to act in what they see as a moral way or on challenging what they see as a government's illegitimate conduct. Demonstrations organized by students, labor unions, and citizen coalitions to demand administrative reform are examples of NGOs voicing their views to a government or a corporation. Other NGOs deliver services, either for the benefit of their members (economic and professional associations) or for various groups, such as homeless people, women, refugees, the elderly, the mentally ill, or illegal immigrants. In recent years, while NPOs in Japan are active in social services areas, NGOs in South Korea are politically active in voicing their opinions, by campaigning against corrupt and ineffective politicians and preventing their reelection to the National Assembly.

Still other NGOs participate in development projects, such as community development, microenterprises, or a sustainable environment. Since the 1990s, the official contributions to development projects on the part of the World Bank, the United Nations Development Program (UNDP), the European Community (EC), the Organization of Petroleum Exporting Countries (OPEC), and all OECD countries have dramatically increased. Development projects are also concerned with issues of sustainable development, land use, growth versus no-growth policy, clean water policy, community planning.

The number of NGOs increased during the Cold War (1945–1990) especially with the rise of peace, human rights, antinuclear, and environmental movements. NGOs are doing much of the ongoing work toward sustainable development; the National Research Council calls them the most recent conceptual focus linking the collective aspirations of the world's peoples for peace, freedom, improved living conditions, and a healthy environment (Henderson, 1996, pp. 22–38). Civil society organizations (CSOs)[1] and NGOs are now forming networks of organizations whose sole function is to link different groups for support, training, research, evaluation, and fundraising.

Because CSOs and NGOs are intermediary organizations between citizens and the state, political development depends upon how effective this relationship is. The relationship "can evolve and reshape political context" (Carroll, 1992; Fisher, 1998). Although relationships vary from country to country, the democratic nature of civil society is greatly related to the degree to which NGOs interact with government as well as citizens'grassroots participation (Heyzer, 1995; Tandon, 1987). Fisher points out that "autonomous NGOs with such attributes as technical skills and a mass base, however, probably have more impact on policy and political context than do other NGOs. Although NGOs have significantly impacted local spaces, subnational government policies, and some national policies, they are only beginning, through networking, to use advocacy and collaboration with government to acquire a major ability to promote sustainable development and responsive government" (Fisher, 1998, p. 159).

In developing countries, centralized governing by the state has prevented local governments from developing the capacity to self-govern. Often a military or civilian elite leads the task of political and economic development. Perhaps the most conspicuous result of the strong state among newly industrializing countries in Asia in the past several decades has been to maintain a high level of stability in society. Policy makers, including higher-level bureaucrats and military leaders, promoted solidarity and citizen responsibility for achieving national goals. For example, during the second half of the twentieth century, the industrializing countries in Asia focused on ways of maintaining citizen solidarity in order to promote national economic prosperity. In addition to the goals of economic development and modernization, South Korea and Taiwan also emphasized national solidarity to fight against Communism between the 1950s and 1980s. Today, citizens are in a state of confusion because South Korea no longer portrays North Korea as an enemy, nor does Taiwan portray China as an enemy. It seems clear that people cannot use old ideologies to resolve new socioeconomic and political problems. Furthermore, people cannot develop civil society by following old Confucian beliefs.

Civil society today has to reflect the changing conditions of the world and people's values. In industrialized Asian countries, with the exception of China, Vietnam, and North Korea, the people at the top can no longer control the process of developing civil society. These powerful people could facilitate the development and involvement of NGOs by providing information, a public forum, and financial resources. The emerging process has to stem from voluntary and participatory actions of citizens and civic organizations. Thus new solidarity has to come forth from citizens' interactions with other citizens through dialogue and discourse.

The idea of civil society can be described in relationship to the degree of social capital and economic development in a country (Fukuyama, 1995; Putnam, 1993). In his essay "Development and Civil Society in Latin America," William Ratliff states that "human capital is a critical factor for launching and sustaining shared economic growth" (1999, p. 94). Neace (1999) states that in his research on four former Soviet republics (Belarus, Kazakhstan, Russia, and Ukrane), he has found that "social capital and trust among entrepreneurs, employees, suppliers, and customers are a vital underpinning resource necessary for creating business networks that lead to sustainable economic growth" (1999, pp. 148–61). These authors insist that social capital and civil society are vital for economic growth. There is little mention of social capital or civil society as concepts that can or should exist except in the context of perpetuating economic growth. Any value system or belief system that does not result in a more productive economic society is seen as insignificant. These authors also assume that civil society and social capital are contingent on the promotion of economic growth and the indicators of increased cooperation among individuals. Many argue, however, that human cooperation for perpetuating an economic system is inherently unjust and damaging to society as a whole and that the presence of social capital and civil society is not necessarily an asset to society but the means used by the ruling elite to assure that a materialistic, socioeconomic system is created and sustained.

In his book *Between Facts and Norms* (1998), Habermas questions the very development of norms in society. If the level of social capital and civil society in the public sphere is determined by the level of economic growth, then we must explore norms and other these belief systems are rooted. The role of civil society should not be one of perpetuating the economic globalization of a consumer-based value system. Civil society must be more than a market and consumer-based society. A healthy, functioning civil society is based in a value system that does not use economic standing as the sole determinant of success. This society is not manipulated by the agenda of the market system but rather acts as an agent that derives its mandate from the community that it serves and advocates for change. It is this kind of civil society that is a truly functioning society.

A CASE OF LOCAL GOVERNANCE:
RESOLVING THE SOUP KITCHEN CONTROVERSY

The city of San Rafael is located in the center of Marin County's eastern corridor, about seventeen miles north of San Francisco.[2] It is an affluent community nestled in valleys surrounded by wooded, grassy hillsides. The business district is a mixture of Victorian buildings, ethnic restaurants, retail stores, and financial institutions, which sustain the city's hometown flavor. Representatives of the St. Vincent de Paul Society's soup kitchen and the city worked for years to resolve issues regarding the soup kitchen's negative impact on downtown merchants, who complained about food lines and homeless people in a commercial district. The limitations of the existing facility combined with escalating operational and criminal problems were such that the city and St. Vincent's jointly resolved to move the soup kitchen to a different location in the city. Throughout the years, numerous discussions were held, and limited cooperative agreements were reached on several issues, yet significant operational problems remained for the soup kitchen, and the relocation issue had not been resolved. Since 1982, the soup kitchen has fed hungry people, but its operation has been an eyesore. Downtown businesses, shoppers, and nearby residents complained about diners' panhandling, public drunkenness, reported drug dealing, verbal abuse, litter, and public urination.

On February 23, 1998, the issue of relocation came to a head. An emergency meeting of the city council had been called after a rancorous city council meeting the week before. The room, built for two hundred, was packed with double that number spilling out into the hallways and outdoors through the side exits. Three well-organized groups representing different sides of the issue had come two hours early to ensure that they would get on the public speakers' list and to secure clustered seating for group cheerleading and booing. In a military manner, they set up numerous boards displaying statistics, facts, and photos, showing sacred turf lines not to be crossed and the opposition's positions and targets (lines of threatened advance). The atmosphere inside the city council chamber was warlike: the mind-set of many was to hold their ground at all costs and to take no prisoners.

Two major groups opposed each other on this issue. The opposition group was made up of the Downtown Business Improvement group, the city's Redevelopment Agency, the Chamber of Commerce, the residents of the surrounding neighborhoods, and the employees and parents at nearby public and private schools. The group in support of the soup kitchen in the core of the downtown retail-shopping district run by St. Vincent de Paul included the "kitchen's" board of advisers, its director, and the not-so-huddled masses of the unkempt, disabled, mentally ill, homeless, and elderly. This latter group filled the city council chamber seats, put up posters, and briefed the members of the newspaper and TV media. They were under direct attack, with nowhere to go and nothing to lose by standing and fighting back for their place of refuge. Joining them, in a surprise stroke of political and symbolic genius, were the priests, ministers, and rabbis of virtually every church and temple in the community. This alliance between a stubborn and independent soup kitchen and the local upper-class religious community suddenly shifted the balance of power in the struggle for the soup kitchen to stay in its downtown location. Until this point, the downtown business community and most voters had encouraged the city council to wage a fight against the drug dealers, child molesters, crazies, litterers, doorway "pissers," and other homeless and suspicious characters of the streets, who were drawn to the downtown shopping area by the kitchen.

The public debate lasted for five hours, from 7 P.M. to 12 A.M., and involved mostly disagreements about relocation. The city manager, Rod Gould, was caught in a bind. He had acted aggressively and made minimum concessions in negotiations, as per the city council's strongly worded public and private direction. Now he could be the head offered up to quiet the uproar if he did not act quickly and carefully. His available options seemed nonviable. If the soup kitchen were to stay at its current site, it would infuriate the business community and embarrass the city council. If he were to force the soup kitchen to move, he would face the wrath of the soup kitchen, the neighborhood to which he moved it, and the entire religious community and still leave the city council with a politically awkward situation. He had to buy time to find a new approach. He suggested that the soup kitchen discussion be tabled and dealt with at a special meeting between the city council and the Redevelopment Agency. This would give him a few days to find a new solution.

At the next city council meeting, the city council members had no choice but to back away from their insistence that the soup kitchen move. The city council decided instead that the soup kitchen could move to the Ritter Street area, a downtown neighborhood that, ironically, the soup kitchen's operators had wanted to explore a year earlier; at the time, the city council had rejected this location. So the city council compromised, and the soup kitchen agreed to operate under a user permit in an attempt to move beyond this conflict. The city council appointed a seventeen-member committee, consisting of business leaders, residents, diners, religious leaders, members of neighborhood associations, representatives of community charity organizations, officials from the St. Vincent de Paul Society, and the city staff. This Ad Hoc Dining Room Committee was responsible for locating an acceptable site in the Ritter Street area, as well as for establishing conditions of operation. The committee spent hours in meetings, consulted many people, and designed a survey and plans for improving the soup kitchen's operation. On June 4, 1998, after researching and reviewing eight sites for relocation and conducting numerous public dialogues, the committee was informed that Pacific Gas and Electric (PG&E) had offered to sell the city a piece of property located in the Ritter Street area and was also interested in redeveloping the entire three-acre block in conjunction with the city. In late August 1999, PG&E announced that Marriott International had been selected as the hotel developer of the new site, and the city of San Rafael, the St. Vincent de Paul Society, and Marriott International were supposed to commence negotiations regarding the development of the new dining facility on sixteen thousand square feet of the three-acre Third Street parcel. Unfortunately, due to the bad California State economy and the decline in hotel business, Marriott decided to abandon the project. Now the Century Theater group plans to build a downtown multiscreen movie theater (or cineplex) at the former hotel site, considering the relocation of the dining room to be included in the construction project. The city government has determined to facilitate the relocation and development of a new dinning facility as the future development project unfolds.

The anticipated result will be a new, improved facility for St. Vincent's, enabling it to continue its mission to feed and serve the needy of the community. The Neighborhood Advisory Committee is convinced that services to the poor will be more efficient through the coordination among the twenty-one nonprofit social services organizations in the community, including Ritter House, Goodwill Industries, Marin Jobs Connection, and the St. Vincent de Paul Society. This case demonstrates that a constructive resolution can emerge from citizens' sense of purpose in building a community-based soup kitchen, one supported by, and accepted by, the surrounding businesses and neighborhood. The process was conducted outside the conventional politics controlled by the city government and powerful interest groups.

This case study suggests some important implications about the responsibility of public officials and administrators in working with local citizens, groups, and organizations. First, in order to explore unknown possibilities in dealing with complex community problems, the democratic process must be continuously exercised through public participation, dialogue, discourse, and deliberation. In this case, people's understanding of one another underwent a major shift. The soup kitchen had a weak organization with no political influence in the community, no rules, and constant problems with its clients who fought, panhandled, drink in public, and committed petty crimes. Even so, these poor and needy residents had as much voice in the city's future as merchants and officials with grand visions for urban renewal. The change came about when it became clear that many believed that no one should be denied food regardless of his or her behavior. After long public deliberation, the city council was persuaded by the religious community.

Another important lesson of this case is that a community can govern itself without hierarchical intervention by government authority. Political and administrative authority played a significant role in the process by providing a public forum so that citizens could disclose their views on the issue at hand. The city manager worked as a facilitator. In civil society, nonhierarchical networking is most effective when citizens, politicians, and administrators volunteer to promote the public good and are willing to be facilitative leaders, to work with citizens' values, listen to citizens' voices, learn from others, and question their own assumptions in a reflexive manner.

Other numerous applications of the governance approach in civil society can be found in the areas of sustainable economic development, environmental protection, community policing, human rights, and community-based social programs, such as those involving education, health, and social welfare. The surge of NGOs worldwide is an example of a governance movement working through networking by citizens, groups, and organizations dealing with various issues, both domestically and internationally.

DESIGNING MODERN DEVELOPMENT PROJECTS

In the process of modernization and industrialization, governments in many countries have played a major role in designing and implementing public policies. The assumption is that the state could and should be the prime mover in economic and national development. The leaders of the rapidly industrializing countries share this perspective. The central government establishes the policy framework for development, designs and enforces development priorities, controls abuses through regulation, and operates major enterprises. In this process, government bureaucrats are the major actors in mobilizing people in business and the local community to participate in the implementation of government policies. As a consequence, these countries have largely neglected the development of civil society. In the following sections, two large development projects are introduced; the Chinese case demonstrates the role of strong government in the absence of business or civil society, and the South Korean case shows the consequences of ineffective pluralistic politics at an early stage of project development and the emerging role of NGOs in the middle of the project.

The Three Gorges Dam: China's Most Ambitious Project since the Great Wall

The Yangtze (Changjiang) is the longest river in China and the third longest in the world. It is 6,300 kilometers in length and empties itself into the East China Sea near Shanghai. The three gorges—the Qutang, the Wuxia, and the Xiling—extend a total of 193 kilometers. The Yangtze River has been plagued with many floods, inundating thousands of square miles and killing more than 300,000 people in the twentieth century alone. In order to put an end to the natural disasters, the Chinese government decided to build a dam east of the three gorges. This water conservation project is known as the Three Gorges Project. When I took a Yangtze River cruise in 1998, I saw firsthand the natural landscapes along the river, including dramatic cliffs and a plethora of cultural and historical relics in the Three Gorges area. Once the dam is complete, many beautiful temples, archaeological sites, and ancient towns will disappear under a vast lake.

The first phase of water storage was completed in June 2003, and everything below 135 meters above sea level, in a 400–kilometer-long section west of the dam along the banks of the Yangtze, was submerged. When the dam is completed in 2009, the water level will reach 175 meters. The inhabitants of 1,400 largely rural towns and villages will be resettled on land either near the reservoir or elsewhere in China at sites chosen by the government. About 2 million people will be displaced as a huge reservoir fills behind the new dam (*National Geographic*, September 1997).

Despite opposition from some Chinese citizens as well as international lending and environmental organizations, the government has launched the project, which will cost at least $17 billion. In November 1997, the dam builders began to pour concrete for the 607–foot-high dam itself, which will run 1.3 miles from the foreground to the far shore and harbor twenty-six of the world's largest turbines, about 400 tons each. The dam will generate 18,200 megawatts of electricity (20 percent of China's electrical power), equivalent to the output of eighteen nuclear power plants, and will also eliminate the burning of some 50 million tons of coal a year. This dam will be the most powerful dam ever built and certainly the biggest project that China has undertaken since the first embankment surrounding the Great Wall went up 2,000 years ago.

From the beginning of the project design, opponents of the dam challenged every aspect of the government's plans. Some of the major criticisms, published in *National Geographic*, follow:

1. The region would be better served by a series of smaller dams on Yangtze tributaries.

2. Sedimentation will make the river's deep-draft harbor unusable and impede the generation of electricity.

3. An annual flow of one quarter trillion gallons of raw sewage, together with effluents flushed from abandoned factories submerged underwater, will kill aquatic species and turn the reservoir into an open sewer.

4. Incalculably valuable relics in unexplored archaeological sites will be forever lost.

5. More than 2 million people will be forced from ancestral homes and farms and relocated elsewhere.

6. Project costs could run as high as $75 million.

7. Some 240,000 acres of cropland will be lost to the dam's 370–mile-long reservoir. (*National Geographic*, p. 8)

In summary, the Chinese government intends to finish the dam regardless of the cost. The people seem to have enthusiasm for and pride in working on a monumental project. Western newspapers and magazines, however, report the various problems of corruption in managing the project funds, the inadequate compensation for the people who are forced to relocate, the shortage of new housing, and the loss of the relics in the region, including many Stone Age ruins. The farmers who move to cities will have to learn new skills and adjust to a new way of life. If this project had been initiated in a democratic country, such as South Korea, Japan, or the United States or a European country, the dam could never have gotten started because of strong opposition on the part of NGOs.

The Fallacy of Changing the Landscape:
Building a Sea Dike in South Korea

During an election campaign, politicians make empty promises that they have problems keeping after they are elected. The construction of a 33 kilometer-long (19.8 mile) sea dike, connecting two harbor cities in the midwestern part of South Korea, began with a political promise. In December 1987, presidential candidate Roh Tae-Woo announced that if elected, he would build a sea dike in order to create new land for agriculture and a large lake to provide a drinking water source. After he became president, his administration did not pursue the project, due to a lack of funds and a lack of urgency: the country was enjoying surplus rice production. The Economic Planning Board, which was then a powerful agency that oversaw the budgetary and planning matters of the central government, recommended not implementing the plan. In 1991, the leaders of the two opposing political parties, Kim Young-Sam (who went on to hold the office of president from 1993 to 1998) and Kim Dae-Jung (who went on to hold the office of president from 1998 to 2003), pressured President Roh to implement the sea dike project. Because of their political pressure, the Roh administration began the project, known as the *Saemangum Project,* in November 1991.

The main goals of the project are (1) to create 23,300 hectares (6,105,841 acres) of agricultural land; (2) to create a freshwater lake of 11,800 hectares (29,157,800 acres) and provide a source for drinking water of 1 billion cubic meters (approximately the same size as the San Francisco-Oakland Bay); and (3) to construct a sea dike to block the tide and provide complete relief from frequent flooding caused by the seawater in the upper stream of two rivers (the Mangyung King River and the Tongjin Kang River basins), to use a new dike as a road to connect the two harbor cities (Gunsan city and Booan city), and to provide employment opportunities for 13,390 people a year during the construction of the project. The traditionally ineffective and corrupt National Assembly supported the president's project without any critical debate, disregarding what would happen to the environment. No strong environmental groups existed to oppose the government policy. Because the Ministry of Agriculture is responsible for executing the project, the bureaucrats in this agency have a vested interest in completing the projects no matter what its cost.

Since 1996, environmental groups and religious organizations have emerged as a critical voice, questioning the environmental impacts of the Saemangum project; they claim that the project was not designed to protect the marshland. They say that it will keep away migratory birds and destroy nature preserves and ecological parks. Furthermore, the dislocation of the inhabitants in the local communities will cause numerous problems, including the disintegration of human relationships and the loss of fishermen's income. These problems would be addressed only inadequately by the government's monetary compensation. By the end of 2002, more than $1.5 billion had been spent. The dike was 73 percent complete. An additional $1 billion was scheduled to be spent on inland development programs related to a new lake and land. In June 2003, three NGOs—the United Environmental Movement, Green Alliance, and the Lawyers Association for a Democratic Society—filed a civil suit against the Ministry of Agriculture and submitted a petition to the Seoul Administrative Court, requesting the immediate stoppage of the dike project until the civil suit was over. On July 15, 2003, to the astonishment of President Roh Moo-Hyun and the Ministry of Agriculture, the court ordered the immediate halt of the project before it could cause further damage to the environment. Because of a joint protest made by the governor of the provincial government where the project was located and the bureaucrats of the Ministry of Agriculture, and because of pressure brought to bear by the president's office, the court has permitted some part of the project to be finished.

The court has heard various environmental reports argued by the Ministry of Agriculture, the Environmental Agency, and the experts representing environmental groups. The Ministry of Agriculture invited an expert witness from the Netherlands to testify about the reasons for completing the dike project, and the environmental groups recruited an environmental advocate from Germany, who advocated converting the Saemangum area into a national park. On February 4, 2005, the court ruled that the project has to be either modified or cancelled. The court, however, allowed the Ministry of Agriculture to continue working on the building of the dike. At this point, nearly 92 percent of the dike project (only 2.7 kilometers left) was completed. Because the dike is likely to be completed in less than two years, the environmental groups have filed another suit to stop the project immediately. Since the dike is likely to be built, the environmental groups will lose in the end. Their defeat, however, could bring the strengthening of their voice and solidarity against any future projects that damage the environment. Furthermore, government's unilateral action would face strong resistance. The political dynamic of this case is different from those of the Chinese case in that NGOs were an influential force in critiquing government policy and protecting the environment. The civic engagement by NGOs in the political and policy process is a truly remarkable change in South Korean politics.

GLOBALIZATION AND DEMOCRATIZATION: A CONTRADICTION

Particularly as a means for the international economic integration of markets for goods, services, and capital, globalization has generated serious unanticipated consequences. As globalization connects countries and markets it tends to create a monoculture. Global marketing strategies attempt to convince people to drink cola, eat fast food, listen to Western rock music, and adopt Western fashions. Many critics argue that a country's distinct political and economic culture is more important than any promised rapid economic growth. Furthermore, these critics do not believe that things will get better if governments can keep improving international trade competition and attract foreign investments that supposedly provide more economic growth and efficiency. Many critics argue that globalization is threatening people's jobs and communities, diminishing democracy, increasing economic anxiety, and stimulating social disintegration, while devouring the last remnants of resources and wilderness. The only beneficiaries seem to be global corporations, which advocate free trade and globalization (Mander and Goldsmith, 1996; Brecher, Costello, and Smith 2000; Cavanagh et al., 2002).

The most common complaints raised by critics of economic globalization are as follows:

• Increased economic globalization greatly contributes to the breakdown of the ecosystem's regenerative capacities and the social fabric that sustains human community.

• The integrated market economy has negatively affected traditional civil society, leading to the destruction of many civic organizations and the minimizing of personal bonds, because of its emphasis on economic relationships. Thus feelings of ethical and moral responsibility have been allowed to decay (Burbach, Nunez, and Kagarlitsky, 1997).

• As U.S. corporations have expanded their global reach, they are better able to put the U.S. workforce in direct competition with foreign workers, thus increasing corporate profits while driving down workers' wages and the general standard of living (Danaher, 1996).

• Global corporations are better able to use technology to downsize their workforce, thus creating anxiety among working people, who no longer feel secure about the future of their jobs.

• As global corporations become less dependent on any particular nation, they have less interest in supporting any government with taxes. This results in a shrinking tax base and what is referred to as a "fiscal crisis of the state" (the tendency for government expenses to outpace revenues).

• Economic globalization has not achieved distributive equity. The richest nations have increased their share of the world gross national product (GNP), while the poorest nations have experienced a decrease in their share of world GNP. The data produced by the UN Development Programs indicate that, between 1960 and 1990, "the richest fifth of all nations had its share of world income rise from 70 per cent to 85 percent, while the poorest fifth of all nations had its share fall from 2.3 per cent to 1.4 percent" (Sandler, 1997, pp. 182–83).

• By using the rationale that maintaining global competition is of the utmost importance, despite driving down the living standards of the majority, the corporate class has shifted more and more wealth from ordinary workers to themselves. This growing inequality is producing resentment and rebellion here and abroad. European countries, who have traditionally placed a high tax burden on their populations, experience difficulty in increasing taxes on corporations, due to the competition and stateless characteristics of globalization and information technology. *The Economist* (1997, p. 15) reports that "over the past decade or so, taxes on capital have already fallen sharply while those on labor have risen. In the future, it will be harder to tax firms or high-earners at high rates because they are the most mobile. The implication is that unskilled labor will have to bear a greater burden."

In his 1996 book *Has Globalization Gone Too Far?* Rodrik argues that economic globalization has produced various side effects in domestic arenas. Globalization has made it easier for firms to move production facilities overseas, substituting low-wage foreign workers for local ones. Thus globalization has created job insecurity through the erosion of nonwage benefits and the weakening of trade unions as free trade conditions threaten workers' rights. Imports to industrializing countries are causing social disruption, including high consumerism, child labor, and a decrease in indigenous production capability. Rodrick suggests that the WTO's rules regarding "safeguards" should be broadened to include rules about sudden surges in imports that create negative effects on society.

The Hunt for "Black Gold" in Ecuador

Texaco's oil exploration in Ecuador between 1972 and 1992 resulted in massive deforestation, oil contamination in the Amazon area, the dislocation of the indigenous people, the destruction of local agriculture, and health hazards for thousands of people. An ABC *Nightline* story in the fall of 1998 also disclosed that, when the oil drilling agreement was reached with Texaco, the weak Ecuadoran government "sold out" the needs of citizens and the ecology of the Orient (the East), an unspoiled land of tumbling brown rivers and humid jungle in the Amazon, in favor of economic development. In 2003, the *Los Angeles Times* reviewed documents, studies, and interviews with current and former Texaco executives and Ecuadoran officials and reported on how the search for oil had wreaked havoc on a remote place and its people. During the oil-drilling operation, Texaco discharged drilling waste into the surface water, which resulted in the destruction of once productive agricultural fields, the death of animals and plants, and health and ecological problems in the area. Because the government had many problems—little money, a large international debt, poverty, and an inability to provide services for its citizens—policy makers did not pay attention to the long-term consequences of the oil exploration or the joint venture with Texaco. Instead, they were eager to make a deal with a well-resourced multinational corporation, counting on bringing in billions of dollars. Because environmental programs had been cut, the Ecuadoran government showed little concern about the impact of Texaco's drilling operations on the environment.

From 1972 to 1992, Texaco pumped 1.5 billion barrels of oil from Ecuador—most of it bound for California markets. Environmentalists estimate that by the time the company pulled out, Texaco had dumped more than 19 billion gallons of waste and spilled 16.8 million gallons of crude oil, one and one-half times the amount spilled by the oil tanker *Exxon Valdez* in Alaska. Within a decade, Texaco had transformed Ecuador. Working with its partner, Gulf Oil, and with the Ecuadoran government, it built a 312–mile-long pipeline traversing the Andes, crisscrossed the jungle with roads, and drilled hundreds of wells. By the time Texaco left, there were more than 600 waste pits pockmarking the region (*Los Angeles Times*, November 30, 2003).

At present, neither the Ecuadoran government nor Texaco is willing to take responsibility for cleaning up the hazardous waste and the environment, and the powerless local people are merely struggling to survive. A 1987 study by the U.S. Environmental Protection Agency found widespread environmental damage in cases in the United States where oil producers poured waste directly into freshwater streams. The study predicted that, in some cases, small wells that dumped no more than one hundred barrels of wastewater a day into streams could slightly increase the risk of cancer among local residents. In the Amazon, Texaco was dumping up to *one hundred thousand* barrels of wastewater a day—one thousand times more (ibid).

It is reasonable to conclude that Texaco knew that its Ecuador operations would not have met standards in the United States and that the company had a responsibility to do more than local laws required. If Texaco had done in the United States what it did in Ecuador, Texaco officials would have been charged with a crime. Former Texaco officials acknowledged that the environment was not as important an issue in the early 1970s as today, but environmentalists contended that Texaco did not keep up with changes in technology as environmental practices improved. A multibillion-dollar lawsuit was filed on behalf of thirty thousand citizens, and the trial began in Ecuador in 2003. Today, U.S. companies such as Los Angles-based Occidental Petroleum are still exploring the region, hoping for a second oil boom.

IMPLICATIONS

Effective democratic governance[3] stems from the psychological commitment of citizens and stakeholders in the community to meet their collective needs, participate in politics, and develop expectations for the future. As illustrated by the cases of China, South Korea, and Ecuador, modern development projects and economic globalization are often the goals of national government; government is doing things "*to* people rather than *by* them" (Cavanagh, et al., 2002, p. 107). Most development projects are driven by an economic ideology promoted by a society's policy makers and business elite. Strengthening civil society is a way to limit the power of a strong government and the market.

The civil society movement is spreading throughout the world, and it will most likely have major social, economic, and political consequences in the twenty-first century. Civil society and democratic governance will transcend the current mode of institutional governing, which is characterized by centralized control, strong hierarchical relationships with citizens and civic organizations, and unethical behavior on the part of big corporations and government. If the development of civil society organizations is appreciated and promoted by political leaders, then a viable civil society and democratic community will emerge. The potential losers are countries that postpone opportunities for developing democratic governance that facilitates civic engagement. Furthermore, civil society organizations and NGOs could be an important social force for socioeconomic and political change in non-Western countries as well, in dealing with citizen needs; sustainable development issues; and the problem of inequality, participation, and people-oriented projects.

As Walter Truett Anderson says, "[G]overnance is not the exclusive monopoly of governments, and it never has been" (Anderson, 1997, p. 18). To really understand the changing nature of governance, we have to go beyond the governing aspect of government and seek not only ways of enhancing civil society, but also ways of actively facilitating civic engagement. The responsibility of public administrators toward NGOs is to understand their purpose and learn to live with the emergence of all types of organizations, including a "citizen agenda for global governance." Public administrators must respect and facilitate the advocacy role of citizen organizations. They must go beyond the idea of establishing a strong central government; instead, they must think of ways to develop a partnership with voluntary organizations and NGOs without jeopardizing these organizations' autonomy or independence. A civil society triangle can also be strengthened by a cooperative and transparent relationship with the business organizations. What is lacking in many countries, however, is a viable civil society. Furthermore, to overcome the inadequacies of today's pluralistic democracy, a large, active, informed, and conscientious body of citizens should participate in public discourse (Gouinlock, 1986, p. 4). Enhancing citizens' capability of self-governance is essential so that in the long run, people gradually raise their consciousness and sense of responsibility for managing their own civic affairs without relying on the directions of the government. The growth of civil society will facilitate the further development of democracy and offer unlimited possibilities for social innovation, particularly through the deliberative process in the public sphere.

CHAPTER 10

Concluding Thoughts

The past century has seen great changes in the development of the governing capability of industrializing and postindustrial countries, such as strong government, management capability, professionalization of public service, scientific and rational ways of designing policies and activities, and coping with diverse political and social conditions. These changes have interacted with political, economic, social, cultural, and technological factors to create the current situation in which we are now keenly aware of the need for democratization, participation, globalization, and an awareness of the interdependence of mutual interests. Since the early 1970s in many Western countries, the United States in particular, we have experienced a critical restructuring of policies and administrative activities: public programs have been reduced; national debts have risen; public finance has changed; agencies have been consolidated; and public entrepreneurship has been promoted. These changes have been brought about by political and social pressures, accompanied by taxpayer revolts, greater equality for people of color and women, and changes in local politics and economies. While Western countries have been restructuring (and reducing) their programs and activities, many industrializing countries in Asia have been expanding government programs and activities—by investing in education and building infrastructures—in order to cope with the rising demands of society.

In dealing with complex problems, policy makers and public administrators tend to rely on instrumental and technical solutions. These changes largely focus on policy revisions, structural and functional adjustments, and procedural modifications. These changes are top-down and management-driven efforts, coupled with various management techniques, such as Program Planning Budgeting System (PPBS), Management by Objectives (MBO), Zero-Based Budgeting (ZBB), Total Quality Management (TQM), Strategic Planning (SP), cost-benefit analysis, performance measurement, and so on. At least three unintended consequences have resulted from these techniques:

235

(1) an increase in the use of rational and instrumental solutions to organizational problems, (2) an increase in centralized decision making, and (3) a decrease in humanistic concerns and values. The solutions that were implemented have led to more managerial power and an increased use of technical tools to control the processes of organizational activities (Jun and Gross, 1996).

In his book *The Technological Society*, Jacques Ellul sees "techniques" (technological or technical tools) as the inevitable product of the rationalizing, order-loving and clarity-loving human consciousness. His view of techniques relates not only to machine technology but also to the standardization of procedures and behavior in order to develop the one best method for the achievement of any result (1964, pp. 3–22). In public administration and policy analysis, the desire of administrators and analysts to achieve goals in the most efficient way motivates them to adopt deterministic and positivistic techniques. Once they adopt a particular technique, their activities become routine and rigid. A technical framework is now reified by human consciousness. The framework is dehumanizing in that it ignores ethical and human implications.

Although a myriad of articles and books have been written about the application of management techniques to promote economy, efficiency, effectiveness, and participation in the public sector, there is little evidence that these techniques have produced the sustained effect of organizational democracy and effective problem solving. Although management techniques and information technology, including the Internet, have improved the management of routine activities and made government activities more transparent, some caution should be used against the abuse of rational-instrumental tools and the neglect of human interaction. Many scholars advance theoretical arguments for participatory management using management techniques. In practice, however, democratic ideas and decentralization in the workplace have produced little equivocal results.

Good techniques can, of course, improve organizational efficiency and rational decision making. But it is equally true that *techniques are only as good as the people who use them*. If management tools are designed to help managers and experts make better decisions and help with organizational performance, why, then, do tools produce only marginal results in most situations, particularly in public organizations? In order to use tools efficiently and effectively, those who are involved in the tool application must have not only technical skills but also human skills so that they are aware of their own biases and the values of others. That is why this book explores the limitations of modern public management and argues for the reconstruction of administrative theory and practice through the perspective of the social construction of reality. One of the ideas of social construction is to turn people's diverse social knowledge into action through people sharing their values and experiences; it is also to go beyond the traditional role of management and not place confidence in technical or functional tools for governing human activities. The social constructionist approach is not a panacea for all administrative problems but is a framework for democratizing governance processes and helping public administrators to think in terms of the broad human context.

RECAPITULATION

I present the concept, practice, and application of the social constructionist perspective as a major theme in order to understand and critically synthesize seemingly disparate aspects of what public administrators do and should do. Underlying the study of contemporary public administration is the idea that democratic governance and collaborative action are necessary if society and administration are to continue to change, innovate, and sustain their vitality. Public administrators and institutions must create opportunities for sharing and learning among organizational members and must facilitate interactive processes between public administrators and citizens so that the latter can voice their problems and opinions. Thus the future role of public administrators will be to transcend the limitations of the management and governing of modern public administration and to explore ways of constructing socially meaningful alternatives through communicative action and the participation of citizens.

More important is to understand individuals in relation to organizational, social, and cultural contexts; as the individual interacts with others and with the diverse environment, the self is always in the process of growth and change. Returning our attention to the problem of individuals helps us explicate why the functionalist and positivistic approaches to management, management-driven change, and the objective requirements of ethics do not produce their intended results.

It also helps us to realize the role of the individual in relation to others in constructing and reconstructing realities. This is one of the merits of the social constructionist perspective on connecting the individual with the organization and creating social settings for interdependence. To understand the problems of the organization and society, we need to use the interactive process, beginning with the individual and proceeding to the group, the organization, society, and the globe. In the interpretive perspective, phenomenology in particular, the individual is conceived as a world-experiencing subject, with human praxis organized around a commonly experienced life-world. It is foundational experience, and it is shared and accessible meaning that most postmodernists reject. Without a reflexive consciousness, a person could not critically examine or understand inner processes or the self (i.e., could not examine the ethical or moral consequences of actions). Thus, understanding ethics through the subjective is more meaningful to individuals than through the objective.

The subjective aspect of relationships is not a significant part of the argument raised by deconstructive postmodernists. The social constructionist perspective explored in this book may be considered constructive postmodern thought (or critical-modernist thought) because it seeks to overcome the limitations of modern public administration, not by neglecting the merits of typified ideas of the administrative (or management) tradition, but by constructing a postmodern public administration that improves human activities. The constructive postmodern view encompasses a critical (and dialectical) synthesis of administration as an art and as a science by turning its attention to people's broadly shared values, interests, and experiences. It is more useful to go beyond dualistic thinking as we study various opposing issues, such as art versus science, administration versus the public, quantitative versus qualitative knowledge, the organization versus the individual, objective and subjective responsibility, governing versus governance. The constructive postmodern view also helps us change old assumptions and design new premises by critically examining the inadequacies of administrative (and management) concepts, scientific methods, and procedures of governing that are commonly espoused in the functionalist and positivist perspectives. In this book, I try to reconstruct public administration from the viewpoint of democratic social construction and stress the importance of relationships that enable organizations to promote the potential in people, rather than devise ways to control and measure their performance. Thus the social constructionist perspective introduced in this book may be interpreted as *critical pragmatism*, in which administrative theory and praxis are grounded in interpretation and understanding of human experiences in relation to broad political, social, economic, and cultural contexts. Social construction is a framework in which people together figure out what is possible and what organizational learning needs to happen.

Another important aspect of the social constructionist perspective is its commitment to change and problem solving through the democratic process, engaging people in discussions of problems and in realizing their values, ideas, and experiences. This process inevitably involves participation, deliberation, and communicative action. In chapters 4 and 5, I provided a critical review of the crisis, rational, and incremental modes of public problem solving. The social design approach to change and problem solving must be practiced through dialogue and discourse in order to understand differences among the participants and construct an intersubjective reality. When we come to an agreement, there is a sense of shared reality, there is learning, and there is mutual respect. Because democratic problem solving involves assent and dissent regarding issues that are difficult to resolve, interactions and negotiations may not produce acceptable decisions among the actors. Even when people fail to reach an agreement in spite of their contested dialogue, the level of intersubjective understanding has been raised. It is important for participants to understand why they were not able to construct a desirable outcome so that their experiences provide a new insight into the next engagement.

The process of social construction encourages people's participation and contribution. When organizations encourage their members to be critical and constructive, then the members find no threat to their autonomy or identity; under these circumstances, most people are willing to experience the process of changing reality. As people engage in the process of sharing their ideas, they can find meaning in their actions. In order to implement a policy or project, the actors involved need to derive a sense of self-worth from and find intrinsic meaning in them. How executives and managers interact with people below them influences greatly the way they motivate them. The social constructionist approach offers an opportunity for people's voluntary participation by mobilizing from below, as opposed to organizational mobilization from the top down in order to gain people's obedience and contributions (Friedmann, 1987, pp. 181–308).

Because democracy demands the participation of people in deliberating diverse viewpoints, social construction as a democratic process is a very complicated activity that cannot be comprehended without understanding how the individuals construct their self-concept in the social (or organizational) world. One of the most common forms in modern and postmodern societies is the structural arrangement of bureaucracy. Although a bureaucratic form of government structures seems to be universal at least in its appearance, the construction of "bureaucratic experience" is quite different from one society to another and from one administrative culture to another. Differences in bureaucratic experience stem from the differences in the social construction of organizational reality as experienced by the organizational members; the construction of organizational elements such as rules and procedures, individual existence, peer relationships, incentives, and future possibilities varies depending on the nature of organizational governance.

In this book, I emphasize the positive aspects of human nature, rather than looking at the negative image of organizational members. Public administrators in general are interested in meaningful action and want to perform good work as ethically and humanely as they can. They are able to reflect on themselves, interpret their life-world, and exercise critical consciousness. When an individual entertains doubts about a choice, the person can discuss his or her ideas with others. In this regard, social construction offers an opportunity for individual self-empowerment as well as "collective self-empowerment" by the actors in particular social settings unveiling or testing individual concerns and knowledge. Michael Barber describes Alfred Schutz's idea of typification and relevance thus: "[O]ur own [original] experiences, as well as any kind of socially derived knowledge, receive additional weight if they are also embraced by other members of our in-group. I tend to believe my own experiences to be correct beyond doubt if others whom my social group considers competent corroborate them" (1988, p. 59).

The changing relationships among government, civil society, and business are also discussed from the social constructionist viewpoint. Globalization has served to bring nations and people closer together: people network, sharing cultural, economic, political, and technological interests. When government and the global market economy obstruct broad human interests and the public good, nongovernmental or civil society organizations act as a counterbalance to government and businesses. Because of the pressing need for economic modernization, governance and development—including global policy making—must go beyond the top-down approach of policymakers and managers. Instead, they must promote the process of bottom-up policy making, involving citizens who will be affected by such global decisions as trade negotiations, economic development projects, and foreign investments. Strengthening civil society by questioning policies and activities is an important way to limit the power of a strong government and the market. As citizens and NGOs improve their communities through discursive practice, they learn how to self-govern. Although a strong civil society is conspicuous in Western countries, many non-Western democratic countries also realize the role that civil society plays in democratizing the governance process.

In the following section, I explore ways to make the process of social construction effective. How can the democratic process be sustained? In what ways can democratic social construction be a significant force for enhancing the potential of individuals as well as involving the public? The answers to these questions require change and innovation in structure, power relationships, and dialogical practice; they also require enhancing trust in people's action skills.

MAKING SOCIAL CONSTRUCTION EFFECTIVE

Democratic social construction provides a framework for developing "collective reasoning," a process in which people work together, seeking collective aims (or public reason) for deciding important activities, policies, or projects (Rawls, 1993; Bohman, 1996; Christiano, 1997; Richardson, 2002; Dryzek, 2000; Hajer and Wagenaar, 2003), such as transportation policy, health care, community planning, economic development, environmental protection, and crime prevention. The democratic social construction of public administration is based on two important assumptions: (1) the value of deliberative democracy, which emphasizes participation in decision making through the process of contested dialogue and discourse, and (2) the value of preventing bureaucratic domination by minimizing hierarchical control.

Although the ideas of democracy and bureaucracy are difficult to reconcile, as long as we are concerned with the *publicness* of public administration, the study of public administration must explore ways to promote a "democratic public" by reconstructing organizational governance and the role of management.[1] This, of course, requires changes in the current practice of public administration. Among many possibilities, I discuss several areas that directly affect process, participation, and interaction.

Decentralization and Power Sharing

Democratic governance and participation mean little if the distribution of governmental power remains undisturbed. This means that government agencies must find ways to share their decision-making power with the public. With a highly centralized government structure, decision-making power resides at the top level of the central government. Japan's first step, as well as South Korea's first step, should be an ongoing effort to decentralize local governments. The next logical step would be for local governments to consider how decentralized authority granted by the central government could be applied to local conditions and how local people could be involved in the democratic process. As the professionalization of local administration increases, there is a tendency to rely on technical skills and rational analysis to solve complex social problems. At the same time, as the informal relationships between government officials and businesses develop, economic and business development projects are initiated without informing citizens, in spite of the environmental damage that could be caused by those projects. If local autonomy is to have public support, then public deliberation and transparency in public meetings are necessary so that citizens can argue for or against development projects and have their words carry weight.

The political and institutional arrangements practiced in Western countries are not readily applicable to other countries, particularly non-Western countries, where politics and administration are highly centralized, the level of professionalization is low, and democracy is new. In those countries, governmental reforms must consider how to develop citizens' capacity for self-governance, as well as how to improve the management capability of local public institutions first, before experimenting with political or administrative decentralization. For example, in many African countries where decentralization programs were introduced, the outcomes were corruption and wasted resources—due largely to a lack of local government capability or civic culture.

Decentralization without power sharing between the higher and lower levels of an institution is simply a structural rearrangement that could create inefficiency if local bureaucrats are passive. When the central authority delegates functions to the local authority without providing sufficient resources, the local authorities are at the mercy of central bureaucrats. Structural change alone does not empower people at the lower echelon of an organization. Democratic governance calls not only for active citizens but also for less hierarchical and more flexible organizations. In Eastern and Western countries, those with administrative responsibilities should act as the facilitators, coordinators, or representatives of agencies. Organizational members should also play an active and deliberative role in the governance process.

Enhancing Discursive Practice

Most change programs initiated by government agencies are the external elements that provide nondiscursive experiences for the participants; they may affect the nature of interactions, participation, and human collaboration. However, resistance to administrative reforms imposed by top management generally comes from nondiscursive aspects of management-driven changes. When management initiates institutional (and structural) improvements of organizational activities, organizational members and citizens may resist these changes. Nondiscursive factors, such as decentralization, changing authority relationships, horizontal networks, and rules of communication, are essential for democratic governance and social construction; external features provide people with nondiscursive experience.[2] Although these nondiscursive aspects can condition the dialogical process, they are not sufficient for facilitating authentic communication. For example, changing authority relationships does not require reciprocal communication—listening, understanding, and feedback—between the management and employees. Management, however, could empower employees by providing them with more autonomy, discretion, and participation and by sharing information. Nondiscursive elements can have a significant influence only if participants see them as intrinsically meaningful to themselves.

Democratic social construction, however, can be effective only when organizational members and citizens demonstrate a psychological commitment, expressing their interest in discursive practice by engaging in open dialogue, discussing issues with others, and interpreting issues collectively. Through a deliberative process, they question hierarchical governing as well as the quality of interactions and participation in a social context. Discursive experience results from communicative action, dialogue and discourse, deliberations that involve contested arguments, and consensus building through understanding, persuasion, learning, and negotiation. People develop mutual respect and intersubjective meaning as they engage in the discursive process by exchanging points of view (Gutmann and Thompson, 1996).

Democratic social construction (i.e., democratic governance, or "discursive democracy") depends on a process that promotes ongoing interactions and continuing relationships, critical and reflexive action, and authentic dialogue and discourse that tolerates opposing voices. As discursive actors (i.e., citizens and administrators) become self-reflexive in their communication, they learn from others, modify their positions, become open to negotiation, and construct new possibilities (Chambers, 1996, pp. 207–08). As Dryzek points out, Habermas emphasizes the procedural requirements of deliberative democracy in reaching public consensus but understates contested elements of discursive democracy (Dryzek, 2000; 1990; also see Chambers, 1996). I agree with his assertion because the dominant influence of the structural and functional elements in public administration, both nondiscursive and discursive experiences, need to be considered as we attempt to democratize the governance process: they are complementary and offer the possibility of democratization. Governance through social construction can be democratic while embracing some important aspects of governing. Public administrators will likely always face organizational and political constraints, such as hierarchical authority, power, and rules. One way of overcoming these constraints is to reflexively critique them through discursive social practice.

The discursive process works better at the community level, because it involves active stakeholders and citizens who are interested in sharing different viewpoints face-to-face; in this situation, there is a greater chance of reaching consensus. However, when large-scale issues are addressed through deliberation and discourse, communication is limited even though it involves debates through various forums and media and among citizens. As John Dryzek points out, "Discursive democracy can embrace difference as well as consensus, the public sphere as well as the state, transnational as well as domestic politics, and nature as well as humanity" (Dryzek, 2000, p. 175). Dryzek further argues that in a pluralistic society, consensus is "unattainable, unnecessary, and undesirable," but participants may agree on a course of action for different reasons.

Promoting Trust and Confidence

Trust is essential to the development of reliable (and authentic) relationships among organizational members and between organizational members and citizens. In recent years, some scholars, however, argue that mutually beneficial cooperative relationships can take place without trust (Cook, Hardin, and Levi, 2005). Although cooperation may be maintained, the development of trusting relationships, however, advances our understanding of what makes people willing or unwilling to take the risks involved in building such relationships and why (Ostrom and Walker, 2005; Kramer and Cook, 2004). Defining the concept of 'trust,' however, is difficult because trust is so nebulous and so inherently tied to so many other concepts that no one definition does justice to its complex nature (Jun and Kim, 2002). When people assign a particular meaning to the notion of trust in institutions or interpersonal relations, the word *trust* is often defined with various synonyms, such as *confidence, faith, trustworthiness, reliance,* or *anticipation of goodwill.* These words convey the "affective attitude" (Jones, 1996) that goes along with an expectation of competence in another person or an institution. Trust is more than confidence, because the latter is more calculating and based more on expectation than the former. If the community faces many unsolved problems, services are delayed, and officials engage in unethical conduct, then citizens' confidence in the government erodes. It is possible for citizens to have confidence in the work of public employees without having full confidence in the government, its institutions, or public service (Warren, 1999).

Trust has an intrinsic application to an analysis of people's interactions with public institutions and vice versa; this includes the interactions of citizens and administration, individuals and bureaucracy, and members of the public and the community. Social interactions may be explained in terms of the exchange between people and institutions with different normative roles in society. These exchanges may involve business contracts, or they may involve some other tool that facilitates trust. So trust is an important element in any exchange involving social interaction, ranging from a calculative and rational exchange to a value exchange. The two broad types of exchanges are "generalized" and "restricted": each is based on some expectations of "trust and solidarity." Janoski points out that restricted exchanges are generally short term because of extensive social mobility of people; generalized exchange works better in a strong community. He also argues that restricted exchange generates little trust because it is based on an individual's cost-benefit calculations to gain personal goods from the market. Whereas restricted exchange does little to further trust in the process of bargaining, "generalized exchange preserves [the] realm of political and economic equality. It requires patience, an ability to look for the larger group or societal results, and the general building of social trust." (1998, p. 91).

An analysis of trust may be applied to individual and institutional levels. Luhmann considers trust in people as distinguished from confidence in institutions (1979). Trust, Luhmann says, is found only in interpersonal relations. Moreover, people may have confidence in institutions, but this is based on their role performance. At the interpersonal level, trust begins with my self-concept. When I trust my ability to learn and change, I am capable of becoming. When I trust another person, I am able to accept him or her into my life experience. However, when I fear someone, I am defensive and do not accept him or her into my life experience. The importance of trust in interpersonal relations is stressed by many humanistic psychologists, such as Carl Rogers, James Bugental, Jack Gibb, and Hubert Otto. They stress that trust and distrust are key to understanding interpersonal relations and human organizations. When trust is high, people collaborate well, and organizations function effectively. When distrust is high, the collaboration and functioning break down. The defensive posture, therefore, becomes one where trust is correspondingly conditioned on the principle of verification.

Interpersonal exchanges between human beings begin with a subjective point of view and are transformed into an intersubjective experience as individuals interact with or take into consideration the experiences of others. Luhmann, a neosystems theorist, also acknowledges the intersubjective construction of meaning and social experience: "A transcendental phenomenological account of the world and its complexity has to take cognizance of the intersubjective nature of such constitution of meaning and world" (1979, p. 18). The limits of empiricism and functionalism in explaining trust are evident from the increase in human science, phenomenology, and hermeneutics. A phenomenological analysis of trust is essential in order to give primacy to the interpretation of meanings and symbolic forms implicit in social relationships.

Interpersonal relationships present the potential for developing solidarity and mutuality that have corresponding values of trust for the individuals involved. The level of solidarity and mutuality is directly tied to this assigned value. People move between roles during these interpersonal exchanges, and this causes a constant redefinition of the relationship and the corresponding levels of trust that they are willing to invest in the process. This can be assessed through the amount of interpersonal competence that people assign to others in their current roles. Regardless of what other factors contribute to confidence in institutions, it is this factor of interpersonal competence that defines interpersonal relationships and differentiates them from interactions associated with institutions.

Trust at the institutional level entails a different meaning. The ideas of trust in interpersonal relations are often difficult to apply to an institutional setting, particularly when people perceive an institution as an objective reality that is separate from their subjective world. As people attempt to understand institutions (and organizations) as objectified reality that they constructed and that always present a possibility for being reconstructed, the issue of trust and distrust may surface as an important subject for discourse. When people view institutions as networks of people with different values and experiences who are engaged in social interactions, transforming low-trust institutions into high-trust ones is possible. However, as long as people engage in instrumental interactions involving technical-functional work relationships and rational exchanges to gain organizational and personal interest, trust will be difficult to develop. Most social relationships at the institutional and political levels tend to be based on instrumental and business interactions. Therefore applying the concepts of 'confidence' and 'reliability' seem to be more appropriate than applying the concept of trust. When members of the public trust a particular institution, they tend to have good interpersonal relationships with the people working in or representing that institution.

The structural relationship with or within the institution is the most difficult to build and in which to sustain trust. This is due not only to role ambiguity of different actors and institutions involved in the interaction process but also to the interactions between actors and institutions, which tend to be political, instrumental-rational, and restricted exchange, if not superficial. Role ambiguity increases the sense of risk; this, in turn, increases fear in predicting the outcome of dependence. This fear can be debilitating, limiting the amount of trust that citizens are willing to invest in the exchange process. Another problem with trust at the institutional level is the source of solidarity. At the interpersonal level, solidarity (and mutuality) is a direct by-product of trust and intimate dialogue. At the institutional level a number of external variables affect the level of solidarity. Institutional solidarity is maintained as people assume a clear sense of organizational obligation and loyalty, commitment, shared interest, pride, roles, and the necessity for survival, growth, or change.

Trust and confidence are more likely to occur when leaders, managers, employees, and institutions demonstrate that they are ethically and morally reliable and confident in carrying out their assumed responsibility. Trust cannot be demanded of people. Although trust and trustworthiness accompanied by ethical responsibility are difficult to promote, they may be the human elements that are the most important to the governance of a democratic society (Hardin, 1998, p. 24; Warren, 1999). As organizations become more confident—and more reliable—in meeting societal needs, organizational members will have a heightened awareness of social trust and display greater interpersonal competence. When government organizations face financial difficulties, executives and managers tend to focus on "urgent things that are really unimportant" that may result in "the disempowerment and alienation of workers" (Covey, 1997). As organizations promote trust and empowerment, organizational members are likely to be committed and take risk in innovation and improvement.

Education for Action Skills

Because of the need to maintain organizational efficiency and productivity, public administration has largely emphasized the technical skills of people working in government organizations. Accordingly, educational programs in public administration in both the East and West focus on the utilization of technical (and functional) and behavioral skills of public employees as the determinant of human resources. Public administration curriculums in Asian countries are largely modeled on Western educational programs, which reflect a functionalist and positivistic approach to the management of public institutions.

Technical skills, such as the functional managerial skills of control, coordination, budgeting, personnel, accounting, planning, scientific research methods, and statistical knowledge, are important in bringing about efficiency in the workplace. Moreover, technical skills and functional skills lend themselves to industrializing societies, which use a wide range of scientific and rational techniques to produce and distribute goods, services, and information. Particularly in the early stages of industrialization, the rational approach works well with regard to centralized planning, control, and functional coordination. Policy makers and planners believe that technical rationality is easy to apply in a hierarchical administration; this, in turn, encourages the continuous improvement of hierarchy and functional coordination. It therefore reinforces itself so that it seems like the only way to accomplish organizational activities rationally. As discussed earlier, the recent emphasis on public management on efficiency, productivity, and performance measurement has focused on instrumental and technical skills and has neglected the intrinsic educational and training values many organizational psychologists and trainers have advocated for years.

Educating new public administrators to go into an environment that is changing rapidly and demands innovative and creative solutions must begin with a new curriculum design. Public administration education needs not only to restructure the traditional courses in public management but also to introduce new courses designed to teach students action skills along with a program to teach them the ethical and democratic dimensions of public administration. Robert Denhardt points out that "action skills are those capabilities that both orient and enable intentional action, those that allow us to act with integrity and consistency in any given situation. Action skills are those that allow us to translate norms and ideas into action" (1986, p. 127). If democratic social construction is to become increasingly meaningful and practiced widely, rather than marginalized, education for action skills must be realized as an essential part of public administration education.

The differences between technical skills and action skills may be explained in terms of how we approach change in public administration. As discussed in other chapters, technical skills are grounded in the concept of instrumental and technical rationality. The process of change is according to the previous experience, rules and procedures, and analytical framework used in technical analysis. Reality can be objectively and empirically measured and evaluated. Change is essentially deterministic, because the application of a particular technical skill is supposed to produce the intended outcome or solve the problem. For example, in the policy science approach, analytical methods are used to determine an optimal solution, based on the rational analysis of alternatives.

Action skills are grounded in interpretive epistemology, which emphasizes understanding the reality of subjects and the hidden aspects of local conditions by paying attention to language, symbols, stories, and values that are unique to a particular culture. Interpretation requires understanding the shared norms, rules, meanings, and expectations that make up our social reality. Interpretation must be used when we encounter something out of the ordinary, something contrary to our beliefs regarding truth or goodness, or something we just do not understand. In terms of organizational change, an important assumption is that actions derived from subjective and intersubjective commitments could present various possibilities for better understanding, problem solving, and change.

The action skills introduced thus far are essentially process driven, as they are applied to the enhancement of interactions between actors. They include reflexive skill, interpersonal and dialogical skills, persuasive skills, therapeutic (listening) skills, and skills in action research. Self-reflexivity is a core skill for an action-oriented administrator. In order for the public administrator to question and, if necessary, change habitual ways of doing things, he or she must assess the appropriateness of his or her own actions. If administrators continually examine their actions, they are likely to engage in responsible actions. As the individual reveals the self to others, he or she engages in an unending process of transcending (and becoming). In order to construct the self and work with others, the individual exercises skills in interpersonal and group interactions. Interactions between people entail "dialogic reverberations" that take place between the different voices (Bakhtin, 1981; Baxter and Montgomery, 1996; Strasser, 1969).

A public administrator also needs persuasive skills in working in the political environment with clients, special interest groups, competing agencies, elected officials, and so on. He or she must overcome resistance to change from conservative peers and be able to advocate innovative ideas through the use of persuasion. A public administrator must also develop the action skills that a group therapist uses. In this regard, the role of the administrator is to not only help to shape the tone of the group process but also to facilitate the process of open dialogue by inviting and listening to different voices. While acting as a therapist, an administrator interacts with the various group members, including minorities, women, the elderly, and the disadvantaged, and also provides a positive setting where people feel free to express their opinions and where support is mutual, both vertically and horizontally. An administrator as a social constructionist and a therapist is one of collaboration and creative relationships with citizens. This viewpoint veers away from the traditionalist's approach of relationships being one of the knower and the ignorant (Gergen, 1999, pp. 167–75). In an era of democratization and globalization, administrators cannot continue to act as experts, the holders of technical knowledge, assuming that citizens must simply follow their decisions. Finally, a public administrator needs to know how to act collectively in dealing with complex problems or project design without giving up his or her identity. In this regard, action research can be a framework of organizational learning in which individual learning is communicated in ways that allow the group to examine problems, goals, actions, and implementation issues. In action research activity, everyone acts as leader, learner, and contributor.

THE TAO OF PUBLIC ADMINISTRATION

Because I completed my higher education in the United States, my understanding of Eastern thought and Western thought is unequal. I do not have rigorous training in Asian philosophy, but I do have a limited knowledge of Confucianism and Taoism and have found that these two philosophies have made a significant contribution to public administration in China, Japan, South Korea, and Singapore. A creative tension between the two makes up the character of Asian thought that will continue to influence people's relationships and ways of governing society and administration. As discussed previously, in spite of some negative interpretations of Confucian thought with regard to human relationships and virtues today, its impact on people's conduct in Asia is immeasurable. One of the most important concepts is "dialectic" in

Taoism. The concept of dialectic is important to many Western philosophers, including Plato, Aristotle, Hegel, Marx, phenomenologists, and critical theorists. An exploration of different views of dialectic is beyond the scope of this book. Dialectical thinking is a conceptual guide for an individual's reflexive vision for constructing more "sane and contended living" in organization and society. Dialectics is a process of understanding "how things swing together from one pole to another" (Cohen, 1981)—for example, how individualism is connected to communitarianism or how autonomy is connected to virtue. The most important intervening element in moving from one stream to another and relating the self to others is an act of self-construction (Kiros, 1998).

In order to compare and contrast Eastern and Western views of dialectic, I next discuss Hegel's idea of reconciling opposites and Lao Tze's view of polarity. Hegel introduced the dialectical method of understanding the process of history by identifying a thesis, its antithesis, and a synthesis. One idea is presented as "the thesis." This calls forth the opposing idea, the antithesis. Eventually, these two give rise to a third idea, the synthesis, which develops out of the relationship of the first two ideas to each other. Furthermore, in the Hegelian sense, the dialectic is a process of searching for a critical synthesis among contradictions, conflicts, and discontinuities in the administrative world.

This Western idea of synthesis may be compared with Watts' explanation of the Eastern dialectic:

> At the very root of Chinese thinking and feeling there lies the principle of polarity, which is not to be confused with the ideas of opposition or conflict. In the metaphors of other cultures, light is at war with darkness, life with death, good with evil, and the positive with the negative, and thus an idealism to cultivate the former and be rid of the latter flourishes throughout much of the world. To the traditional way of Chinese thinking, this is as incomprehensible as an electric current without both positive and negative poles, for polarity is the principle that plus (+) and minus (−), north and south, are different aspects of one and the same system, and that the disappearance of either one of them would be the disappearance of the system. (1975, pp. 19–20)

One of the most fundamental polarities in Taoism is yin and yang, as discussed in chapter 7. Yin and yang represent not a dualism, but rather "an explicit duality expressing an implicit unity" (Watt, 1975, p. 26).

Eastern mysticism emphasizes a "basic oneness," but this does not mean that all things are the same. And the individuality of a thing is important, but "all differences and contrasts are relative within an all-embracing unity" (Capra, 1975, p. 145). Western synthesis happens when two opposing things combine to make a third. The Eastern perspective sees the two sides as already connected. What these two views have in common is the principle of mutual arising: the thesis calls its antithesis into being; the foreground and the background are distinguished simultaneously. They also share the qualities of nonsummativity and wholeness.

Nonsummativity is described in the phrase *The whole is greater than the sum of its parts.* If we can quantify or process the elements of the thesis and the antithesis, their value to us when they are creatively synthesized is greater than their value as unrelated forces taken together. The principle of nonsummativity can be observed when individuals relate to each other dialectically, for example, when they engage in collaborative conflict-resolution or decision-making processes. These processes are characterized by an outcome that could not be predicted by simply examining the information that each person brings to the conversation. The conversation itself is what is important, and a successful conversation can produce outcomes that take care of each member and simultaneously enable each member to take care of the others. What is agreed or disagreed upon emerges after much communication and discussion, and therefore the solution proposed tends to be accepted by the parties involved. Moreover, even if the participants do not agree on anything, from the interpretive perspective, they are likely to gain a new understanding of one another.

According to tai chi chuan instructor Elizabeth Jensen, the principle of nonsummativity appears in Taoism.[3] In the martial art of tai chi chuan, you blend your movements with the opponent's movements in order to maintain your equilibrium and unbalance the other. The two-person practice, *peng lu chi ahn*, begins as a choreographed form in which the practitioners aim to first yield, and then follow, and finally gain the superior position. The outcome of the contest is more than the sum of its parts. One of the pair is able to channel the kinetic energy of both practitioners' movements and use this force against the other. The movements alone would not produce any result, but the movements together cause one of them to fly across the floor.

Another quality of the dialectical process that the East and the West share is wholeness. In a sense, wholeness is nonsummativity looked at from the other direction. It is the principle that things cannot be reduced to their component parts. In administrative theory, as I discussed in chapter 6, both the functionalist and the interpretive perspectives are reductionistic: each has a one-sided view of human action and social reality. Public administration is too complex to be reduced to mechanical subsystems as assumed in systems theory. At the same time, we cannot focus just on the interpretive problems of studying administrative phenomena. The dialectic deals with this by focusing on the complexity of administrative reality, comprehending it as a whole. For example, when people that make up the parts of an organization think dialectically, they critically reflect on their relationship to the whole (Benson, 1977). As Watts points out, our conception of something is distinct from the thing itself and is only an abstract representation of it. Any model or theory can only partially represent reality, so it tends to violate the principle of wholeness (Watts, 1975, pp. 43–44).

We can see the holistic nature of Taoism in the Taoist's inclusive perspective. For example, an individual studies tai chi chuan with a teacher from a Taoist lineage. That person receives instruction on how to balance every element of his or her life. This includes the individual's body: posture, diet, and the rhythm of daily activities. It also includes the student's relationship with spouse, family, friends, relationships with work, play, practice, and the rest of society. Taoists recognize that for optimum health and long life, we need to consider the whole human being and not sacrifice any part of the person for the sake of any other part. Each element is granted a right to be and a right to be nurtured. The integrity of the whole is more important than any of its parts.

There are other important conceptual comparisons between Taoist and Western philosophy as applied to an understanding of the human mind in the administrative world, such as action and nonaction, rational mind and nonintellectual intelligence, linear thinking and nonlinear thinking, and continuity and discontinuity. Dialectic turns from one issue to the next, making connections between them and bringing everything together in a way that transforms consciousness and generates possibility. Dialectical thinking includes challenging assumptions, allowing theories to act as critiques of one another, acknowledging the reality of contradictions and conflicts, and using these as points of inquiry instead of ignoring them. A dialectically inclined person (and a theorist) does not try to solve these problems by simply applying a theory, method, or technique with more force or greater precision but recognizes that each solution works for only a specific range of problems and that each solution is another set of variables, that may well be problems in themselves. The dialectician allows all parts of the organization and its environment to be, recognizing that any theory or model necessarily distorts reality because it cannot represent the full complexity of social reality.

The Taoist spins the spiral in the other direction, beginning with the assumption that there never was a division in the first place, that you can never wander from the path or deviate from the Tao: any appearance of that is only another facet of the Tao. In practical application, the Taoist finds the balance in each apparent dichotomy that she encounters, beginning in the center with herself, and gradually expanding this principle to include everything in her world. We need to enhance dialectical thinking to discover the limits of each administrative dimension, and we need to develop strategies for overcoming those limits. We can do this through dialectical discourse among participants and by creating new possibilities. If we do this, we can transform the stagnant situation that our current level of functionalist and positivistic thinking got us into. This process needs to begin within the individual and expand outward to the interpersonal, group, organization, societal, and global levels.

To conclude the Taoist view of contemporary public administration and society, once again we turn to the idea of mutual learning and respect through communication and participation. This allows us to go beyond the explicit notion of duality, such as the administration and the public, the self and the organization, the scientific methods and human science, explanation and understanding, globalization and antiglobalization, and East and West. Public administration in each country needs to find ways to build better governance and to make organizations more innovative, more oriented to change. The role of government is not only to improve public services to citizens but also to create a context for "value creation" through effective politics (Kirlin, 1996) and human interaction. At the same time, each country has unlimited possibilities when it comes to learning from others concerning new policy design, such as delivery of services, health care policy, distribution of wealth, organizational reform, improving the quality of working life, and ways of enhancing citizen participation. In the past, countries in the East looked to the West, emulating the Western model of modernization and industrialization. Since the 1980s, however, globalization has created not only the reverse transaction but also the exchange of mutual interests, despite radical criticisms of the rich nations controlling the dominant economic forces. We are not likely to halt the forces of globalization. If globalization is to promote economic prosperity and democracy throughout the world, policy makers and administrators must exercise a critical consciousness, examining policies and their implications in light of human consequences.

In cross-cultural learning, interpreting the cultural dynamics of the East and the West means understanding the hidden dimensions of the administrative culture of each country. Each administrative culture has an organizational norm (or a certain value) that constitutes reality to its members. These norms define the larger context for people's organizational lives, giving meaning and providing a guide for behavior and ethical conduct. For example, Confucianism influences the behavior of administrators in Far East Asian countries, just as the Protestant ethic influences the behavior of administrators in many Western countries. However, as people become more self-reflexive, learn to participate in the organizational process, and interact with the external world, they begin to reinterpret the meaning of the old culture in light of a new emerging culture and a new work ethic. Korean, Japanese, and Singaporian administrative cultures can be carried to the extreme of denying selfhood. As young people bring their new values, learned largely from the West, to organizations, they seek a new identity, demanding recognition as individuals with critical voices. New workers demand rewards for individual performance, as opposed to the traditional recognition of group performance.

With regard to the Confucian ethic among the Far East Asian countries, the attitude of public administrators is changing. The traditional virtues of loyalty, diligence, and commitment were long viewed as a countervailing influence to Western materialism. But the thousands of students who return home after studying in the West question old values, thinking more of their private realm than their responsibility for the public realm. Moreover, the traditional cultural value of maintaining social order, with each person understanding his or her roles and responsibilities in society, has already been transforming.

Likewise, we may also scrutinize the Western orientation of individual rights as opposed to societal responsibility: a dynamic civil society demands an ongoing balance between individualism and communitarianism. To Americans, Asian administrators may say that because of our emphasis on individual rights, we run the risk of breaking the bonds that hold organizations and communities together. American administrators may say to Asian administrators that they run the risk of hampering individual development, which is the strength of any innovative organization and society.

The strength of American culture is, however, multiculturalism: the attitudes, values, experiences, and differences of diverse groups of people in the workplace and society contribute to the vitality of American society. To value diversity is to recognize and understand individual differences "so that we can take one another's perspective into account when making moral judgments" (Young, 1997, p. 52). As other countries become multicultural because of changes in demography (e.g., due to the migration of workers), they can also learn ways of appreciating and coping with changing cultural contexts from the United States and other Western countries.

Theories regarding administrative phenomena must be reflexively grounded in the concept of the social construction of administration and democratic governance. In the everyday life of an organization, both the functionalist perspective and the interpretive perspective of public administration are valid and useful: the first explains the importance of structure, policy, and management from a macro viewpoint; and the second looks at the meanings of people's experiences, language, and culture from a micro viewpoint. The functionalist perspective is that these two views of the administrative world are unrelated: the organization and the individual (object and subject) are treated as separate and independent of each other. The interpretive perspective— and the subjective view of phenomenology in particular—emphasizes that action in an organization must be understood in terms of the individual's meanings and intentions. How individuals engage in their activities in constructing reality (e.g., role and function) is important. The critical perspective helps us explore alternatives by critically reflecting on opposing views and conflicts in relation to broad human, cultural, and political contexts, and sharing diverse knowledge and experiences.

The Tao of public administration (as well as the social construction of public administration) rejects the duality of administrative phenomena. Instead, it considers both sides of a problem, such as the objective view and the subjective view. Shunning duality, it embraces relationships, interdependence, reciprocity, and dialectic. These ideas can be seen in both the Eastern view and the Western view of social reality. The Eastern perspective emphasizes harmony, coexistence, unity, and wholeness; the Western perspective emphasizes participation, deliberation, critical reflexivity, and communication. To renew our effort to construct (and reconstruct) a societal vision and democratic organizations, we need both perspectives. Moreover, both Eastern and Western public administration must find ways to improve democratic governance without sacrificing the unique individuality or autonomy of each person. Public administrators must facilitate the process of changing organizations by relating the organization and the individual, the administration and citizens, and objectivity and subjectivity, rather than separating them. They must learn the problems and learn the values of organizational members and citizens if they are to comprehend their responses to changes that originate with the administration.

NOTES

CHAPTER 1

1. The concept of the positivistic and functionalist epistemology is discussed in chapter 3. Epistemology is a theory of knowledge that is concerned with the investigation of the origin, structure, methods, and validity of knowledge.

2. On the critique of the role of experts, see also G. Benveniste, *The Politics of Expertise* (Berkeley, Calif.: Glendessary, 1972); L. May, *The Socially Responsive Self: Social Theory and Professional Ethics* (Chicago: University of Chicago Press, 1996); J. A. Rhor, *Public Service, Ethics and Constitutional Practice* (Lawrence: University Press of Kansas, 1998).

3. According to James Bohman, hyperrationality is "an excessive rationalism to the extent that it ignores conditions that could make a satisfactory outcome of deliberation impossible, such as uncertainty and lack of information. [It] is thus an inability to recognize failures of rationality, as when deliberators ignore uncertainty, ambiguity and lack of full information and yet demand uniquely rational decisions" (J. Bohman, *Public Deliberation: Pluralism, Complexity, and Democracy* [Cambridge, Mass.: MIT Press, 1996], p. 157).

4. Ontology is concerned with the theory of being insofar as being. It concerns the issue of whether social reality is given to the individual or the product of the individual. (G. Burrel and G. Morgan, *Sociological Paradigms and Organizational Analysis*, 1979, p. 1). Social construction focuses on how the individual constructs reality with others.

5. "Subjectivity" refers to the experiences, cogitations, motives, and intuitions of an individual. Subjective meaning inherent in action is always the meaning that the acting person ascribes to his or her action.

6. Objectivity is the character of a real object existing independently of the knowing mind in contrast to subjectivity. Everything apprehended is independent of his or her interpretation.

5. According to Husserl, bracketing is a methodological device of phenomenological inquiry, consisting in a deliberate effort to set all ontological judgments about the "nature" and "essence" of things, events, and so on. Thereby, the "reality" of things and events is not denied but "put into brackets." This procedure is called "phenomenological reduction." Through bracketing of all judgments about the ontological nature of the perceived objects, Husserl wanted to reduce the observed phenomenon to its own features without out preconceived interpretation.

CHAPTER 2

1. For Max Weber, functional rationality, or instrumental rationality, is attained by the elaboration (on the basis of scientific knowledge) of rules that try to direct, from the top, all behavior toward maximum efficiency. Weber's rationalization is the product of the scientific specialization and technical differentiation peculiar to Western culture, and Weber sometimes associates it with the notion of intellectualization.

2. In *Paths of Change: Strategic Choices for Organizations and Society* (1992), Will McWhinney illustrates that the process of conventionalization is the tendency toward centralization of knowledge in order to bring about change.

3. Although deconstruction as argued by some postmodernists, such as Jacques Derrida and Michel Foucault, emphasizes "negative critical capacity," reinterpretation as discussed here implies a positive reconstruction of meaning.

CHAPTER 3

1. G. Burrel and G. Morgan (1979) consider the interpretive approach to be a separate paradigm, one that is in opposition to the functional paradigm.

2. Although the terms *social constructionism* and *social constructivism* are often used interchangeably, their meanings are different. Kenneth Gergen describes the difference: "For constructivists the process of world construction is psychological; it takes place 'in the head.' In contrast, for social constructionists what we take to be real is an outcome of social relationships." (See K. Gergen, *An Introduction to Social Construction* [Thousand Oaks, Calif.: Sage, 1999], pp. 236–37.)

3. The life-world is the concrete reality of an individual's lived experience, in contrast to the interpretation of that reality made by the scientist (Husserl and Schutz).

4. As P. L. Berger and T. Luckmann describe, we are born into an objectified world, a society created and maintained by people as they live their lives and interpret subjectively their surroundings. This objectified world is often taken for granted as being "real" when it is maintained and modified by a common language and social practices.

CHAPTER 4

This chapter is a revised version of a book chapter "Public Administration as Social Design," in J. S. Jun, *Public Administration: Design and Problem Solving* (New York: Macmillan, 1985).

1. In their book *Reframing Organizations* (1997), L. Bolman and T. Deal introduce four frames as metaphors for explaining the organizations. In *Images of Organization* (1997), G. Morgan discusses eight metaphors, exploring their implications for thinking about the nature of organization.

2. The idea of change making and design is emphasized by Allan Cahoon and C. H. Levin, "Designed Change: A Post Minnowbrook Perspective for the 'New' Public Administration," a paper presented at the National Conference of the American Society for Public Administration, Syracuse, N.Y., May 6, 1976.

3. On using a system of relationships in achieving an organizational goal, also see C. W. Churchman. 1968. *The Systems Approach.* New York: Dell.

4. Proposition 13 was intended to

1. limit property taxes to 1 percent of the full cash value of the property;
2. require counties to levy the 1 percent tax and apportion it according to law to the districts within the counties;
3. establish as a basis for full cash value of a property the county assessor's appraised value as of March 1, 1975 (property subsequently sold or improved would be reappraised);
4. limit increases in fair market value to 2 percent per annum; and
5. require an affirmative vote of two-thirds of the qualified electors of any respective taxing entity to raise city, county, or special-district taxes.

For a detailed discussion of the background and implications of Proposition 13, see J. S. Jun, *Public Administration: Design and Problem Solving*, pp. 202–05.

The rational-economic model generally involves seven steps for the rational actors to take:

1. define the problem to be solved;
2. define goals and objectives to be achieved;
3. search for all information relevant to the goals and objectives sought;
4. analyze and organize information into meaningful categories;
5. find the alternative courses of action that are most economical and and efficient;
6. evaluate and compare perceived consequences of each alternative; and
7. select the best or preferred choice, given the goals and objectives.

For similar steps in rational design, see H. Simon, *Administrative Behavior*, 2d ed. (New York: Macmillan, 1961); E. S. Quade, *Analysis for Public Decisions,*

2nd ed. (New York: Elsevier, 1982); G. T. Allison, *Essence of Decision* (Boston: Little, Brown, 1971).

6. Considering these and other criticisms, C. Lindblom formulated "disjointed incrementalism" (see: "The Science of Muddling Through," *Public Administration Review*, vol. 19 (Spring 1959): 79–88). He considers incrementalism a strategy used for problem solving, decision making, policy design, and analysis. The essence of the incremental strategy is as follows:

1. Emphasis is on small changes within already existing structures. Such changes may be repetitive, something that has been done again and again; or nonrepretitive, small steps in a sequence that is indefinite.
2. Analysis of policies involves minor adjustments to the status quo. The only alternatives compared and considered are those similar to existing policy.
3. Alternative and their expected results differ from each other only Incrementally.
4. Means and ends are not separable. The ends/means dichotomy in rational problem solving is considered limited or unjustifiable.
5. Incremental policies or decisions are reactive, subjective, and give a strong consideration to values.
6. The future is thought to be an extension of past policies and Experiences, to be approached slowly and cautiously.

CHAPTER 5

1. Robert Peel, a wealthy member of Britain's Parliament in 1829, was influential in passing the Metropolitan Police Act. He emphasized this principle: "The police are the public, and the public are the police." His belief was that police were, first and foremost, members of the larger society.

2. Because meeting participants came from different cities, the meeting was shorter than the two-and-one-half-day conference that is the usual length of future search conferences.

3. See *The Economist* (August 23, 2003): pp. 19–20.

4. U.S. Conference of Mayors,—1998 (December 1998).

5. See Catherine Burke. *Innovation and Public Policy* (Lexington, Mass.: Lexington Books, 1979), especially chapters 2, 4, and 11. Burke's chapters illustrate the social design process of the transit system.

6. The summary discussion of the Clinton health care plan and its demise was largely derived from issues of the *New York Times* between August 29, 1994, and September 27, 1994.

CHAPTER 6

1. Talcott Parsons states the following: "A social system is only one of three aspects of the structuring of a completely concrete system of social action. The other two are the personality systems of the individual actors and the cultural system which is built into their action. Each of the three must be considered to be an independent focus of the organization of the elements of the action system in the sense that no one of them is theoretically reducible to terms of one or a combination of the other two" (*The Social System* [New York: Free Press, 1951], p. 6).

2. Alasdair MacIntyre in his book *After Virtue* (1984) discusses the two competing grounds for making moral judgments: rational, or principled, versus emotive arguments. Although the former emphasizes the universality of principles, the latter is based on the premise of subjective and individual preferences in making a moral judgment.

3. The discussion of praxis and change is based on my previous publications: J. S. Jun. 1994. "On Administrative Praxis" *Administrative Theory and Praxis*, vol. 16, no. 2, pp. 201–07; J. S. Jun and R. VrMeer. "Aesthetics and Changing Human Organizations" in J. S. Jun. *Philosophy of Administration* (Seoul: Daeyoungmoonhwa International, 1994), pp. 206–25.

4. Many articles published in the journal of *Administrative Theory and Praxis* deal with the problems and concepts of human relationships, actions, discourse, reflexivity, and governance, relating to the interpretive and critical theory perspectives.

5. The idea of sensemaking is developed by K. E. Weick. *Sensemaking in Organizations* (Thousand Oaks, Calif.: Sage, 1995); Barbara Czarniawska discusses the appeal of functionalism (or a functionalist device) to engineers in her book *A Tale of Three Cities* (Oxford: Oxford University Press, 2002).

6. To learn about the future search conference method, see: M. Emery, *The Search Conference: A Powerful Method for Planning Organizational Change and Community Action* (San Francisco: Jossey-Bass, 1996); M. R. Weisbord and S. Janoff, *Future Search* (San Francisco: Berrett-Koehler, 1995).

CHAPTER 7

1. To understand institutions, society, and the world, people need to change their minds (human consciousness). I recommend two stimulating books: H. Smith, *Beyond the Post-Modern Mind* (New York: Crossroad, 1982); W. Harman, *Gobal Mind Change* (San Francisco: Berrett-Koehler, 1998).

2. On the social contract theory of Thomas Hobbes and John Locke, see: Thomas Hobbes, *Leviathan* (1651; reprint, London: Penguin, 1968); John

Locke, *An Essay concerning Human Understanding* (1690; reprint. Oxford: Clarendon, 1957).

3. Samuel Huntington states, "The West, and especially the United States, which has always been a missionary nation, believe that the non-Western peoples should commit themselves to the Western values of democracy, free markets, limited government, human rights, individualism, the rule of law, and should embody these values in their institutions." As a result, the United States is likely to continue to have "difficulties in defending its interest against those of non-Western societies." Samuel P. Huntington, *The Clash of Civilizations and the Remaking of World Order* (New York: Touchtone Book, 1996), p. 184.

4. Although Islam has influenced many regions in the East, I am not able to discuss it here largely because of my lack of knowledge. Islam as a religion focuses more on a "personal submission to God as Islam" than submission to rituals, beliefs, and customs (Turner, 1994).

5. Virtues for self-cultivation include *jen* (benevolence) and *li* (propriety). *Jen* is a personal quality that comes from a person's inwardness: it is not a product of biological, social, or political forces. It is linked with "the self-reviving, self-perfecting, and self-fulfilling process of an individual." *Li* is propriety, good manners, politeness, ceremony, worship, the external exemplification of eternal principles, the feeling of respect and reverence. According to Tu Wei-ming, the function of *li* is to act as the externalization of *jen* in a specific social context and to actualize *jen* so that the person can be of use to society in the real world. See Wei-ming Tu, *Confucian Thought: Selfhood as Creative Transformation* (Albany: State University of New York Press, 1985).

6. I did not go into the discussion of the self and sociality in the East because Eastern thought, such as Confucianism, Taoism, Hinduism, and Buddhism, does not put much emphasis on dialogue but puts a high value on relationships, selflessness, no boundaries, compassion, humility, restraints, and virtue. Moreover, Western views of sociality stress the importance of communication, dialogue, sharing, and learning.

7. For further readings on interpersonal relationships, see Chris Argyris's books *Interpersonal Competence and Organizational Effectiveness* (Homewood, Ill.: Dorsey, 1962) and *Integrating the Individual and the Organization* (New York: Wiley, 1964); Carl R. Rogers, *On Becoming a Person: A Therapist's View of Psychotherapy* (Boston: Houghton Mifflin, 1961) and *Carl Rogers on Personal Power* (New York: Dell, 1977). Argyris is much more directive in integrating the individual and organization, but Rogers as a humanistic psychologist is more nondirective in his approach to interpersonal relationships.

8. I deliberately avoid a discussion of the self in the transcendental tradition, as argued by Immanuel Kant and Edmund Husserl, because their philosophical positions relate more closely to the problem of consciousness and the critique of science.

CHAPTER 8

1. Examples from Irving Janis's *Victims of Groupthink* and from the Richard Nixon presidential administration between 1969 and 1974 indicate the negative consequences of unquestioned loyalty.

2. I am not implying that laws are easier to implement than a code of ethics. Because of the broad content and ambiguity in legalistic text, laws also invite different interpretations. Many professional associations have a code of ethics, but codes of ethics are guidelines for professional conduct.

3. In *Responsibility as Paradox*, Michael Harmon critically reviews the decision of Horatio Hornblower, commander of H.M. Sloop *Hotspur*, a British ship, in handling his steward, Doughty, who was charged with mutiny and striking a superior officer. Harmon says that by making his irresponsible sentimental decision to let Doughty escape, "Hornblower failed at genuine self-reflexive understanding, but he succeeded in spite of himself in acting on humane instinct."

4. There have been a number of criticisms of the Confucians emphasis on family structure and authority relationships, particularly how it is extended to the relationship between the ruler and the ruled. Paternalistic relationships are emphasized by autocratic leaders in Asia, who demand loyalty and social obligations to the government. In his book *The Country Can Survive When Confucius Dies*, K. I. Kim forcefully argues that many of Korea's social and political problems originate in Confucian tradition. For other discussions, see A. C. Graham, *Disputers of the Tao* (LaSalle, Ill.: Open Court, 1989).

CHAPTER 9

1. The term *civil society organizations* (CSO)s) is used by the UN Public Administration Development Program.

2. This case study is a revised article published by J. S. Jun, "New Governance in Civil Society: Changing Responsibility of Public Administration," in *Rethinking Administrative Theory: The Challenge of the New Century*, ed. J. S. Jun (Westport, Conn.: Praeger, 2002), pp. 295–98.

3. The strategies for making governance and social construction effective are discussed in chapter 10.

CHAPTER 10

1. Because bureaucracy is designed to promote organizational efficiency, it appears inevitably to be in an "antagonistic encounter" with the characteristics of democracy. Dwight Waldo points out that "the principle of hierarchy

stands against the principle of equality and the principle of liberty stands against discipline, precision, and rules" (1978, p. 7).

2. For the philosophical argument of nondiscursive experience, see R. Shusterman, *Practicing Philosophy: Pragmatism and the Philosophical Life* (New York: Routledge, 1997), chapter 6.

3. Elizabeth Jensen, a martial arts instructor and a former student of mine, provided insightful guidance regarding the application of Taoism to martial arts and to the life perspective.

REFERENCES

Abel, C. F., and Sementelli, A. J. (2003). *Evolutionary Critical Theory and Its Role in Public Affairs*. Armonk, N.Y.: M. E. Sharpe.

Ackoff, R. (1978). *The Art of Problem Solving*. New York: Wiley.

Adams, G. B., and Balfour, D. L. (1998). *Unmasking Administrative Evil*. Thousand Oaks, Calif.: Sage.

Adorno, T. W., and Horkheimer, M. (1979). *Dialectic of Enlightenment*. Trans. J. Cumming. London: NLB.

Albrow, M. (1996). *The Global Age*. Stanford, Calif.: Stanford University Press.

Alexander, J. C. (1988). *Action and Its Environments: Toward a New Synthesis*. New York: Columbia University Press.

Alexander, J. C. (1982). *Positivism, Presuppositions, and Current Controversies*. Vol. 1. Berkeley: University of California Press.

Allan, G. (1990). *The Realization of the Future*. Albany: State University of New York Press.

Allan, K. (1998). *The Meaning of Culture: Moving the Postmodern Critique Forward*. Westport, Conn.: Praeger.

Allen, D. (Ed.). (1997a). *Culture and Self*. Boulder, Colo.: Westview.

Allen, D. (1997b). "Social Constructions of Self: Some Asian, Marxist, and Feminist Critiques of Dominant Western Views of Self." In *Culture and Self: Philosophical and Religious Perspectives, East and West*. Boulder, Colo.: Westview, pp. 3–26.

Allison, G. T. (1971). *Essence of Decision: Explaining the Cuban Missile Crisis*. Boston: Little Brown.

Anderson, W. T. (1997). "Governance Tomorrow: Global or Local? Corporate or Citizen?" *The Futurist*. (May-June), pp. 18–19.

Arendt, H. (1958). *The Human Condition*. Chicago: University of Chicago Press.

Arendt, H. (1964). *Eichmann in Jerusalem*. (Rev. ed.). New York: Viking.

Arendt, H. (1971). "Thinking and Moral Considerations." *Social Research*. Vol. 38, no. 3 (Autumn), pp. 417–46.

Argyris, C. (1962). *Interpersonal Competence and Organizational Effectiveness*. Homewood: Dorsey.

Argyris, C. (1964). *Integrating the Individual and the Organization*. New York: Wiley.

Argyris, C. (1968). "Conditions for Competence Acquisition and Therapy." *The Journal of Applied Behavioral Science*. Vol. 4, no. 2, pp. 1–19.

Argyris, C., Putnam, R., and Smith, D. M. (1985). *Action Science: Concepts, Methods, and Skills for Research and Intervention*. San Francisco: Jossey-Bass.

Argyris, C., and Schön, D. (1978). *Organizatonal Learning: A Theory of Action Perspective*. Reading, Mass.: Addison-Wesley.

Atkinson, J. M., and Heritage, J. (Eds). (1984). *Structures of Social Action: Studies in Conversation Analysis*. Cambridge: Cambridge University Press.

Bakhtin, M. M. (1981). *The Dialogic Imagination: Four Essays by M. M. Bakhtin*. Trans. M. Holquist, ed. C. Emerson and M. Holquist. Austin: University of Texas Press.

Barber, B. (1984). *Strong Democracy: Participatory Politics for a New Age*. Berkeley: University of California Press.

Barber, B. R. (1999). "Clansmen, Consumers, and Citizens: Three Takes on Civil Society." In R. K. Fullinwider (Ed.), *Society, Democracy, and Civic Renewal*. Oxford: Rowman & Littlefield.

Barber, M. D. (1988). *Social Typifications and the Elusive Other: The Place of Sociology of Knowledge in Alfred Schutz's Phenomenology*. London: Bicknell University Press.

Baudrillard, Jean. (1975). *The Mirror of Production*. St. Louis: Telos.

Baudrillard, Jean. (1983). *Simulations*. New York: Semiotext(e).

Bauman, Z. (1993). *Postmodern Ethics*. Cambridge, Mass.: Blackwell.

Baxter, L. A., and B. M. Montgomery. (1996). *Relating: Dialogues and Dialectics*. New York: Guilford.

Beck, U. (1994). "Towards a Theory of Reflexive Modernization." In U. Beck, A. Giddens, and S. Lash (Eds.), *Reflexive Modernization: Politics, Tradition and Aesthetics in the Modem Social Order*. Stanford: Stanford University Press. 1–55.

Becker, H. S., and McCall, M. M. (1990). *Symbolic Interaction and Cultural Studies*. Chicago: University of Chicago Press.

Bellah, R., Madsen, R., Sullivan, W., Swidler, A., and Tipton, S. M. (1985). *Habits of the Heart*. Berkeley: University of California Press.

Benson, J. K. (1977). "Organizations: A Dialectical View." *Administrative Science Quarterly*. Vol. 22, no. 1, pp. 1–21.

Benveniste, G. (1972). *The Politics of Expertise*. Berkeley: Glendessary.

Berger, P. L., and Luckmann, T. (1967). *The Social Construction of Reality*. Garden City: Doubleday.

Bernstein, R. J. (1971). *Praxis and Action*. Philadelphia: University of Pennsylvania Press.

Bernstein, R. J. (1983). *Beyond Objectivism and Relativism: Science, Hermeneutics, and Praxis*. Philadelphia: University of Pennsylvania Press.

Bernstein, R., and Munro, R. H. (1997). *The Coming Conflict with China.* New York: Vintage Books.

Bezold, C. (Ed.). (1978). *Anticipatory Democracy: People in the Politics of the Future.* New York: Vintage.

Birenbaum, A. (1997). *Managed Care.* Westport, Conn.: Praeger.

Blumer, H. (1969). *Symbolic Interactionism: Perspectigve and Method.* Englewood Cliffs, N.J.: Prentice-Hall.

Bogason, P. (2002). "Postmodern Public Administration Research: American and Northwest European Perspectives." In J. S. Jun. (Ed.), *Rethinking Administrative Theory: The Challenge of the New Century.* Westport, Conn.: Praeger, pp. 53–74.

Bohman, J. (1996). *Public Deliberation: Pluralism, Complexity, and Democracy.* Cambridge, MA: MIT Press.

Bohman, J., and W. Rehg. (Eds.). (1997). *Deliberative Democracy.* Cambridge, MA: MIT Press.

Bolman L. G., and Deal, T. E. (1997). *Reframing Organizations: Artistry, Choice, and Leadership.* Francisco: Jossey-Bass.

Bosserman, P. (1968). *Dialectical Sociology: An Analysis of the Sociology of Georges Gurvitch.* Boston: Sargent.

Boulding, E. (1990). "Building a Global Civic Culture." *Development.* 2:39.

Bourdieu, P. (1990). *In Other Words: Essays toward a Reflexive Sociology.* Stanford: Stanford Univeristy Press.

Bourdieu, P., and Wacquant, L. J. D. (1992). *An Invitation to Reflexive Sociology.* Chicago: University of Chicago Press.

Bowie, M. (1991). *Lacan.* Cabridge, Mass.: Harvard University Press.

Box, R. C. (1998). *Citizen Governance: Leading American Communities into the 21st Century.* Thousand Oaks, Calif.: Sage.

Boxill, B. (1998). "Majoritarian Democracy and Cultural Minorities." In A. M. Melzer, J. Weinberger, and M. R. Zinman (Eds.), *Multiculturalism and American Democracy.* Lawrence: University Press of Kansas.

Boyer, B. D. (1973). *Cities Destroyed for Cash: The Scandal at FHA.* Chicago: Follet.

Braithwaite, V. (1998). "Institutionalizing Distrust, Enculturating Trust." In V. Braithwaite and M. Levi (Eds.), *Trust and Governance.* New York: Sage Foundation, pp. 343–44.

Braithwaite, V., and M. Levi. (Eds.). (1998). *Trust and Governance.* New York: Sage Foundation.

Braybrooke, D., and Lindblom, C. E. (1963). *A Strategy of Decision: Policy Evaluation as a Social Process.* New York: Free Press.

Brecher, J., Costello, T., and Smith, B. (2000). *Globalizaztion from Below.* Cambridge, Mass.: South End.

Buber, M. (1958). *I and Thou.* Trans. R. G. Smith. New York: Scribner's Sons.

Bunting, H. (1996). "A Single True Morality? The Challenge of Relativism." In D. Archard (Ed.), *Philosophy and Pluralism*. Cambridge: Cambridge University Press, pp. 73–85.

Burbach, R., Nunez, O., and Kagarlitsky, B. (1997). *Globalization and Its Discontents*. London: Pluto.

Burke, C. (1979). *Innovation and Public Policy*. Lexington, Mass.: Lexington Books.

Burrell, G., and Morgan, G. (1979). *Sociological Paradigms and Organizational Analysis*. London:

Heinemann.

Caldwell, L. K. (1975). Managing the Transition to Post-modern Society. *Public Administration Review* 35(6): 567–72.

Callinicos, A. (1990). *Against Postmodernism: A Marxist Critique*. New York: St. Martin's.

Canovan, M. (1992). *Hannah Arendt: A Reinterpretation of Her Political Thought*. Cambridge: Cambridge University Press.

Capra, F. (1975). *The Tao of Physics*. Berkeley: Shambhala.

Carnevale, D. G. (1995). *Trustworthy Government: Leadership and Management Strategies for Building Trust and High Peformance*. San Francisco: Jossey-Bass.

Carr, D. (1999). *The Paradox of Subjectivity: The Self in the Transcendental Tradition*. Oxford: Oxford University Press.

Carroll, T. F. (1992). *Intermediary NGOs: The Supporting Link in Grassroots Development*. West Hartford, CT: Kumarian.

Cavanagh, J. et al. (2002). *Alternative to Economic Globalization: A Better Wold Is Possible*. The International Forum on Globalization. San Francisco: Berrett-Koehler.

Chambers, S. (1996). *Reasonable Democracy: Jürgen Habermas and the Politics of Discourse*. Ithaca, N. Y.: Cornell University Press.

Cheng, C. Y. (1991). *New Dimensions of Confucian and Neo-Confucian Philosophy*. Albany: State University of New York Press.

Chin, R., and Benne, K. D. (1984). "General Strategies for Effecting Changes in Human Systems." In W. G. Bennis, K. D. Benne, and R. Chin. (Eds.), *The Planning of Change*. 4th ed. New York: Holt, Rinehart, and Winston, pp. 22–45.

Chong, K. C., S. H. Tan, and C. L. Ten. (Eds.). (2003). *The Moral Circle and the Self: Chinese and Western Approaches*. Chicago: Open Court.

Christiano, T. (1997). "The Significance of Public Deliberation," in J. Bohman and W. Reheg, (Eds.). *Deliberative Democracy: Essays on Reason and Politics*. Cambridge, Mass.: MIT Press, pp. 243–77.

Christopher, R. C. (1983). *The Japanese Mind: The Goliath Explained*. Tokyo: Tuttle.

Churchman, C. W. (1968). *The Systems Approach*. New York: Dell.

Churchman, C. W. (1971). *The Design of Inquiring Systems: Basic Concepts and Organization*. New York: Basic Books.

Clark, J. (1991). *Democratizing Development: The Role of Voluntary Organizations*. West Hartport, Conn.: Kumarian.

Cohen, H. (1981). *Connections: Understanding Social Relationships*. Ames: Iowa State University Press.

Collin, F. (1997). *Social Reality*. London: Routledge.

Cook, K. S., Hardin, R., and Margaret, L. (2005). *Cooperation without Trust?* New York: Sage Foundation.

Cooper, T. L. (1990, 3rd ed.) and (1998, 4th ed.). *The Responsible Administrator: An Approach to Ethics for the Administrative Role*. San Francisco: Jossey-Bass.

Covey, S. R. (1997). *The 7 Habits of Highly Effective Families*. New York: Covey-Golden Books.

Cox, T., Jr. (1993). *Cultural Diversity in Organizations: Theory, Research, and Practice*. San Francisco: Berrett-Koehler.

Crocker, D. A. (1977). "Markovic's Concept of Praxis as Norm." *Inquiry*. Vol. 20, pp. 1–43.

Cunliffe, A., and Jun, J. S. (2005). "The Need for Refelexivity in Public Administration." *Administration and Society* (March).

Czarniawska-Joerges, B. (1992). *Exploring Complex Organizations: A Cultural Perspective*. Newbury Park, Calif.: Sage.

Czarniawska-Joerges, B. (2002). *A Tale of Three Cities or the Glocalization of City Management*. Oxford: Oxford University Press.

Czempiel, E. (1992). "Governance and Democratization." In J. Rosenau, and E. Czempiel (Eds.), *Governance without Government: Order and Change in World Politics*, pp. 250–71.

Dagger, R. (1997). *Civic Virtues: Rights, Citizenship, and Republican Liberalism*. Oxford: Oxford University Press.

Danaher, K. (Ed.). (1996). *Corporations Are Gonna Get Your Mama: Globalization and the Downsizing of the American Dream*. Monroe, ME: Common Courage Press.

Dasgupta, P., and Serageldin, I. (Eds.). (1999). *Social Capital: A Multifaceted Perspective*. Washington, D.C.: World Bank.

Deetz, S. A. (1992). *Democracy in an Age of Corporate Colonization: Developments in Communication and the Politics of Everyday Life*. Albany: State University of New York Press.

Denhardt, R. B. (1981). *The Shadow of Organization*. Lawrence: University Press of Kansas.

Denhardt, R. B. (1986). "Action Skills in Public Administration Education." In R. Denhardt and L. Jennings, *Renewing Public Administration*. Columbus: University of Missouri Press.

Denhardt, R. B. (1993). *The Pursuit of Significance*. Belmont, Calif.: Wadsworth.

Denhardt, J., and Denhardt, R. B. (2003). *The New Public Service: Serving, Not Steering*. Armonk, N.Y.: Sharpe.

De Oliveira, M. D., and Tandon, R. (Eds.). (1994). *Citizens Strengthening Civil Society*. Washington, D.C.: CIVICUS (World Alliance for Citizen Participation).

Derrida, J. (1970). "Structure, Sign, and Play in the Discourse of the Human Sciences." In R. Macksby and E. Donato (Eds.), *The Languages of Criticism and the Sciences of Man*. Baltimore: Johns Hopkins University Press, pp. 247–65.

Derrida, J. (1973). *Speech and Phenomena*. Trans. D. B. Allison. Evanston, Ill.: Northwestern University Press.

Derrida, J. (1976). *Grammatology*. Trans. G. Spivak. Baltimore: Johns Hopkins University Press.

Derrida, J. (1978). *Writing and Difference*. London: Routledge and Kegan Paul.

Derrida, J. (1988). *The Ear of the Other*. New York: Schocken.

Derrida, J. (1981). *Dissemination*. Chicago: University of Chicago Press.

Dewey, J. (1916). *Democracy and Education*. New York: Macmillan.

Dewey, J. (1929). *The Quest for Certainty: A Study of the Relation of Knowledge and Action*. New York: Capricorn Books.

Dewey, J. (1934). *Art as Experience*. New York: Minton, Balch.

Dewey, J. (1963). *Liberalism and Social Action*. New York: Putnam's Sons. (Original work published in 1935).

Dickens, D. R., and Fontana, A. (Eds.). *Postmodernism and Social Inquiry*. New York: Guilford.

Dilthey, W. (1961). *Pattern and Meaning in History: Thoughts on History and Society*. Edited with an introduction by H.P. Rickman. London: Allen and Unwin.

Dilthey, W. (1977). *Descriptive Psychology and Historical Understanding*. Hague: Nijhoff.

Dilthey, W. (1996). *Hermeneutics and the Study of History*. Edited with an introduction by R. A. Makkreel and F. Rodi. Princeton, N.J.: Princeton University Press.

Douglas, J. D. (Ed.). (1970). *Understanding Everyday Life*. Chicago: Aldine.

Dreyfus, H. (Ed.). (1982). *Husserl, Intentionality, and Cognitive Science*. Cambridge, Mass. MIT Press.

Dryzek, J. S. (1990). *Discursive Democracy: Politics, Policy, and Political Science*. Cambridge: Cambridge University Press.

Dryzek, J. S. (2000). *Deliberative Democracy and Beyond: Liberals, Critics, Contestations*. Oxford: Oxford University Press.

Durkheim, E. (1938). *The Rules of Sociological Method*. Glencoe, Ill.: Free Press.

Edwards, D. (1973). *Creating a New World Politics.* New York: McKay, 1973.

Ehrenberg, J. (1999). *Civil Society: The Critical History of an Idea.* New York: New York University Press.

Ellul, J. (1964). *The Technological Society.* New York: Vintage Books.

Elster, J., (Ed.) (1998). *Deliberative Democracy.* Cambridge, U.K.: Cambridge University Press.

Etzioni, A. (1993). *The Spirit of Community: Rights, Responsibilities, and the Communitarian Agenda.* New York: Crown.

Etzioni, A. (1995). *New Communication Thinking: Persons, Virtues, Institutions and Communities.* Charlottesville: University Press of Virginia.

Farmer, D. J. (1995). *The Language of Public Administration: Bureaucracy, Modernity, and Postmodernity.* Tuscaloosa: University of Alabama Press.

Farmer, D. J. (Ed.). (1998). *Papers on the Art of Anti-Administration.* Burke, VA.: Chatelaine.

Feibleman, J. K. (1976). *Understanding Oriental Philosophy.* New York: New American Library.

Fischer, F., and Forester, J. (Eds.) (1993). *The Argumentative Turn in Policy Analysis and Planning.* Durham, N.C.: Duke University Press.

Fisher, F. (1980). *Politics, Values, and Public Policy: The Problem of Methodology.* Boulder, Colo.: Westview.

Fisher, J. (1998). *Nongovernments: NGOs and the Political Development of the Third World.* West Hartford, Conn.: Kumarian.

Forber, D. (1975). *Hume's Philosophical Politics.* Cambridge, Mass.: Cambridge University Press.

Forester, J. (1985). (Ed.). *Critical Theory and Public Life.* Cambridge, Mass.: MIT Press.

Forester, J. (1999). *The Deliberative Practitioner.* Cambridge, Mass.: MIT Press.

Foster, P. M. (1976). "The Theory and Practice of Action Research in Work Organizations." In A. W. Clark (Ed.), *Experimenting with Organizational Life: The Action Research Approach.* London: Plenum, pp. 64–65.

Foucault, M. (1970). *The Order of Things: An Archaeology of the Human Sciences.* New York: Vintage.

Foucault, M. (1980). *Power/Knowledge.* Ed. and trans. C. Gordon. New York: Pantheon.

Foucault, M. (1982). *The Archaeology of Knowledge.* New York: Pantheon.

Foucault, M. (1984). *The Foucault Reader.* New York: Pantheon.

Foweraker, J., and Craig, A. L. (1990). *Popular Movements and Political Change in Mexico.* Boulder, Colo.: Rienner.

Fox, C. J., and Miller, H. T. (1996). *Postmodern Public Administration: Toward Discourse.* Thousand Oaks, Calif.: Sage.

Freire, P. (1970). *Pedagogy of the Oppressed.* New York: A Continuum Book, Seabury.

Freire, P. (1973). *Education for Critical Consciousness*. New York: A Continuum Book, Seabury.

Freund, J. (1968). *The Sociology of Max Weber*. New York: Pantheon Books.

Friedmann, J. (1973). *Retracking America: A Theory of Transactive Planning*. Garden City, N.Y.: Doubleday.

Friedmann, J. (1987). *Planning in the Public Domain: From Knowledge to Action*. Princeton, N.J.: Princeton University Press.

Fukuyama, F. (1995). *Trust: The Social Virtues and the Creation of Prosperity*. New York: Free Press.

Gabel, J. (1975). *False Consciousness: An Essay on Reification*. Trans. M. A. Thompson and K. A. Thompson. New York: Harper & Row.

Gadamer, H-G. (1976). *Philosophical Hermeneutics*. Trans. and ed. D. E. Linge. Berkeley: University of California Press.

Gadamer, H-G. (1980). *Dialogue and Dialectic: Eight Hermeneutical Studies on Plato*. Trans. P. Christoper Smith. New Haven, Conn.: Yale University Press.

Gadamer, H-G. (1989). *Truth and Method*. 2nd edition. Trans. J. Weimsheimer and D. G. Marshall. London: Sheed & Ward.

Galston, W. (1991). *Liberal Purposes: Goods, Virtues, and Duties in the Liberal State*. Cambridge: Cambridge University Press.

Gardner, N. (1974). "Action Training and Research: Something Old and Something New." *Public Administration Review*. Vol. 34, no. 2 (March/April), pp. 108–15.

Garfinkel, H. (1967). *Studies in Ethnomethodology*. Englewood Cliffs, N.J.: Prentice Hall.

Gawthrop, L. C. (1984). "Civis, Civitas, and Civilitas: A New Focus for the Year 2000." *Public Administration Review*. Vol. 44 (March).

Geertz, C. (1973). *The Inerpretation of Culture*. New York: Basic Books.

Geertz, C. (1983). *Local Knowledge: Further Essays in Interpretive Anthropology*. New York: Basic Books.

Gergen, K. J. (1999). *An Invitation to Social Construction*. Thousand Oaks, Calif.: Sage.

Gerth, H. H., and Mills, C. W. (1946). *From Max Weber: Essays in Sociology*. New York: Oxford University Press.

Gibb, J. R. (1978). *Trust: A New View of Personal and Organizational Development*. Cardiff, Calif.: Omicron.

Giddens, A. (1990). *Then Consequences of Modernity*. Stanford, Calif.: Stanford University Press.

Giddens, A. (1998). *The Third Way*. Cambridge: Polity.

Glazer, Nathan. (1997). *We Are All Multiculturalists Now*. Cambridge, Mass.: Harvard University Press.

Goldman, R., and Papson, S. (1994). "The Postmodernism That Failed." In

D. Dickens and A. Fontana (Eds.). *Postmodernism and Social Inquiry*. New York: Guilford, pp. 224–53.

Goldstein, H. (1979). "Improving Policing: A Problem-Oriented Approach." *Crime and Delinquency*. Vol. 25: pp. 241–43.

Goldstein, H. (1990). *Problem-Oriented Policing*. New York: McGraw-Hill.

Golembiewski, R. T. (1972). *Renewing Organizations: The Laboratory Approach to Planned Change*. Itasca: Peacock.

Goodsell, C. T. (1983). *The Case for Bureaucracy: A Public Administration Polemic*. Chatham, N.J.: Chatham House.

Gouinlock, J. (1978). "Dewey's Theory of Moral Deliberation." *Ethics*. Vol. 88, no. 3, pp. 218–28.

Gouinlock, J. (1986). *Excellence in Public Discourse: John Stuart Mill, John Dewey, and Social Intelligence*. New York: Columbia University Press.

Gouldner, A. W. (1970). *The Coming Crisis of Western Sociology*. New York: Basic Books.

Greenwood, D. J., and Levin. M. (1998). *Introduction to Action Research: Social Research for Social Change*. Thousand Oaks, Calif.: Sage.

Gross, R., and Osterman, P. (Eds.). (1971). *Individualism: Man in Modern Society*. New York: Dell.

Gunnell, J. G. (1987). *Political Theory: Tradition and Interpretation*. Lanham, NY.: University Press of America.

Gutmann, A. (1987). *Democratic Education*. Princeton, NJ: Princeton University Press.

Gutmann, A., and Thompson, D. (1996). *Democracy and Disagreement*. Cambridge, MA: Harvard University Press.

Gutmann, A., and Thompson, D. (2004). *Why Deliberative Democracy?* Princeton, N.J.: Princeton University Press.

Haber, H. F. (1994). *Beyond Postmodern Politics*. London: Routledge.

Habermas, J. (1971). *Knowledge and Interests*. Trans. J. J. Shapiro. Boston: Beacon.

Habermas, J. (1973). *Theory and Practice*. Boston: Beacon.

Habermas, J. (1975). *Legitimation Crisis*. Boston: Beacon.

Habermas, J. (1984). *The Theory of Communicative Action: Reason and the Rationalizaton of Society*. Vol. 1. Trans. T. McCarthy. Boston: Beacon.

Habermas, J. (1987). *The Philosophical Discourse of Modernity*. Boston: MIT.

Habermas, J. (1990). *Moral Consciousness and Communicative Action*. Trans. C. Lenhardt and S. W. Nicholsen. Cambridge, MA: MIT Press.

Habermas, J. (1998). *Between Facts and Norms: Contributions to a Discourse Theory of Law and Democracy*. Trans. W. Rehg. Cambridge, Mass.: MIT Press.

Habermas, J. (2003). *The Future of Human Nature*. Cambridge, UK: Polity.

Hacker, A. (1961). *Political Theory: Philosophy, Ideology, Science*. New York: Macmillan.

Hajer, M. A., and Wagenaar, H. (Eds.). (2003). *Deliberative Policy Analysis: Understanding Governance in the Network Society.* Cambridge: Cambridge University Press.

Hall, D. L., and Ames, R. T. (1987). *Thinking through Confucius.* Albany: State University of New York Press.

Handy, C. (1994). *The Age of Paradox.* Boston, Mass.: Harvard Business School Press.

Hardin, R. (1996). "Trustworthiness." *Ethics.* Vol. 107 (October), pp. 26–42.

Hardin, R. (1998). "Trust in Government." In V. Braithwaite and M. Levi (Eds.), *Trust and Governance.* New York: Sage Foundation.

Hardin, R. (2004). *Trust and Trustworthiness.* New York: Sage Foundation.

Harman, W. W. (1974). "The Coming Transformation in Our View of Knowledge." *The Futurist.* 8(2).

Harmon, M. M. (1981). *Action Theory for Public Administration.* New York: Longman.

Harmon, M. M. (1995). *Responsibility as Paradox.* Thousand Oaks, Calif.: Sage.

Harmon, M. M., and Mayer, R. T. (1986). *Organization Theory for Public Administration.* Boston: Little, Brown.

Hassard, J., and Parker, M. (Eds.). *Postmodernism and Organizations.* Newbury Park, Calif.: Sage.

Hayes, M. (1992). *Incrementalism and Public Policy.* New York: Longman.

Hegel, G. W. F. (1952). *Hegel and the Human Spirit: A Translation of the Jena Lectures on Philosophy of Spirit* (1805–1806) *with Commentary.* Trans. L. Rauch. Detroit: Wayne State University Press.

Hegel, G. W. F., (1967). *The Phenomenology of Mind.* New York: Harper-Torch Books.

Heidegger, M. (1962). *Being and Time.* Trans. J. Macquarrie and E. Robinson. New York: Harper & Row.

Heirich, M. (1998). *Rethinking Health Care: Innovation and Change in America.* Boulder, Colo.: Westview.

Henderson, H. (1996). *Building a Win-Win World: Life beyond Global Economic Warfare.* San Francisco: Berrett-Koehler.

Heyzer, N. (1995). Toward New Government-NGO Relations for Sustainable and People-Centered Development. In *Government-NGO Relations in Asia.* Ed. N. Heyzer, J. V. Riker, and A. Quizon. New York: St. Martin's.

Hiley, D. R., Bohman, J. F., and Shusterman, R. (Eds.). (1991). *The Interpretive Turn: Philosophy, Science, Culture.* Ithaca, N.Y.: Cornell University Press.

Hill, D. M. (1994). *Citizens and Cities: Urban Policy in the 1990s.* New York: Harvester.

Hirshman, Albert O. 1970. *Exit, Voice, and Loyalty*. Cambridge, Mass.: Harvard University Press.

His Honiness the Dalai Lama. (1999). *Ethics for the New Millennium*. New York: Riverhead Books.

Hobbes, T. (1946). *The Leviathan*. Edited with an introduction by M. Oakeshott. Oxford: Blackwell.

Holzner, B. (1968). *Reality Construction in Society*. Cambridge, Mass. Schenkman.

Howard, M. W. (1992). "The Self, Difference, and Democratic Theory." *Contemporary Philosophy*. Vol. 14, no. 1, pp. 6–9.

Howell, J., and Pearce, J. (2001). *Civil Society and Development: A Critical Exploration*. Boulder, Colo.: Rienner.

Hoy, D. (1985). "Derrida." In Q. Skinner (Ed.), *The Return of Grand Theory in the Human Sciences*. Cambridge: Cambridge, U.K.: University Press, pp. 41–64.

Hume, D. (1975/1777). *Philosophical Essays concerning Human Understanding*. (Reprint), New York: Clarendon.

Hummel, R. P. (1994). 4th ed. *The Bureaucratic Experience: A Critique of Life in the Modern Organization*. New York: St. Martin's.

Husserl, E. (1962). *Ideas: General Introduction to Pure Phenomenology*. Trans. W. R. Boyce Gibson. New York: Collier Books.

Husserl, E. (1970). *Logical Investigations*. 2 vols. Trans. J. N. Findlay. New York: Humanities.

Husserl, E. (1973). *Experience and Judgment*. Trans. J. S. Churchill and K. Americks. Evanston, Ill.: Northwestern University Press.

Husserl, E. (1975). *Introduction to the Logical Investigations. Draft of a Preface to the Logical Investigations*. (Ed.) E. Fink. Trans. P. J. Bossert and C. H. Peters. The Hague: Nijhoff.

Ingram, D. (1987). *Habermas and the Dialectic of Reason*. New Haven, Conn.: Yale University Press.

Issac, J. C. (1993). "Civil Society and the Spirit of Revolt." *Dissent*. (Summer), pp. 356–61.

Ivanhoe, P. J. (1990). 2nd ed. *Ethics in the Confucian Tradition: The Thought of Mengzi and Wang Yangming*. Indianapolis: Hackett.

Jacoby, N. H. (1973). *Corporate Power and Social Responsibility*. New York: Macmillan.

Janis, I. (1972). *Victims of Groupthink: A Psychological Study of Foreign Policy Decisions and Fiascos*. Boston: Houghton Mifflin.

Janoski, T. (1998). *Citizenship and Civil Society*. Cambridge: Cambridge University Press.

Jantsch, E. (1975). *Design for Evolution*. New York: Braziller.

Jaspers, K. (1957). *Socrates, Buddha, Confusius, and Jesus*. New York: A Harvest Book, Harcourt Brace.

Jay, M. (1973). *The Dialectical Imagination*. London: Heinemann.

Jay, M. (1985). "Habermas and Modernism." In R. Bernstein (Ed.). *Habermas and Modernity*. Cambridge, Mass.: MIT Press.

Joachim, H. H. (1951). *Aristotle: The Nicomachean Ethics—A Commentary*. Oxford, U.K.: Clarendon.

Johnson, J. P. (1997). "Spirituality and Community." *The Journal of Speculative Philosophy*. Vol. 11, no. 1, pp. 20–39.

Jonas, H. (1984). *The Imperative of Responsibility: In Search of an Ethics for the Technological Age*. Chicago: University of Chicago Press.

Jones, K. (1996). "Trust as an Affective Attitude." *Ethics*. Vol. 107 (October), pp. 4–25.

Jun, J. S. (1986). *Public Administration: Design and Problem Solving*. New York: Macmillan.

Jun, J. S. (1994a). "On Administrative Praxis." *Administrative Theory and Praxis*. Vol. 16, no. 2, pp. 201–07.

Jun, J. S. (1994b). *Philosophy of Administration*. Seoul: Daeyoungmoonhwa International.

Jun, J. S. (1996). "Tool Tropism in Public Administration: The Pathology of Management Fads." *Administrative Theory and Praxis*. Vol. 18, no. 2, pp. 108–18.

Jun, J. S. (1997). "Phenomenology of Administrative Communication." In J. L. Garnett and A. Kouzmin (Eds.), *Handbook of Administrative Communication*. New York: Marcel Dekker, pp. 141–152.

Jun, J. S. (1999). "The Need for Autonomy and Virtues: Civic-minded Administrators in a Civil Society." *Administrative Theory and Praxis*. 21(2):218–23.

Jun, J. S. (2002). "New Governance in Civil Society: Changing Responsibility of Public Administration." In J. S. Jun (Ed.), *Rethinking Administrative Theory: The Challenge of the New Century*. Westport, Conn.: Praeger, pp. 289–307.

Jun, J. S. (Ed.). (2002). *Rethinking Administrative Theory: The Challenge of the New Century*. Westport: Praeger.

Jun, J. S., and Campodonico, L. (1998). "Globalization and Democratic Governance: A Contradiction." *Administrative Theory and Praxis*. Vol. 20, no. 4, pp. 478–90.

Jun, J. S., and Kim, T. Y. (2002). "Distrust as a Hindrance to Democratic Governance in South Korea." *Asian Journal of Political Science*. Vol. 10, No. 1 (June), pp. 1–16.

Jun, J. S., and Park, M. S. (2001). "Crisis and Organizational Paralysis: The Lingering Problem of Korean Public Administration." *Journal of Contingencies and Crisis Management*. Vol. 9, no. 1 (March), pp. 3–13.

Jun, J. S., and Rivera, M. (1997). "The Paradox of Transforming Public

Administration: Modernity Versus Postmodernity Arguments." *American Behavioral Scienists.* Vol. 41. no. 1, pp. 132–147.

Jun, J. S., and Storm, W. B. (Eds.). (1973). *Tomorrow's Organizations: Challenges and Strategies.* Glenview, Ill.: Scott, Foresman.

Jun, J. S., and Wright, D. S. (Eds.). (1996). *Globalization and Decentralization: Institutional Contexts, Policy Issues, and Inter-governmental Relations in Japan and the United States.* Washington, D. C.: Georgetown University Press.

Jun, Jong S., and Hiromi Muto. (1995). "The Hidden Dimensions of Japanese Administration: Culture and Its Impact." *Public Administration Review.* Vol. 55, no. 2 (March/April), pp. 125–34.

Kafka, F. (1948). *The Trial.* Trans. W. and E. Muir. New York: Knopf.

Kant, I. (1956). *Critique of Practical Reason.* Trans. L. W. Beck. New York: Liberal Art.

Kass, H. D., and Catron, B. L. (Eds.). (1990). *Images and Identities in Public Administration.* Newbury Park, Calif.: Sage.

Kass, H., (Ed.). (1999). "Community Capacity, Social Trust and Public Administration." *Administrative Theory and Praxis.* Vol. 21, no. 1, pp. 10–119.

Katsiaficas, G., and Kiros, T. (Eds.). (1998). *The Promise of Multiculturalism: Education and Autonomy in the 21st Century.* New York: Routledge.

Kaufman, H. (1981). "Fear of Bureaucracy: A Raging Pandemic." *Public Administration Review.* Vol. 41, no. 1 (January/February), pp. 1–9.

Keane, J. (1998). *Civil Society: Old Images, New Visions.* Stanford, CA: Stanford University Press.

Kettl, D. F. (2002). *The Transformation of Governance: Public Administration for Twenty-First Century America.* Baltimore: Johns Hopkins University Press.

Khademian, A. M. (2002). *Working with Culture: The Way the Job Gets Done in Public Programs.* Washington, D.C.: CQ.

King, C., and Stivers, C. (Ed.). (1998). *Government Is Us.* Thousand Oaks, Calif.: Sage.

Kirlin, J. J. (1996). "What Government Must Do Well: Creating Value for Society." *Journal of Public Administration Research and Theory.* Vol. 6, no. 1, pp. 161–85.

Kiros, T. (1998). *Self-construction and the Formation of Human Values: Truth, Language, and Desire.* Westport, Conn.: Greenwood.

Kiss, E. (1992). "Democracy without Parties?" *Dissent.* (Spring), pp. 222–31.

Klemm, D. E., and Zöller, G. (1997). *Figuring the Self: Subjecrt, Absolute, and Others in Classical German Philosophy.* Albany: State University of New York Press.

Kooiman, J. (Ed.). (1993). *Modern Governance: New Government-Society Interactions.* Thousand Oaks, Calif.: Sage.

Korten, D. (1990). *Getting to the 21st Century: Voluntary Action and the Global Agenda*. West Hartford, Conn.: Kumarian.

Korten, D. C. (1995). *When Corporations Rule the World*. West Hartford, Conn.: Kumarian.

Kramer, R. M., and Cook, K. S. (Eds.). (2004). *Trust and Distrust in Organizations: Dilemmas and Approaches*. New York: Sage Foundation.

Krut, R. (1997). *Globalization and Civil Society: NGO Influence in International Decision-Making*. Geneva, Switzerland: United Nations Research Institute for Social Development (UNRISD).

Kymlicka, W. (1995). *Multicultural Citizenship*. Oxford: Oxford University Press.

Laçan, J. (1982). *Écrits: A Selection*. Trans. Alan Sheridan. New York: Norton.

Lakoff, G., and Johnson, M. (1980). *Metaphors We Live By*. Chicago: University of Chicago Press.

Landau, M. (1972). *Political Theory and Political Science*. New York: Macmillan.

Lao Tsu. (1972). *Tao Te Ching*. Trans. G. Feng and J. English. New York: Vintage Books.

Lash, S. (1993). "Pierre Bourdieu: Cultural Economy and Social Change." In C. Calhoun, E. LiPuma, and M. Postone (Eds.), *Bourvieu: Critical Perspectives*. Chicago: University of Chicago Press, pp. 193–211.

Laudan, L. (1977). *Progress and Its Problems: Toward a Theory of Scientific Growth*. Berkeley: University of California Press.

Lawson, H. (1985). *Reflexivity: The Postmodern Predicament*. La Salle, Ill.: Open Court.

Lewin, K. (1947). "Frontiers in Group Dynamics: Part II, Channels in Group Life, Social Planning, Action Research." *Human Relations*. Vol. 1, no. 2, pp. 143–53.

Lewin, K. (1951). *Field Theory and Social Science*. New York: Harper and Brothers.

Lieberman, J. K. (1970). *The Tyranny of the Experts*. New York: Walker.

Lindblom, C. E. (1965). *The Intelligence of Democracy*. New York: Free Press.

Lindblom, C. E. (1968). *The Policy-Making Process*. Englewood Cliffs, N.J.: Prentice-Hall.

Lindblom, C. E. (1977). *Politics and Markets*. New York: Basic Books:

Linstead, S. (1993). "Deconstruction in the Study of Organizations." In J. Hassard and M. Parker (Eds.), *Postmodernism and Organizations*. Newbury Park, Calif.: Sage, pp. 49–70.

Livernash, R. (1992). "The Growing Influence of NGOs in the Developing World." *Environment*. Vol. 34, no. 5, pp. 12–20, 41–43.

Lobkowicz, N. (1967). *Theory and Practice*. Notre Dame: University of Notre Dame Press.

Luard, E. (1990). *The Globalization of Politics: The Changed Focus of Political Action in the Modern World*. New York: New York University Press.

Luhmann, N. (1979). *Trust and Power*. New York: Wiley and Sons.

Lynch, T. D., and Lynch, C. E. (1999). "Spiritual Wisdom and Public Administration: Are They Compatible?" *International Journal of Organization Theory and Behavior*. Vol. 2, nos. 3 & 4, pp. 273–302.

Lyotard, J. (1984). *The Postmodern Condition: A Report on Knowledge*. Trans. G. Benington and B. Massouri. Minneapolis: University of Minnesota Press.

Macann, C. (1993). *Four Phenomenological Philosophers: Husserl, Heidegger, Satre, and Merleau-Ponty*. London: Routledge.

Macedo, S. (1990). *Liberal Virtues: Citizenship, Virtue, and Community*. Oxford: Oxford University Press.

Macedo, S., (Ed.). (1999). *Deliberative Politics: Essays on Democracy and Disagreement*. Oxford: Oxford University Press.

MacIntyre, A. (1981). *After Virtue: A Study in Moral Theory*. 2nd ed. Notre Dame, Ind.: Notre Dame University Press.

Madison, G. B. (1988). *The Hermeneutics of Postmodernity: Figures and Themes*. Bloomington: Indiana University Press.

Mander, J., and Goldsmith, E. (Eds.). (1996). *The Case against the Global Economy: And for a Turn toward the Local*. San Francisco: Sierra Club Books.

Mannheim, K. (1940). *Men and Society in an Age of Reconstruction*. New York: Harcourt, Brace, and World.

Marsh, J. L., Caputo, J., and Westphal, M. (Eds.). (1992). *Modernity and Its Discontents*. New York: Fordham University Press.

March, J. G., and J. P. Olsen. (1995). *Democratic Governance*. New York: Free Press.

Marković, M. (1974). *From Affluence to Praxis: Philosophy and Social Criticism*. Ann Arbor: University of Michigan Press.

Mavima, P., Satran, J., Snyder, M., Tao, J., Wilson, J. J. III, (1997). "NGOs, National Governments, and Intgernational Donors: The New Triumvirate?" *SICA Occasional Paper Series* (June).

May, L. (1996). *The Socially Responsive Self: Social Theory and Professional Ethics*. Chicago: University of Chicago Press.

McCarthy, T. (1981). *The Critical Theory of Jürgen Habermas*. Cambridge, Mass.: The MIT Press.

McClellan, G. S. (Ed.). (1979). *The Quality of Federal Policymaking: Programmed Failure in Public Housing*. Columbia: University of Missouri Press.

McCollough, T. E. (1991). *The Moral Imagination and Public Life*. Chatham, N.J.: Chatham House.

McSwite, O. C. (1997). "Jacques Lacan and theTheory of the Human Subject." *American Behavioral Scientist*. Vol. 41, No. 1 (September), pp. 43–63.

McSwite, O. C. (1997). *Legitimacy in Public Administration: A Discourse Analysis*. Thousand Oaks, Calif.: Sage.

McWhinney, W. (1992). *Paths of Change: Strategic Choices for Organizations and Society*. Thousand Oaks, Calif.: Sage.

Mead, G. H. (1934). *Mind, Self and Society*. Chicago: University of Chicago Press.

Mead, G. H. (1938). *The Philosophy of the Act*. Chicago: University of Chicago Press.

Melzer, A. M., Weinberger, J., and Zinman, M. R. (1998). *Multiculturalism and American Democracy*. Lawrence: University Press of Kansas.

Merleau-Ponty, M. (1962). *The Phenomenology of Perception*. Trans. C. Smith. London: Routledge & Kegan Paul.

Merleau-Ponty, M. (1968). *The Visible and the Invisible*. Trans. A. Lingis. Evanston, Ill.: Northwestern University Press.

Merleau-Ponty, M. (1973). *Adventures of the Dialectic*. Evanston, Ill.: Northwestern University Press.

Merton, R. K. (1957). *Social Theory and Social Structure*. New York: Free Press.

Miyamoto, M. (1994). *Straitjacket Society: An Insider's Irreverent View of Bureaucratic Japan*. Tokyo: Kodansha International.

Morales, I., De Los Reyes, G., and Rich, P. (Eds.). (1999). "Civil Society and Democratization." *The Annals of the American Academy of Political and Social Science*. Vol. 565.

Morgan, G. (1997). 2nd ed. *Images of Organization*. Thousand Oaks, Calif.: Sage.

Morton, L. W. (2001). *Health Care Restructuring: Market Theory vs. Civil Society*. Westport, Conn.: Auburn House.

Mosher, F. C. (1868). *Democracy and the Public Service*. New York: Oxford University Press.

Mulgan, G. (1997). *Connexity: How to Live in a Connected World*. Boston: Harvard Business School Press.

Münch, R. (1987). *Theory of Action: Towards a New Synthesis Going beyond Parsons*. London: Routledge & Kegan Paul.

Muramatsu, M. (1997). *Local Power in the Japanese State*. Trans. B. Scheiner and J. White. Berkeley: University of California Press.

Myrdal, G. (1968). *Asian Drama: An Inquiry into the Poverty of Nations*. New York: Twentieth Century Fund.

Nader, R. (Ed.). (1972). *Whistle-Blowing*. New York: Grossman.

Natanson, M. (1970). *The Journeying Self: A Study in Philosophy and Social Role*. Reading, Mass.: Addison-Wesley.

Natanson, M. (1973). *The Social Dynamics of George H. Mead*. The Hague: Nijhoff.

Neace, M. B. (1999). "Entrepreneurs in Emerging Economies: Creating Trust, Social Capital, and Civil Society." In I. Morales, G. De Los Reyes, and P.

Rich (Eds.), *Civil Society and Democratization*. The Annals of the American Academy of Political and Social Science. Thousand Oaks, Calif. Sage, pp. 148–61.

Neal, P. (1997). *Liberalism and Its Discontents*. New York: New York University Press.

Noggle, R. (1997). "The Public Conception of Autonomy and Critical Self-Reflection." *The Southern Journal of Philosophy*. Vol. 35, no.4. pp. 495–515.

Norris, P. (1999). *Critical Citizens: Global Support for Democratic Government*. Oxford: Oxford University Press.

Norris, P. (2001). *Digital Divide: Civic Engagement, Information Poverty, and the Internet Worldwide*. Cambridge, U.K.: Cambridge University Press.

Norris, P. (Ed.). (1999). *Critical Citizens: Global Support for Democratic Governance*. Oxford: Oxford University Press.

Nozick, R. (1974). *Anarchy, State, and Utopia*. New York: Basic Books.

Nye, J. S., and Donahue, J. D. (2000). *Governance in a Globalizing World*. Washington, D.C.: Brookings Institution Press.

O'Connell, B. (1999). *Civil Society: The Underpinnings of American Democracy*. Hanover, N.H.: Tufts University Press.

Offe, A. C. (1999). "How Can We Trust Our Fellow Citizens?" In Warren (Ed.), *Democracy and Trust*, pp. 42–87.

O'Neill, J. (1995). *The Poverty of Postmodernism*. London: Routledge.

Osborne, D., and Gaebler, T. (1992). *Reinventing Government: How the Entrepreneurial Spirit Is Transforming the Public Sector*. Reading, Mass.: Addison-Wesley.

Ostrom, E. (1993). *Social Capital and Development Projects*. Prepared for social capital and economic development, American Academy of Arts and Sciences. Cambridge, Mass. 30–31 July.

Ostrom, E., and Walker, J. (Eds.). (2005). *Trust and Reciprocity: Interdisciplinary Lessons for Experimental Research*. New York: Sage Foundation.

Palmer, R. E. (1969). *Hermeneutics*. Evanston, I.L.: Northwestern University Press.

Panitch, L. (1996). "Rethinking the Role of the State." In J. H. Mittleman (Ed.), *Globalization: Critical Reflections*. London: Rienner.

Parsons, T. (1949). *The Structure of Social Action*. New York: Free Press.

Parsons, T. (1951). *The Social System*. New York: Free Press.

Parsons, T. (1978). *Action Theory and the Human Condition*. New York: Free Press.

Parsons, T., and Shils, E. (Eds.). (1951). *Toward a General Theory of Action*. Cambridge, Mass.: Harvard University Press.

Pateman, C. (1970). *Participation and Democratic Theory*. Cambridge: Cambridge University Press.

Payton, S. (1998). "The Politics of Comprehensive National Health Care Reform: Watching the 103rd and 104 Congresses at Work." In M. Rosenthal and M. Heirich (Eds.), *Health Policy: Understanding Our Choices from National Reform to Market Forces.* Boulder, Colo.: Westview, pp. 211–36.

Peak, K., and Glensor, R. W. (1996). *Community Policing and Problem Solving: Strategies and Practices.* Englewood Cliffs, N. J.: Prentice Hall.

Peters, B. G. (1996). *The Future of Governing: Four Emerging Models.* Lawrence: The University Press of Kansas.

Peterson, R. T. (1996). *Democratic Philosophy and the Politics of Knowledge.* University Park: Pennsylvania State University Press.

Phillipson, M. (1972). "Phenomenological Philosophy and Sociology." In P. Filmer, M. Phillipson, D. Silverman, and D. Walsh. (Eds.). *New Directions in Sociological Theory.* Cambridge, Mass.: MIT Press.

Pirages, D. C. (Ed.). (1996). *Building Sustainable Societies: A Blueprint for a Post-Industrial World.* New York: Sharpe.

Polkinghorne, D. (1983). *Methodology for the Human Sciences: Systems of Inquiry.* Albany: State University of New York Press.

Putnam, H. (1978). *Meaning and the Moral Sciences.* London: Routledge & Kegan Paul.

Putnam, R. (1993). *Making Democracy Work: Civic Traditions in Modern Italy.* Princeton, NJ: Princeton University Press.

Putnam, R. (1995). "Bowling Alone: America's Declining Social Capital." *Journal of Democracy.* Vol. 6, no. 1, pp. 65–78.

Quade, E. S. (1975). *Analysis for Public Decisions.* New York: Elsevier.

Quah, Jon S. T. (2003). *Curbing Corruption in Asia: A Comparative Study of Six Countries.* Singapore: Eastern Universities Press.

Ramos, A. G. (1981). *The New Science of Organizations: A Reconceptualization of the Wealth of Nations.* Toronto: University of Toronto Press.

Rand, A. (1961). *The Virtue of Selfishness.* New York: New American Library.

Ratliff, W. (1999). "Development and Civil Society in Latin America and Asia." In I. Morales, G. De Los Reyes, and P. Rich (Eds.), *Civil Society and Democratization.* The Annals of the American Academy of Political and Social Science. Thousand Oaks, Calif.: Sage, pp. 91–112.

Rawls, J. (1971). *A Theory of Justice.* Cambridge, Mass.: Harvard University Press.

Rawls, J. (1993). *Political Liberalism.* New York: Columbia University Press.

Redford, E. S. (1975). *Democracy in the Administrative State.* New York: Oxford University Press.

Reed, S. (1993). *Making Common Sense of Japan.* Pittsburgh, Penn.: University of Pittsburgh Press.

Reich, C. A. (1970). *The Greening of America.* New York: Random House.

Rein, M. (1976). *Social Science and Public Policy*. New York: Penguin Books.

Rein, M. (1983). *From Policy to Practice*. New York: Sharpe.

Rhodes, R. A. W. (1997). *Understanding Governance*. Buckingham, U.K.: Open University Press.

Richardson, H. S. (2002). *Democratic Autonomy: Public Reasoning about the Ends of Policy*. Oxford: Oxford University Press.

Richardson, W. D. (1997). *Democracy, Bureaucracy, and Character*. Lawrence: University Press of Kansas.

Ricoeur, P. (1991). *From Text to Action*. Trans. Kathleen Blamey and J. E. Thompson. Evanston, Ill.: Northwestern University Press.

Riordon, W. (1963). *Plunkitt of Tammany Hall*. New York: Dutton.

Ro, C. H., Frederickson, H. G., and Hwang, S. D. (Eds.). (1997). *Confucian Thought and Bureaucracy in East Asia*. Seoul: Korea Institute of Public Administration.

Robertson, R. (1992). *Globalization: Social Theory and Global Culture*. Thousand Oaks, Calif.: Sage.

Rodrik, D. (1996). *Has Globalization Gone Too Far?* Washington, D.C.: Institute for International Economics.

Roetz, H. (1993). *Confucian Ethics of the Axial Age*. Albany: State University of New York Press.

Rogers, C. R. (1968). "Interpersonal Relationships: U.S.A. 2000." *The Journal of Applied Behavioral Science*. Vol. 4, no. 3 (July/August/Semptember), pp. 265–80.

Rohr, J. A. (1998). *Public Service, Ethics and Contitutional Practice*. Lawrence: University Press of Kansas.

Rorty, R. (1982). *Consequences of Pragmatism: Eassys, 1972–80*. Minneapolis: University of Minnesota Press.

Rorty, R. (1989). *Contingency, Irony, and Solidarity*. New York: Cambridge University Press.

Rorty, R. (1991). *Objectivity, Relativism, and Truth*. New York: Cambridge University Press.

Rosenau, J. N. (1992). "Governance, Order, and Change in World Politics." In J. N. Rosenau and E. Czempiel (Eds.), *Governance Without Government: Order and Change in World Politics*. Cambridge, U.K.: Cambridge University Press.

Rosenau, P. M. (1992). *Post-Modernism and the Social Sciences: Insights, Inroads, and Intrusions*. Princeton, N.J.: Princeton University Press.

Rosenbloom, D. H. (2002). "Administrative Reformers in a Global World: Diagnosis, Prescription, and the Limits of Transferability." In J. S. Jun (Ed.), *Rethinking Administrative Theory: The Challenge of the New Century*. Westport, Conn.: Praeger, pp. 217–31.

Roy, W. G. (2001). *Making Societies*. Thousand Oaks, Calif.: Pine Forge.

Rudolph, S. H. (2002). "In Defense of Diverse Forms of Knowledge." *PS* (Political Science & Politics). Vol. 35, no. 2, pp. 193–95.

Sachs, J. (1998). "Global Capitalism," *The Economist*, September 28, pp. 23–25.

Sahlins, M. (1982), "Individual Experience and Cultural Order." In W. H. Kruskal (Ed.), *The Social Sciences: Their Nature and Uses*. Chicago: The University of Chicago Press, pp. 35–48.

Sandel, M. (1982). *Liberalism and the Limits of Justice*. Cambridge: Cambridge University Press.

Sandel, M. (1996). *Democracy's Discontent*. Cambridge, MA: Harvard University Press.

Sandler, T. (1997). *Global Challenges: An Approach to Environmental, Political, and Economic Problems*. Cambridge: Cambridge University Press.

Sartre, J. (1976). *The Critique of Dialectical Reason*. Trans. A. Sheridan-Smith. London: New Left Books.

Sarup, M. (1988). *An Introductory Guide to Post-Structuralism and Postmodernism*. 2nd ed. Athens: University of Georgia Press.

Sarup, M. (1992). *Jacques Lacan*. Toronto: University of Toronto Press.

Schachter, H. L. (1997). *Reinventing Government or Reinventing Ourselves*. Albany: State University of New York Press.

Schein, E. (1970). 2d. ed. *Organizational Psychology*. Englewood Cliffs, N.J.: Prentice-Hall.

Schön, D. (1971). *Beyond the Stable State*. New York: Norton.

Schön, D. (1983). *The Reflective Practitioner*. New York: Basic Books.

Schön, D., and Rein, M. (1994). *Frame Reflection: Toward the Resolution of Intractable Policy Controversies*. New York: Basic Books.

Schroyer, T. (1973). *The Critique of Domination: The Origins and Development of Critical Theory*. New York: Braziller.

Schutz, A. (1962). *Collected Papers I: The Problem of Social Reality*. Ed. and introduced by M. Natanson. The Hague: Nijhoff.

Schutz, A. (1967). *The Phenomenology of the Social World*. Trans. G. Walsh. Evanston, Ill.: Northwestern University Press.

Schwedler, J. (Ed.). (1995). *Toward Civil Society in the Middle East? A Primer*. Boulder, Colo.: Rienner.

Searle, J. R. (1995). *The Construction of Social Reality*. New York: Free Press.

Seligman, A. (1990). "Toward a Reinterpretation of Modernity in an Age of Postmodernity." In B. S. Turner (Ed.), *Theories of Modernity and Postmodernity*. Newbury Park, Calif.: Sage.

Seligman, A. B. (1992). *The Idea of Civil Society*. New York: Free Press

Seligman, A. B. (1997). *The Problem of Trust*. Princeton: Princeton University Press.

Sharp, E. B. (1980). "Toward a New Understanding of Urban Services and Citizen Participation: The Coproduction Concept." *Midwest Review of Public Administration*. Vol. 14, no. 2, p. 110.

Sheridan, A. (1980). *Michael Foucault: The Will to Truth*. New York: Tavistock.

Shigeru, T. (2003). "The Emergence of NPOs and the Implications for Local Governance." In F. Shun'ichi and M. Toshihiro (Eds.), *Japan's Road to Pluralism: Transforming Local Communities in the Global Era*. Tokyo: Japan Center for International Exchange, pp. 161–78.

Shotter, J. (1993). *Conversational Realities: Constructing Life through Language*. Thousand Oaks, Calif.: Sage.

Shotter, J., and Cunliffe, A. L. (2002). "Managers as Practical Authors: Everyday Conversations for Action." In D. Holman and R. Thorpe. (Eds.), *Management and Language: The Manager as Practical Author*. London: Sage.

Shuman, M. H. (1998). *Going Local: Creating Self-Reliant Communities in a Global Age*. New York: Free Press.

Silverman, D. (1970). *The Theory of Organizations*. London: Heinemann.

Silverman, H. J. (1984). "Phenomenology: From Hermeneutics to Deconstruction. In *Research in Phenomenology*. Vol XIV: pp. 19–34.

Simon, H. A. (1945 and 1957). 2nd ed. *Administrative Behavior*. New York: Macmillan.

Simon, H. A. (1977). *The New Science of Management Decisions*. Englewood Cliffs, N.J.: Prentice-Hall.

Sirianni, C., and Friedland, L. (2001). *Civic Innovation in America*. Berkeley: University of California Press.

Smith, A. (1937/1776). *An Inquiry to the Nature and Causes of the Wealth of Nations*. New York: Modern Library.

Smith, A. (1966/1853). *The Theory of Moral Sentiments*. (Reprint), New York: Macmillan.

Smith, H. (1982). *Beyond the Post-Modern Mind*. New York: Crossroad.

Smith, H. (2001). *Why Religion Matters: The Fate of the Human Spirit in an Age of Disbelief*. San Francisco: Harper San Francisco.

Smith, H., and Novak, P. (2003). *Buddhism: A Concise Introduction*. New York: Harper San Francisco.

Sokolowski, R. (2000). *Introduction to Phenomenology*. Cambridge: Cambridge University Press.

Stillman, II, R. J. (1987). *The American Bureaucracy*. Chicago: Nelson-Hall.

Stillman, II, R. J. (1991). *Preface to Public Administration: A Search for Themes and Direction*. New York: St. Martin's.

Stivers, C. (1993). *Gender Images in Public Administration: Legitimacy and the Administrative State*. Newbury Park, Calif.: Sage.

Stokey, E., and Zeckhauser, R. (1978). *A Primer for Policy Analysis*. New York: Norton.

Strasser, S. (1969). *The Idea of Dialogical Phenomenology*. Pittsburgh, Pa.: Duquesne University Press.

Stringer, E. T. (1996). *Action Research: A Handbook for Practitioners*. Thousand Oaks, Calif.: Sage.

Ströker, E. (1999). *Husserl's Transcendental Phenomenology*. Stanford, CA: Stanford University Press.

Suler, J. R. (1993). *Contemporary Psychoanalysis and Eastern Thought*. Albany: State University of New York Press.

Surber, J. P. (1998). *Culture and Critique: An Introduction to the Critical Discourses of Cultural Studies*. Boulder, Colo.: Westview.

Swartz, D. (1997). *Culture and Power: The Sociology of Pierre Bourdieu*. Chicago: University of Chicago Press.

Tandon, R. (1987). *NGO Government Relations: A Source of Life or a Kiss of Death*. New Delhi: Society for Participatory Research in Asia.

Taylor, C. (1985a). "Interpretation and the Sciences of Man." *Philosophy and the Human Sciences: Philosophical Papers 2*. Cambridge: Cambridge University Press.

Taylor, C. (1985b). *Philosophy and the Human Sciences: Philosophical Papers 2*. Cambridge: Cambridge University Press.

Taylor, C. (1989). *Sources of the Self*. Cambridge, MA: Harvard University Press.

Taylor, C. (1995). *Philosophical Arguments*. Cambridge, Mass.: Harvard University Press.

Taylor, F. W. (1967). *The Principles of Scientific Management*. New York: Norton.

Thomason, B. C. (1982). *Making Sense of Reification: Alfred Schutz and Constructionist Theory*. Atlantic Highlands, N.J.: Humanities.

Thurman, W., Zhao, J., and Giacomazzi, A.(2001). *Community Policing in a Community Era: An Introduction and Exploration*. Los Angeles: Roxbury.

Tu, W. M. (1985). *Confucian Thought: Selfhood as Creative Transformation*. Albany: State University of New York Press.

Turbayne, C. M. (1971). *The Myth of Metaphor*. Columbia: University of South Carolina Press.

Turner, B. S. (1994). *Orientalism, Postmodernism, and Globalism*. London: Routledge.

Tyler, T. R. (1998). "Trust and Democratic Governance." In V. Braithwaite and M. Levi (Eds.), *Trust and Governance*.

Urban Mass Transportation Administration. (1991). *ADA Paratransit Handbook*. Washington, D.C.: U.S. Department of Transportation.

Uslaner, E. M. (1999). "Democracy and Social Capital." In M. E. Warren (Ed.), *Democracy and Trust*, pp. 121–50.

Vazquez, A. S. (1977). *The Philosophy of Praxis.* London: Merlin.

Ventriss, C. (2002). "A Democratic Public and Administrative Thought: A Public Perspective." In J. S. Jun (Ed.), *Rethinking Administrative Theory: The Challenge of the New Centur.* Westport, Conn.: Praeger, pp. 93–104.

Waldo, D. (1978). "Democracy, Bureaucracy and Hypocracy." Royer Lecture, given at the University of California, Berkeley, May 13, 1978, on the occasion of Professor Emeritus ceremonies for Victor Jones.

Waldo, D. (1948). *The Administrative State.* New York: Ronald.

Walzer, M. (1973). "The Problem of Dirty Hands." *Philosophy and Public Affairs* (Winter), pp. 160–80.

Waltzer, M. (1983). *Spheres of Justice: A Defense of Pluralism and Equality.* New York: Basic Books.

Warren, M. E. (Ed.). (1999). *Democracy and Trust.* Cambridge: Cambridge University Press.

Warren, R. et al. (1982). "Citizen Participation in Production of Services: Methodological and Policy Issues in Coproduction Research." *The Southwestern Review.* Vol. 14, no. 3, pp. 41–55.

Watts, A. (1975). *TAO: The Watercourse Way.* New York: Pantheon Books.

Watts, A. (1997). *Taoism: Way beyond Seeking.* Edited transcripts. Boston: Tuttle.

Weaver, R. K., and Stares, P. B. (2001). *Guidance for Governance: Comparing Alternative Sources of Public Policy Advice.* Tokyo: Japan Center for International Exchange.

Weber, M. (1947). *The Theory of Social and Economic Organization.* Trans. A. M. Henderson and T. Parsons, ed. with an introduction by T. Parsons. New York: Free Press.

Weick, K. (1995). *Sensemaking in Organization.* Thousand Oaks, Calif. Sage.

Weil, A., and Finegold, K. (Eds.). (2002). *Welfare Reform: The Next Act.* Washington, D.C.: Urban Institute.

Weinstein, D. (1979). *Bureaucratic Opposition.* New York: Pergamon.

Weisband, E., and Franck, T. M. (1975). *Resignation in Protest: Political and Ethical Choices between Loyalty to Team and Loyalty to Conscience in American Public Life.* New York: Grossman.

Weisbord, M. (1992). *Discovering Common Ground.* San Francisco: Bernett-Koehler.

Weisboard, M. R., and S. Janoff. (1995). *Future Search: An Action Guide to Finding Common Ground in Organizations and Communities.* San Francisco: Berrett-Koehler.

White, D. R., and G. Hellerich. (1998). *Labyrinths of the Mind: The Self in the Postmodern Age.* Albany: State University of New York Press.

Whitehead, A. N. (1927). *Symbolism: Its Meaning and Effects*. New York: Macmillan.

Whitehead, A. N. (1929). *Process and Reality: An Essay in Cosmology*. New York: Macmillan.

Whyte, W. H., Jr. (1965). *The Organziation Man*. New York: Simon & Schuster.

Whyte, W. F., Jr. (1984). *Learning from the Field: A Guide from Experience*. Beverly Hills: Sage.

Wilber, K. (1979). *No Boundary: Eastern and Western Approaches to Personal Growth*. Boulder: Shambhala.

Wildavsky, A. (1979). *Speaking Truth to Power: The Art and Craft of Policy Analysis*. Boston: Little, Brown and Company.

Williams, T. A. (1982). *Learning to Manage Our Futures*. New York: Wiley.

Wilshire, B. (1968). *William James and Phenomenology*. Bloomington: Indiana University Press.

Wilson, D., (Ed.). (1997). "Globalization and the Changing U.S. City." *The Annals of the American Academy of Political and Social Science*. Vol. 551.

Wilson, J. Q. (1968). *Varieties of Police Behavior: The Management of Law and Order in Eight Communities*. Cambridge, Mass.: Harvard University Press.

Wilson, J. Q. (1989). *Bureaucracy: What Government Agencies Do and Why They Do It*. New York: Basic Books.

Wilson, W. (1887). "The Study of Administration." *Political Science Quarterly*. Vol. 2, no. 2, pp. 197–220.

Winch, P. (1958). *The Idea of a Social Science*. London: Routledge and Kegan Paul.

Winter, G. (1966). *Elements for a Social Ethic*. New York: Macmillan.

Wisband, E., and T. M. Franck. (1975). *Resignation in Protest: Political and Ethical Choices between Loyalty to Team and Loyalty to Conscience in American Public Life*. New York: Grossman.

Wolfe, A. (1989). *Whose Keeper? Social Science and Moral Obligation*. Berkeley: University of California Press.

Woll, P. (1963). *American Bureaucracy*. New York: Norton.

Wrong, D. H. (1961). "The Oversocialized Conception of Man in Modern Sociology." *American Sociological Review*. Vol. 26, pp. 183–93.

Yalom, I. D. (1985). *The Theory of Practice of Group Psychotherapy*. New York: Basic Books.

Yanow, D. (1996). *How Does a Policy Mean? Interpreting Policy and Organizational Action*. Washington, D.C.: Georgetown University Press.

Yezzi, R. (1986). *Directing Human Actions: Perspectives on Basic Ethical Issues*. Lanham, Md.: University Press of America.

Young, I. M. (1997). *Intersecting Voices: Dilemmas of Gender, Political Philosophy, and Policy*. Princeton, N.J.: Princeton University Press.

Young, I. M. (2000). *Inclusion and Democracy*. New York: Oxford University Press.

Zaner, R. (1970). *The Way of Phenomenology*. New York: Pegasus.

Zanetti, L. A. (1997). "Advancing Praxis: Connecting Critical Theory with Practice in Public Administration. *American Review of Public Administration*. Vol. 27, no. 2, pp. 145–67.

INDEX